Drive Around

Vancouver
and British Columbia

YOUR GUIDE TO GREAT DRIVES

Titles in this series include:

For further information about these and other Thomas Cook publications, write to Thomas Cook Publishing, PO Box 227, The Thomas Cook Business Park, 15–16 Coningsby Road, Peterborough PE3 8SB, United Kingdom.

Drive Around

Vancouver
and British Columbia

The best of Vancouver's big city
attractions plus Victoria's heritage
buildings and the magnificent scenery
of British Columbia's mountains,
forests and rivers

Maxine Cass and Fred Gebhart

Thomas Cook
Publishing

www.thomascookpublishing.com

Published by Thomas Cook Publishing,
a division of Thomas Cook Tour Operations Limited
PO Box 227
The Thomas Cook Business Park
15–16 Coningsby Road
Peterborough PE3 8SB
United Kingdom

Telephone: +44 (0)1733 416477
Fax: +44 (0)1733 416688
E-mail: books@thomascook.com

For further information about
Thomas Cook Publishing, visit our website:
www.thomascookpublishing.com

ISBN 1-841574-74-0

Text: © 2005 Thomas Cook Publishing
Maps and diagrams:
Road maps supplied and designed by Lovell Johns Ltd, OX8 8LH
Road map data © Map Quest.com Inc., Mountville PA 17554
City maps prepared by RJS Associates, © Thomas Cook Publishing

Head of Thomas Cook Publishing: Chris Young
Series Editor: Charlotte Christensen
Production/DTP Editor: Steven Collins
Project Administrator: Michelle Warrington

Written, researched and updated by:
Maxine Cass and Fred Gebhart

About the authors

In the years since **Maxine Cass** was born on the Stanford University campus in Palo Alto, California, she has studied Medieval European History at the University of California, Santa Barbara, lived in Greece and Senegal and become a widely published photojournalist and writer. Maxine is the author of the *AAA Photo Journey to San Francisco* and *Time for Food: San Francisco*, and contributes to travel and business publications in Europe, the US, Canada and Asia, as well as collaborating with other authors on the *Drive Around Guides, On the Road Around* and *Discover Guides* series. Between research trips around the world and exploring every corner of the West, and Mexico, Maxine gardens and shares the indulgences of two pampered cats with her husband and co-author, Fred Gebhart, at their home in San Francisco.

Fred Gebhart has lived in the West for more than 40 years, interrupted by extended sojourns in Europe and West Africa. He has travelled BC as a teenager as well as an adult, exploring by bicycle, kayak, rail, horseback, helicopter, sailboat and cruise ship, as well as by car. A freelance photojournalist for two decades, Fred covers the western side of North America for publications in Asia and Europe, and Australasia for North American readers. Fred has written eight Thomas Cook titles with his wife, Maxine Cass, including *Drive Around Guide: California, Discover Guide: California* and *Discover Guide: Florida*. Fred's passion is scuba diving.

Acknowledgements

The authors and publishers would like to thank the following people and organisations for their assistance during the preparation of this book: John Bateman; Super, Natural British Columbia; Catherine Callary, Tourism Kelowna; Monica Campbell-Hoppé, Canadian Tourism Commission; Michelle Comeau, Tourism Whistler; Teresa Davis, Tourism North Central Island; Anthony Everett, Tourism Victoria; Fairmont Hotels & Resorts; Lou Gebhart; Michael & Manon Hobbs and the *Duen*; Laurel Point Inn, Victoria; Kate Colley Lo, Tourism Vancouver; Paul & Virginia McCarthy; Mendo; Pan Pacific Hotel, Vancouver; Mary Ellen Quesada; Panther; Prince George Development Corp; Miranda Richter & Dick Griffith, Air Canada; The Rocky Mountaineer; Mika Ryan, Janice Greenwood and Cindy Burr, Tourism British Columbia; Krista Rodger, Jasper Tourism & Commerce; Laura Serena; Liz Steele, Gabriola Island Chamber of Commerce; Doug Treleaven, BC Ferries; Linda Trudeau, Thompson Okanagan Tourism; Vancouver, Coast & Mountains Tourism Region; VIA Rail; Westin Resort & Spa, Whistler; and Bruce Wishart, Tourism Prince Rupert.

Contents

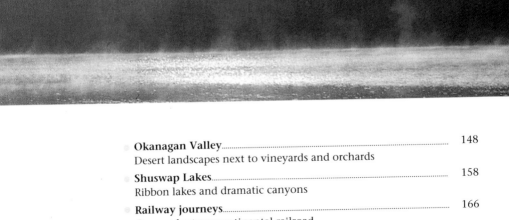

About Drive Around Guides

Thomas Cook's Drive Around Guides are designed to provide you with a comprehensive but flexible reference source to guide you as you tour a country or region by car. This guide divides Vancouver and British Columbia into touring areas – one per chapter. Major cultural centres or cities form chapters in their own right. Each chapter contains enough attractions to provide at least a day's worth of activities – often more.

Star ratings

To make it easier for you to plan your time and decide what to see, the principal sights and attractions are given a star rating. A three-star rating indicates an outstanding sight or major attraction. Often these can be worth at least half a day of your time. A two-star attraction is worth an hour or so of your time, and a one-star attraction indicates a site that is good but often of specialist interest.

Chapter contents

Every chapter has an introduction summing up the main attractions of the area, and a ratings box, which will highlight the area's strengths and weaknesses – some areas may be more attractive to families travelling with children, others to wine-lovers visiting vineyards, and others to people interested in finding churches, nature reserves or good beaches.

Each chapter is then divided into an alphabetical gazetteer, and a suggested tour. You can select whether you just want to visit a particular sight or attraction, choosing from those described in the gazetteer, or whether you want to tour the area comprehensively. If the latter, you can construct your own itinerary, or follow the authors' suggested tour, which comes at the end of every area chapter.

The gazetteer

The gazetteer section describes all the major attractions in the area – the villages, towns, historic sites, nature reserves, parks or museums that you are most likely to want to see. Maps of the area highlight all the places mentioned in the text. Using this comprehensive overview of the area, you may choose just to visit one or two sights.

One way to use the guide is simply to find individual sights that interest you, using the index, overview map or star ratings, and read what our authors have to say about them. This will help you decide whether to visit the sight. If you do, you will find plenty of practical information, such as the street address, the telephone number for enquiries and opening times.

Alternatively, you can choose a hotel, perhaps with the help of the

Symbol Key

- **ℹ** Tourist Information Centre
- **⮂** Advice on arriving or departing
- **Ⓟ** Parking locations
- **Ⓡ** Advice on getting around
- **➲** Directions
- **Ⓜ** Sights and attractions
- **Ⓒ** Accommodation
- **⑪** Eating
- **◖** Shopping
- **⑨** Sport
- **⌂** Entertainment

Practical information

The practical information in the page margins, or sidebar, will help you locate the services you need as an independent traveller – including the tourist information centre, car parks and public transport facilities. You will also find the opening times of sights, museums, churches and other attractions, as well as useful tips on shopping, market days, cultural events, entertainment, festivals and sports facilities.

accommodation recommendations contained in this guide. You can then turn to the overall map on pages 10–11 to help you work out which chapters in the book describe those cities and regions that lie closest to your chosen touring base.

Driving tours

The suggested tour is just that – a suggestion, with plenty of optional detours and one or two ideas for making your own discoveries, under the heading *Also worth exploring*. The routes are designed to link the attractions described in the gazetteer section, and to cover outstandingly scenic coastal, mountain and rural landscapes. The total distance is given for each tour, as is the time it will take you to drive the complete route, but bear in mind that this indication is just for the driving time: you will need to add on extra time for visiting attractions along the way.

Many of the routes are circular, so that you can join them at any point. Where the nature of the terrain dictates that the route has to be linear, the route can either be followed out and back, or you can use it as a link route, to get from one area in the book to another.

As you follow the route descriptions, you will find names picked out in bold capital letters – this means that the place is described fully in the gazetteer. Other names picked out in bold indicate additional villages or attractions worth a brief stop along the route.

Accommodation and food

In every chapter you will find lodging and eating recommendations for individual towns, or for the area as a whole. These are designed to cover a range of price brackets and concentrate on more characterful small or individualistic hotels and restaurants. In addition, you will find information in the *Travel facts* chapter on chain hotels, with an address to which you can write for a guide, map or directory. The price indications used in the guide have the following meanings:

$ budget level
$$ typical/average prices
$$$ de luxe.

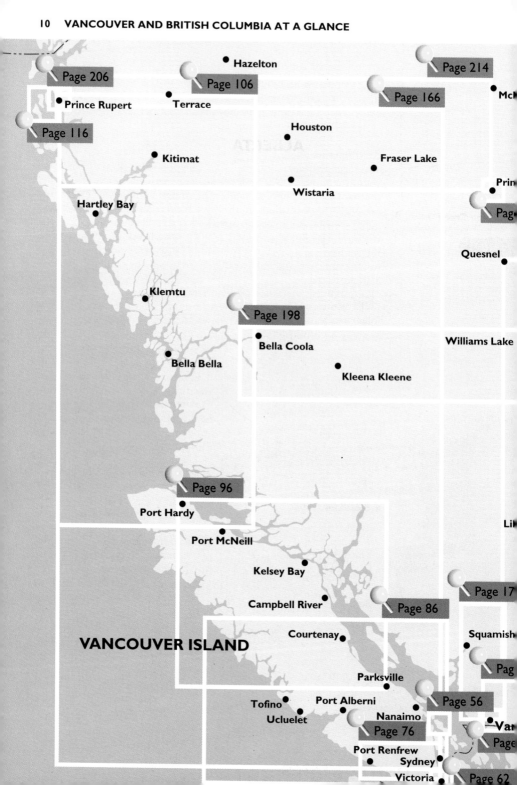

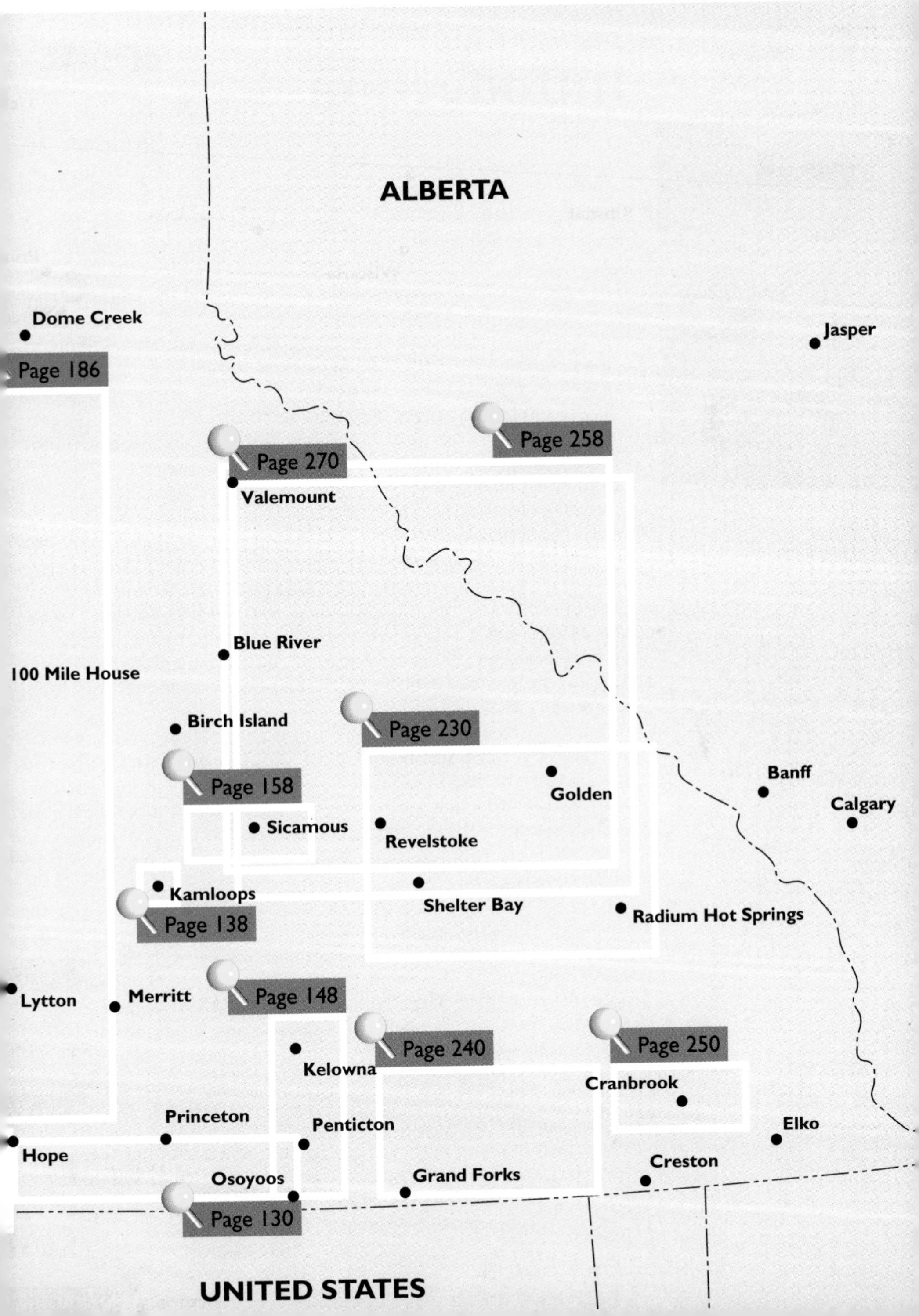

ALBERTA

Dome Creek

Jasper

Page 186

Page 270

Page 258

Valemount

Blue River

100 Mile House

Birch Island

Page 230

Page 158

Golden

Banff

Sicamous

Calgary

Revelstoke

Kamloops

Shelter Bay

Page 138

Radium Hot Springs

Lytton

Merritt

Page 148

Page 240

Page 250

Kelowna

Cranbrook

Princeton

Penticton

Elko

Hope

Osoyoos

Grand Forks

Creston

Page 130

UNITED STATES

Introduction

Above
Fraser River

Even if you've been to British Columbia before, you may have missed the best the province has to offer. If this is your first visit, chances are that you'll still miss some of the most amazing country to be found in North America. BC is simply too big, too grand and too empty to take in at one visit. It's not that the province doesn't try. The provincial tourist authority calls itself Super, Natural British Columbia, trying to convey the immense variety bursting from within its boundaries. But the grand sense of space and discovery that comes from so few people scattered across such an immense territory is also BC's biggest stumbling block. Beyond Vancouver, BC's economic heartland, Victoria, its political capital, and a handful of smaller population centres, the province is almost empty.

British Columbians are justifiably proud of the rolling grasslands of the Chilcotin Plateau stretching westward from Williams Lake, but few have actually *seen* the vast prairies and the occasional rough-hewn fence snaking along the only road for 200km in any direction. The magnificently decaying totem poles that still dot the Queen Charlotte Islands a century after smallpox decimated the population are famous around the globe. But more Americans, Britons, Germans, Italians and Japanese actually visit Gwaii Haanas National Park each year than Canadians.

That's not to deny BC's obvious urban allure. Vancouver is one of the cleanest, most scenic and most walkable big cities in North America, a combination of late 19th-century urban planning and late 20th-century affluence, surrounded by snow-capped mountains and sparkling ocean inlets. Victoria is a classic capital that has adapted to the modern era without sacrificing its grand façades, open views or British style.

BC is schizophrenic. Greenpeace was born of ecological angst in Vancouver, yet both city and province remain heavily dependent on the continuing exploitation of forest, fish and mineral resources that are rapidly disappearing. The sea otters and fur seals that first lured outsiders to the BC coast have been hunted to extinction. Coastal and interior rainforests that once stretched for days in any direction are being systematically reduced to scattered holdings in isolated parklands.

Seemingly endless shoals of silvery salmon that gave coastal and interior First Nation groups the wealth and leisure to produce some of the finest art the world has seen have been reduced to annual trickles by overfishing at sea and clearcutting (the practice of cutting down every tree, leaving the landscape barren) on land. Toxic run-off from mining operations in the Kootenays and other regions that have been closed for three generations continues to poison the land.

The unrelenting and very public battle between preservation and continued exploitation gives BC a sense of tension and endless struggle. Look carefully from viewpoints such as Meadows in the Sky, vast wildflower fields at the top of Mount Revelstoke, and it's easy to believe that nature reigns supreme and serene. Turn your gaze beyond park boundaries and entire mountainsides have been shorn of trees and riven with erosion scars.

It seems a miracle that any sense whatsoever of the natural grandeur of forest, lake and mountains, the isolation and unabashed awe recorded by travellers less than 150 years ago, can still be found. It's more a testament to commercial and political avarice than to any far-sighted policy of preservation.

Early businessmen and politicians contrived to turn immense tracts of crown lands into semi-private playgrounds along railways and roadways and called them National Parks. Banff, Glacier, Jasper and Yoho may have been created for the enjoyment of the rich and the enrichment of the Canadian Pacific Railway, but all have become spiritual and physical refuges for the public.

It's not the first time that private enrichment schemes have backfired. BC's original First Nation inhabitants were systematically deprived of land, liberty and tradition by government policies designed to open the land to White settlers, loggers and miners. But the traditions and peoples that generations of government agents worked so hard to suppress have re-emerged as potent political, economic and cultural forces – fuelled in large part by modern angst over those not-so-long-ago transgressions.

Change has become a permanent part of the BC landscape. The First Nations were overtaken by fur traders and explorers in the 18th century, who were themselves displaced by lumbermen followed by farmers in the 19th century, only to be overtaken by First Nations claims in the 20th century.

Nature continues a tug-of-war, with points won and lost on all sides. The once-mighty Columbia River has long-since been banished into a series of placid lakes behind a series of dams extending south into the United States. At Rogers Pass, railway builders abandoned the surface to unrelenting snowfall and endless avalanches and drove tunnels nearly 400m beneath the inhospitable pass. Faced with similar problems in the Cascades, the Kettle Valley Railway simply gave up and closed.

Whether resource industries simply give up or find new routes in the 21st century remains to be seen. The battle between exhausting natural resources or preserving them for future uses is already straining BC's social and economic fabric. Either way, the outcome will mean the passing of traditional ways of life that someone holds dear. If BC finally breaks with tradition to favour conservation, the awe-inspiring scenery that has been creating legends for the last 100 centuries will still be around for another visit.

Travel facts

Accommodation

Chain hotels and motels provide the most reliable accommodation, while bed and breakfast may be good value outside major cities. Expect to pay $100–200 per night in major cities, $40–100 in smaller towns, single or double occupancy.

Whether you're considering a hotel, motel, bed & breakfast, houseboat, dude ranch (equipped for horse riding), guest ranch, or fishing camp, to book accommodation, contact **Super, Natural British Columbia,** *tel: (800) 435-5622 [800-HELLOBC] or (250) 387-1642; www.hellobc.com* and **Travel Alberta,** *tel: (800) 252-3782 or (780) 427-4321; www1.travelalberta.com.* Both provinces have lodging information and can make bookings. Local tourist offices also have lists of area accommodations.

Prices vary as much as 50 per cent from value season to high season (about mid-May to early September, and winter at ski resorts), when cities and tourism areas are booked out months in advance.

Airports

Most international visitors arrive at Vancouver International Airport (YVR). Calgary International Airport (YYC) provides access to the Rocky Mountain National Parks from Alberta. For flight information and bookings, contact individual airlines, not the airport. Luggage trolleys are free for international arrivals; expect to pay $1–2 at local airports. Major airports have foreign exchange and banking services as well as car hire/rental facilities. Airport Improvement Tax of $5–15 is levied unless passengers have same-day flight connections.

Children

Most attractions offer reduced prices for children (or students). Major hotels and motels can arrange for babysitters, a pricey service. Children stay free in their parents' room with many motel chains.

Picnics offer mealtime flexibility, so does a small cooler filled with cold drinks and snacks. Most towns have roadside restaurants with long hours, cheap children's menus and familiar names.

Climate

Western Canadians are proud of the damp coastal weather that nurtures lush forests and the dramatic climate that transforms the interior with a snowy winter blanket or sizzling summer temperatures. Weather and temperature can vary widely along the coast, fog one hour, drizzle the next, crisp blue sky followed by scudding clouds. Prepare for rain and snow from October to April, and plunging temperatures and heavy snow any month in the Canadian Rockies. Coastal BC climate is moderated by the Pacific Ocean. Victoria and the Gulf Islands are famed as Canadian sun spots, sheltered by Vancouver Island's mountains and Washington's Olympic Mountains.

Currency

Canadian dollars come in denominations of $1 and $2 coins, and $5, $10, $20, $50 and $100 notes (bills). Bills vary in colour, but are the same size. There are 100 cents to the dollar. Coins are: 1 cent (penny), 5 cents (nickel), 10 cents (dime), 25 cents (quarter), 1 dollar (loonie) and 2 dollars (toonie).

The safest forms of money are traveller's cheques and credit or debit cards. Carry at least one, preferably two, major credit cards, such as **American Express, MasterCard (Access)** or **Visa**. Car hire companies, hotels and motels require a credit card or a substantial cash deposit, even if the bill has been prepaid or will be settled in cash. Some shops, motels, restaurants and petrol (gas) stations will accept only cash.

Thomas Cook Bureaux provide full foreign exchange facilities and will change currency and traveller's cheques (free of commission in the case of Thomas Cook Traveller's Cheques). They can also provide emergency assistance in the event of loss or theft of Thomas Cook Traveller's Cheques.

Banks can exchange foreign currency or traveller's cheques, but expect delays at small town branches. Traveller's cheques from well-known issuers such as Thomas Cook are acceptable everywhere. To report Thomas Cook Traveller's Cheque losses and thefts; *tel: (800) 223-7373* (freephone, 24-hour service).

Customs allowances

Visitors to Canada may bring 1.14 litres of spirits, 200 cigarettes, 50 cigars and 200g of loose tobacco. All rules may change. Check limits before travelling. Check with customs officials at home for returning duty-free allowances. Because of taxes, alcohol is cheaper at duty-free shops. Tobacco and perfume are cheaper at supermarkets and department stores than at airport and duty-free shops.

Drinking laws

The minimum drinking age is 19 in British Columbia and 18 in Alberta and it is strictly enforced. Beer, wine and spirits can be purchased in BC-owned Liquor Stores; beer and wine are also available in privately owned beer and wine stores. Look for beer, wine and

Electricity

Canada uses 110 volt, 60 hertz current with two- or three-prong plugs. Power and plug converters are seldom available.

Beware of buying electrical equipment – it probably won't operate on the 220v 50 Hz power the rest of the world uses. Exceptions are battery-operated items such as radios, cameras and portable computers.

Be equally wary of pre-recorded videotapes. Canada uses the NTSC format while most other countries use PAL or SECAM. When buying pre-recorded videos, check the box for compatibility. If no system is listed, it's probably NTSC.

spirits in provincially licensed private Liquor Stores in Alberta. Licensed establishments, bars, lounges, saloons, taverns or pubs may open between 0800 and varying times after midnight.

Laws against drinking and driving are severe and strictly enforced (see Drinking and driving laws, pages 25 and 26).

Eating out

Canadians enjoy eating out as an occasion, a chance for social mixing and to see how the rest of the world lives. Even in casual spots, smart-casual clothing and footwear are required.

Salmon and berry dishes have been part of the Western Canadian diet for generations, and are dependable. Very few things from Canada on any menu are expensive, though imported foodstuffs or exotic game such as caribou will reflect availability and transport costs. Portions are hearty, in keeping with pioneer traditions of serving without stint.

Breakfast often includes rashers of Canadian bacon or sausages with hash browns (shredded fried potatoes), eggs, pancakes and toast. Bagels, fruit or bran muffins, scones or English muffins (crumpets), porridge or cereal are other possibilities. A 'Continental breakfast' is juice, coffee or tea and bread or pastry.

Lunch and dinner menus feature appetisers (starters), salads, soups, pastas, entrées (main courses) and desserts. Salads come at the beginning of the meal. Sunday brunch (usually 1100–1400), self-service buffets piled high with hot and cold dishes, can be good value for hearty eaters. Many fast-food outlets have drive-up windows. Look for A&W, Burger King, KFC (Kentucky Fried Chicken), Little Caesar's, McDonald's, Pizza Hut and Taco Bell.

Coffee and tea are widely available and, except when served at coffee shops or coffee houses in major cities, often weaker than that served in Europe. Iced tea may be sweet; ask if you prefer it plain, without sugar and unflavoured. Plain water is served free of charge upon request.

Entry formalities

US citizens must present photographic identification such as a driving licence, and proof of citizenship such as a birth certificate or a passport. Formal clearance is easier for passport holders. Non-Canadian visitors generally need a passport and may be required to obtain a visa before arrival. Check with the Canadian Embassy or Consulate (and www.cic.gc.ca/english/visit/visas.html) for passport, visa and proof of return travel requirements before departing for Canada.

Canada prohibits revolvers, pistols, fully automatic firearms and other weapons and self-defence sprays such as mace and pepper spray. Firearms such as hunting rifles and shotguns must be declared at entry. Narcotics and certain pharmaceutical products may not be imported. Carry documentation such as a doctor's prescription to prove that medications are legitimate.

Opposite
Victoria Parliament Building

Festivals

Western Canada's events are the mirror of the community, from wine festivals (Okanagan Spring (Apr–May) and Fall (Oct) Wine Festivals) and fruit (Peach Festival, Penticton – Aug), to boating events (Classic Boat Festival, Victoria Inner Harbour – Sept), rodeos (Cloverdale Rodeo – May) and First Nations powwows (Squilax Pow Wow, Squilax, North Shuswap – Jul; Kamloopa Pow Wow, Kamloops – Aug) and sophisticated music, film and theatre festivals in Vancouver (TD Canada Trust Vancouver International Jazz Festival – late Jun–early Jul; Vancouver Folk Music Festival – mid-Jul; HSBC PowerSmart Celebration of Light (fireworks) – late Jul–early Aug; Vancouver International Film Festival – late Sept–early Oct) and Victoria (Shakespeare in the Summer – mid-Jul–mid-Aug; Victoria Fringe Theatre Festival – Aug; Vancouver Island Blues Bash – early Sept).

Food

Rich, delicate salmon is king on any Western Canadian menu, from raw to grilled, broiled, poached, creamed, sauced or doused with Eastern Canada's contribution, maple syrup. Fish is delicious whether farmed or wild. Alberta contributes lean beef and buffalo for meat-eaters; autumn brings caribou, venison and elk (wapiti) to the menu.

The Okanagan Valley's fruitbasket grows peaches, pears, apples, cherries, plums, nectarines, grapes and vegetables, while the Lower Fraser Valley produces berries – blueberries, raspberries, blackberries, gooseberries and huckleberries.

Health

In the event of a life-threatening emergency, telephone 911 for an ambulance. If a life is at stake, treatment will be swift and professional, as government-run health programmes cover everyone. Non-Canadians pay for treatment, and non-emergency care cost is reasonable, though emergency care can be exorbitant. Most travel agents selling international travel offer travel insurance policies covering Canadian medical costs.

Bring prescription medication for the entire trip, plus a few extra days. Carry a copy of the prescription showing the generic (chemical) name and formulation, not just a brand name.

Canada is basically a healthy place. No inoculations are required and common sense is enough to avoid most health problems. Eat sensibly and don't drink water that hasn't come from the tap or a bottle. Most ground water is contaminated with *Giardia lamblia*, which results in a severe bacterial infection of the gut.

Sunglasses, broad-brimmed hats and sunscreen help prevent sunburn, sunstroke and heat prostration. Drink plenty of non-alcoholic liquids, especially in warm weather.

Information

Tourism British Columbia *mailing: PO Box 9830 Stn Prov Govt, Victoria, BC V8W 9W5; business: 1166 Alberni St, Suite 600, Vancouver BC V6E 3Z3; walk-in visitor information centre: Plaza Level, 200 Burrard St, Vancouver, BC V6C 3L6; tel: (800) 435-5622 or (250) 387-1642; www.hellobc.com.* In UK via **Canadian Tourism Commission** *Canada House, Pall Mall East, Trafalgar Square, London SW1Y 5BJ; tel: (020) 7258-6478.*

Travel Alberta *mailing: PO Box 2500, Edmonton, AB T5J 2Z4; walk-in visitor information centre: 999 8th St SW, Suite 760, Calgary, AB T2R 1J5; tel: (800) 252-3782 or (780) 427-4321; www1.travelalberta.com*

Parks Canada for Alberta and British Columbia *Suite 552, 220 4th Ave SE, Calgary, AB T2G 4X3; tel: (800) 748-7275; http://parkscanada.pch.gc.ca.* (Provincial) **BC Parks** *all information through http://wlapwww.gov.bc.ca/bcparks*

Insurance

Travel insurance should cover you, your belongings and your holiday. Buy cover for delayed or cancelled flights, as well as weather problems and medical evacuation.

Language

Canada is officially bi-lingual in English and French; all public signage and documents will be in both languages (see *also* page 282).

Maps

The **Canadian Automobile Association** (CAA) prints useful road maps in conjunction with the **American Automobile Association** (AAA), free to members at CAA offices. The RAC and other automobile clubs have reciprocal agreements with the CAA. **MapArt** *70 Bloor St E, Oshawa, ON L1H 3M2; tel: (905) 436-2525; www.mapart.com,* produce easy-to-use regional and city maps. Detailed, 3-dimensional maps of Rocky Mountain National Parks are designed by **Gem Trek Publishing** *#6, 245 2nd Ave E., Cochrane, AB T4C 2B9; tel: (403) 932-4208 or (877) 688-6277; www.gemtrek.com*

Museums

Most museums charge an entry fee, and are closed one day a week. Rural museums sometimes open only on weekends or in summer.

National and Provincial Parks

National Parks and Historic Heritage Sites charge daily entry fees per person. Camping fees are extra. Save money and purchase the personal **National Parks Pass** ($45), **National Historic Sites** ($35), or both passes in the **Discovery Package** ($59), for entry to 28 parks and 74 historic sites. Fees are less for seniors over 64 years, children 6 to 16, and family groups. **BC Provincial Parks** fees vary, and differ seasonally.

Opening times

Standard office and business hours are 0830/0900–1630/1700 Mon–Fri. Most banks are open Mon–Fri 1000–1600, and Sat mornings. ATMs are open 24 hours. Shops are open Mon–Wed and Sat 0900/1000–1800, and Thur and Fri until 2100. Sun hours are 1100/1200–1700.

Tourist offices outside Vancouver and Victoria have limited hours or may be closed from mid-Sept–mid-May. Petrol (gas) stations are open long hours, but may close between 2200 and 0630. Pub, saloon and restaurant hours vary greatly between areas, but are likely to close earlier in winter. Call churches, synagogues, temples or mosques in advance for services and opening hours.

Packing

Outside a handful of restaurants in the major cities and resorts that require business attire, dress is casual and practical. Take rainwear and at least one change of warm clothing (sweater/pullover and jacket) and sturdy shoes, or consider buying them at one of Canada's fine-quality outdoor outfitters.

Public holidays

The following public holidays are observed in British Columbia and Alberta:

New Year's Day (I Jan);
Alberta Family Day (Mon
    in mid-Feb);
Good Friday (Mar/Apr);
Easter Monday (Mar/Apr);
Victoria Day (Mon on
    or prior to 24 May);
Canada Day (I Jul);
BC Day and Alberta
    Heritage Day (first Mon
    in Aug);
Labour Day
    (first Mon in Sept);
Thanksgiving Day
    (second Mon in Oct);
Remembrance Day
    (II Nov);
Christmas (25 Dec)
    and Boxing Day (26 Dec).

Post offices and government offices close on public holidays.

Dress in layers as temperatures can change dramatically during the day, especially in the mountains and near the ocean. A backpack can be pre-packed or stocked upon arrival with a hat, sunscreen, insect repellent, sunglasses, prescription medicine, contraceptives, an umbrella, raincoat, electricity adaptor, alarm clock and a camera.

Postal services

Every town has at least one **Canada Post/Postes Canada** office, listed in the phone directory blue pages. Most are open Mon–Fri 0900–1700. Hotel concierges, drug stores and tourist shops often sell stamps.

Letters or parcels sent abroad (even to the USA) should go airmail to avoid delays. Domestic letters generally arrive in three to seven days.

Public transport

• **BC Transit** have extensive bus and related systems throughout the province, including Vancouver, *tel: (604) 953-3333; www.translink.bc.ca,* and for Victoria and beyond, *tel: (250) 995-5639; www.transitbc.com*
• **BC Ferries**, *tel: (250) 386-3431* or *(888) 223-3779; www.bcferries.com,* serve Victoria, Vancouver Island, the Gulf Islands and Queen Charlotte Islands, Prince Rupert and Bella Coola, with stops along Inside Passage, and other BC coastal areas.

Reading

• *Backroading Vancouver Island,* by Rosemary Neering, 1996, Whitecap Books, Vancouver.
• *The BC Fact Book,* by Mark Zuehlke, 1995, Whitecap Books, Vancouver.
• *The Big New Beautiful British Columbia BC Travel Guide,* by Bryan McGill et al, 1999, Beautiful British Columbia, Victoria.
• *The Greater Vancouver Book,* by Chuck Davis et al, 1997, the Linkman Press, Surrey, BC.
• *Haida Gwaii: Journeys Through the Queen Charlotte Islands,* by Ian Gill, 2004, Raincoast Books, Vancouver.
• *Handbook of the Canadian Rockies,* by Ben Gadd, 1999, Corax Press, Jasper.
• *Looking at Indian Art of the Northwest Coast,* by Hilary Stewart, 1979, Douglas & McIntyre, Vancouver/Toronto.
• *More English than the English: A Social History of Victoria,* by Terry Reksten, 1986, Orca Book Publishers, Victoria.
• *Native Peoples and Cultures of Canada,* by Alan D McMillan, 1995, Douglas & McIntyre, Vancouver.
• *Native Sites in Western Canada,* by Pat Kramer, 2002, Altitude Publishing Canada Ltd, Canmore, Alberta.
• *Official Guide to Pacific Rim National Park Reserve,* by JM MacFarlane et al, 1996, Blackbird Naturegraphics, Inc, Calgary.

• *Raven Steals the Light,* by Bill Reid and Robert Bringhurst, 1996, Douglas & McIntyre Ltd, Vancouver.
• *Totem Poles,* by Pat Kramer, 2004, Altitude Publishing Canada Ltd, Canmore, Alberta.
• *Touring the Canadian Rockies,* by Fred Gebhart and Maxine Cass, 1998, Thomas Cook Publishing, Peterborough, UK.
• *A Traveller's Guide to Aboriginal BC,* by Cheryl Coull, 1996, Whitecap Books, Vancouver.
• *A Traveller's Guide to Historic British Columbia,* by Rosemary Neering, 2002, Whitecap Books, Vancouver.

• *The West Beyond the West: A History of British Columbia*, by Jean Barman, Revised Edition 1996, University of Toronto Press, Toronto.

Safety and security

• Dial 911 on any telephone for free emergency assistance from police, fire and medical authorities.
• Never discuss travel plans or valuables in public. Walk with assurance in well-lit places and give the impression that you are not worth robbing (eg don't wear expensive jewellery). A wallet in a back pocket or an open handbag is an invitation to theft. Report incidents to local police immediately, and get a report for your insurance company.
• Unwatched luggage can vanish in an instant and is subject to confiscation by authorities. Hotel bell staff may keep guest luggage for a few days, but always get receipts.
• If your car breaks down, turn on the flashing emergency lights, raise the bonnet and wait inside the vehicle. Have your keys out to unlock car doors before entering a car park on foot, and check around and inside the vehicle before entering. Don't pick up hitchhikers and never leave the car with the engine running.
• Lock room doors, windows and sliding glass doors from the inside. Ground-floor rooms are convenient but easier to break into. When leaving the room at night, leave a light on. When someone knocks at the door, use the peephole to see who it is. If someone claims to be on the hotel staff, check with the front desk. Money, cheques, credit cards, passports and keys should be with you or in the hotel safe deposit box. Photocopy the important pages of your passport and visas. Carry the copies and extra passport photos separately from the documents themselves.

Stores

Major department store chains include The Bay Company. Among discount chains are Kmart and Wal-Mart.

Shopping

Food souvenirs include smoked or tinned salmon; local Okanagan Valley wines; dried cherries, berries, and apples; berry conserves and syrups.

Canadian-made clothing and footwear are well made, attractive and practical. Outdoor outfitters and discount stores carry a wide range of goods, many sport-specific. Mountie (RCMP) souvenirs come in wood, on tea towels or as stuffed bears or beavers.

First Nations artwork is usually pricey; ask for the artist's certificate of authentication when you purchase an artefact. Aboriginal peoples produce masks; baskets; stone, wooden and soapstone carvings; jewellery; paintings; and hand-made grey or white Cowichan sweaters.

Sport

Vancouver offers several professional sports: NLL Vancouver Ravens lacrosse; NHL Vancouver Canucks hockey and WHL Vancouver Giants hockey; CFL BC Lions football; USL Vancouver Whitecaps men's and NWL Vancouver Canadians baseball. Playing fields abound throughout British Columbia. Golf, marathons, bicycling, fishing, alpine and Nordic skiing, sailing, windsurfing and the very Canadian sport of curling are popular for individual recreation. Vancouver, Whistler and Victoria are the principal venues for the 2010 Winter Olympics and Paralympic Winter Games, *www.vancouver2010.com/Default.htm*, and visitors will see signs of construction and refurbishment in the southwestern region of the province until then.

Time

Most of British Columbia is on Pacific Standard Time (PST), GMT –8. Alberta and roughly the Rocky Mountain section of BC are on Mountain Standard Time (MST), GMT –7. Both provinces jump ahead to Daylight Time (PDT) GMT –7/(MDT) GMT –6, from the first Sunday in April until the last Sunday in October.

Tipping

Tipping is standard except in the very rare restaurant where a service charge is added. Servers expect 15 per cent of the food and drink charge; bartenders at least 50¢ per drink.

Hotel porters get $1 per bag and the bellperson who shows you your room several dollars more. Expect to pay $1–5 for valet parking each time your car is delivered. Don't tip ushers in cinemas, theatres and similar establishments.

Toilets

Canadians know them as washrooms. Restrooms, bathrooms and toilet are terms imported from the USA. Men and Women are also common designations. Ultra-trendy bars, parks and recreational areas may have unisex washrooms.

Taxes

British Columbia's provincial sales tax is 7.5 per cent; Alberta has none. Most services are subject to a Canadian Goods and Services Tax, or GST, of 7 per cent, though purchases of goods, including accommodation, of over $50 per transaction can have the GST rebated upon application to *Revenue Canada Visitor Rebate Programme, Summerside Tax Centre, Canada Customs and Revenue Agency, Suite 104, 275 Pope Rd, Summerside, PE C1N 6C6; tel: (800) 668-4748 or (902) 432-5608*. Both provinces charge a room tax.

Telephones

Public telephones (pay phones) are marked by a white telephone on a blue background. Dialling instructions are posted on the telephone or in the telephone directory white pages. Local calls cost 50¢; toll-free (800, 877 and 888 area codes) and 911 (emergency) calls are free. To talk to an operator, dial 0. To locate local numbers, dial 411. For long-distance information, dial 1 + area code + 555-1212. There is a charge for all information calls.

Talking Super Pages, *tel: (local area code) 299-9000*, has information on entertainment, attractions and shopping.

Many hotels and motels add steep surcharges to phone calls, even calling toll-free numbers from rooms; use a pay phone in the lobby. Prepaid phone cards are widely available, and maybe a bargain.

For international enquiries or assistance, dial 00. For international calls, dial 011 (access code) + country code + city code (omit the first zero if there is one) + local number.

Travellers with disabilities

While Federal and provincial laws require that public business and services be readily accessible by handicapped persons, not all are. For specific information, contact **SATH** (Society for Accessible Travel & Hospitality), *347 5th Ave, Suite 610, New York, NY 10016; tel: (212) 447-7284; www.sath.org*. RADAR, *12 City Forum, 250 City Rd, London EC1V 8AF; tel: (020) 7250-3222; www.radar.org.uk*, publishes a useful annual guide, *Holidays and Travel Abroad*, with details of facilities abroad.

Wheelchair accessibility information is free from the **Canadian Paraplegic Association** *780 SW Marine Dr, Vancouver, BC V6P 5Y7; tel: (800) 720-4933 or (877) 324-3611; #305, 11010–101 St, Edmonton, AB T5H 4B9; tel: (780) 424-6312; www.canparaplegic.org*. **Access Canada** (criteria: *www. tourismvictoria.com/content/EN/1155.asp*) certifies agility, mobility, vision and hearing-impaired, disabled-designated accommodations, and senior need, Canada-wide. SPARC *201-221 E. 10th Ave, Vancouver BC, V5T 4V3; tel: (604) 718-7733; www.sparc.bc.ca/parkingpermit/index.html*, provide disabled parking permits on a province-wide basis.

Driver's guide

Automobile Clubs

There are no reciprocal agreements between the AA and RAC, and the equivalent CAA in Canada. You should ensure that you purchase sufficient insurance when you hire a car.

Autoroutes

The Coquihalla Highway between Hope and Kamloops is BC's only toll road, with a standard $10 toll for a car or RV. The tollbooth accepts some credit cards as well as cash.

Accidents

Legally, you must STOP if involved in a collision or accident and call the local police or Royal Canadian Mounted Police (RCMP). For most areas in BC, the emergency number is 911 to alert the police or emergency medical services. You can also dial 0 to be directed to the authorities. Emergency service numbers are listed inside the phone directory front cover. Call your own insurance company and, if in a hired car, your car rental company. Collisions in BC resulting in death, injury or property damage apparently exceeding $1000 are the responsibility of the driver, who is personally responsible for alerting police and, within 24–48 hours depending on the jurisdiction, the Insurance Corporation of British Columbia (ICBC): *tel: (800) 910-4222 or (604) 520-8222; www.icbc.com*. ICBC, whose offices are listed in the telephone directory, is the province's issuer of driving licences as well as the provider of accident insurance. If you are involved in an accident, British Columbia and Alberta require you to produce your driving licence, vehicle licence number, vehicle registration number, insurance carrier and cover policy number along with your contact information to police and other parties to the incident. Exchange your information with the other driver(s) and get the names and contact information of any witnesses. Note as many details as you can, such as the time, location and weather. Photographs can be helpful later. You should remain at the accident site until police arrive and the law requires you to render all reasonable assistance. Pull over to the side of the roadway if possible and set out emergency triangles to warn other drivers.

Right
Kabuki Kabs, Victoria

Documents

Your home-country driving licence is valid in British Columbia and Alberta. You should always carry it while driving and have your picture identification with you at all times.

The vehicle registration, proof of liability and collision insurance coverage, with any rental car contract, must be in the car and accessible at all times.

The minimum driving age is 16 in British Columbia and 18 years of age in Alberta. Provisional licences are not valid. Car rental companies require that all drivers be at least age 25.

Drinking and Driving

Driving while impaired (DWI), often called DUI (driving under the influence of alcohol or drugs) is illegal. The criminal blood alcohol limit is .08 mg. Strict enforcement permits a breath sample to be taken by a police officer; a blood sample may be required later. Police and the RCMP establish random checkpoints and may be particularly attentive near winery tasting rooms and entertainment venues. Penalties include fines and imprisonment.

If your vehicle collides with a parked vehicle, leave a note with your name, address, licence plate number and insurance information securely affixed to the other vehicle. For a collision with an animal – 10 per cent of all BC accidents are with animals – do not try to move it but call the nearest humane society or authorities.

Breakdowns

If you have a breakdown, stop your vehicle on the hard shoulder, getting it as far to the right as possible. On ordinary roads, consider using the verge but beware of roadside ditches. Turn hazard lights on and raise the bonnet. If it's dark or visibility is limited, place flares and reflective warning triangles where they can be seen by other drivers. (Remember, it can be very dangerous to walk on the hard shoulder of any freeway or highway.) Place an SOS note on the windscreen. You and your passengers may be safer out of the vehicle and well up the verge away from the traffic, but for security, stay in the locked car if you are in an isolated area, it is night-time, or it is hard to see for any reason.

You may call for a breakdown lorry, called a tow truck, usually dispatched from a local petrol (gas) station. Breakdown insurance is strongly recommended and one phone call is all it takes to hand the whole problem over to an operator who is expert in sorting things out. Your insurance company may call a towing service it has under contract for emergency roadside assistance repairs or towing to a repair garage. You are responsible for payment or for signing the form that affirms to your insurance company that you have had the service. Most car-hire companies either pay for repairs directly or reimburse the cost shown on repair receipts. If a hire car is going to be out of service for more than a few hours, ask the hire company for a replacement vehicle.

Caravans and camper vans (Trailers and RVs)

Recreational vehicles or RVs, often called motorhomes, are a popular way to travel in Western Canada, though hire companies restrict access to some highways and may limit cross-border travel to the USA. Hire options include a choice of daily kilometre limits and seasons; high season is Jul–Aug.

The higher cost of renting and operating an RV is offset by savings on accommodation and meals, and the convenience of not packing and unpacking at each stop.

Maintenance takes time and attention away from touring. Check the vehicle inside and out for its condition. Get operating manuals and a full demonstration for all systems before leaving with a hired RV. Buy a pair of sturdy rubber gloves to handle emptying the waste holding tanks and wear old clothes for the task. For sanitary and

Essentials

You should travel with three red, reflective warning triangles, road flares, a torch, a first aid kit and a jack for tyre repair. If the vehicle has a spare tyre, make sure that it is properly inflated. Have chains for snow season travel.

Fines

Drivers can be fined for moving violations like speeding, illegal turns or other infractions, for parking violations, and for DWI, driving while impaired under the influence of alcohol or illegal drugs. Police authorities will issue a citation, often called a ticket, on the spot. The citation specifies the police authority, jurisdiction (city, town), legal code reference number, a short description of the violation, the vehicle reference, the police officer's identification, your information if it is a moving violation, and where and how the ticket can be paid or challenged.

On-the-spot fine payments are *never* made, and anyone offering to pay a fine when cited may be assumed to be offering a bribe to a police officer, an extremely serious offence.

Citations are registered in a computer database by car licence that is linked to the vehicle identification number. The car or RV rental company will be notified of any citations issued to its vehicles.

environmental reasons, sewage system disposal must be done at authorised dump stations.

The size of an RV or trailer cannot exceed 12.5 metres (41 feet) in length. These vehicles drive more like lorries than cars and are generally treated as lorries by traffic laws. They are blown about more by the wind than cars and are more subject to rollover and drift. Taller and wider dimensions can create hazards at gas stations, tollbooths, parkades and with low-hanging trees and signs. On BC Ferries, the cost of passage for RVs is based on vehicle length.

Woodall's (*www.woodalls.com*) is a fine reference for 14,000 camping spots in North America; the Canada listings are also in *Woodall's Canadian Campground Guide*. There are private RV parks and camping in some National Parks and BC (provincial) Parks during the summer, generally Apr to Sept. To book a BC Parks camping pitch, *tel: (800) 689-9025; www.discovercamping.ca*. Travel Alberta handles camping information requests; *www1.travelalberta.com/content/camping*.

Wherever you park along the side of a road or on city streets, the vehicle must always be pulled off the roadway and should only be parked in a safe, well-lit place in view of passers-by. Always lock the vehicle. Canada's wonderful outdoors presents the challenge of bears searching for easy food supplies. Observe all provincial and park recommendations for storing and carrying food to avoid temptation for the bear and an unpleasant confrontation.

Driving in British Columbia and Alberta

Major roads across Canada are superbly maintained and most signs are in both in English and French, with distances in kilometres. The greatest challenge, other than winter driving, is that pedestrians always have the right-of-way at zebra crossings (crosswalks) and intersections.

Away from the coast in winter, blowing snow can reduce visibility to zero and snow, ice and wet roadways slow or halt traffic for hours. Highways require mandatory use of chains (traction devices) between 1 Nov and 30 Apr and the speed limit lowers to 40–50kph. It's wise to keep the petrol (gas) tank at least half full at all times. Carry extra water, food, warm clothing and a torch if driving in winter or marginal weather conditions outside of urban areas. Useful snow country equipment includes an ice scraper and small shovel. Parked cars should be equipped with a front engine compartment plug, plugged into an electrical source and the engine block heater turned on when temperatures fall to –10°C.

The green sign with a white maple leaf marks the Trans-Canada Highway (Highway 1) that runs 7821km from Victoria on Vancouver Island to Kamloops, Golden, Banff National Park, Calgary, and on to St John's, Newfoundland in the east. The Yellowhead Highway, with its road sign of a silhouette of the Iroquois fur trapper, Tête Jaune (Yellow Head), is a northern alternative to some of the Trans-Canada

Lights

Headlights must be on at all times. Driving only with parking lights is illegal.

Mobile phones

Mobile or cell(ular) phone use while driving is not illegal, but a hands-free device is recommended over one that requires dialling and distracts attention from the road. A cell phone can be useful to call 911 in an emergency or for breakdown assistance.

Road information

British Columbia Ministry of Transport and Highways InfoLine; *tel: (900) 451-4997 (75 cents);* *www.bchighway.com/report/,* and in Alberta, on the Internet, *www.tu.gov.ab.ca/Roads/RoadConditions.asp,* has road condition information. Local radio stations also broadcast weather and driving information. In urban areas, most stations have regular traffic reports during morning and evening rush hours.

Government of Canada Weather Information numbers are in the telephone directory blue pages. Check weather online for British Columbia at *http://weatheroffice.ec.gc.ca/forecast/textforecast_e.html#BC* and for Alberta at *http://weatheroffice.ec.gc.ca/forecast/textforecast_e.html#AB*

Highway. The Yellowhead (Highway 16) leaves Highway 1 west of Winnipeg, and is the main route through Edmonton, Jasper, Prince George and ends at Prince Rupert. Highway 3, the Crowsnest Highway, is marked with a black crow on a white signpost and crosses the BC–Alberta boundary in the south. The Icefields Parkway, with hanging and walk-on glaciers, alpine lakes, waterfalls and river vistas between Lake Louise and Jasper, is one of Canada's most scenic drives. Vancouver, Whistler and Victoria are the principal venues for the 2010 Winter Olympics and Paralympic Winter Games and drivers will encounter road construction on the Sea-to-Sky Highway between Horseshoe Bay (Vancouver) and Whistler up till 2009.

Driving rules

Traffic drives on the right in Canada. Car headlights must be on at all times while driving, even in daylight. Horns are seldom used.

When cars arrive at an intersection at nearly the same moment, the vehicle to the right proceeds first. Unless otherwise posted, a vehicle can turn right from the right-hand lane after a full stop. Before turning, drivers should, but don't always, signal the direction of the intended turn. Buses stopping at the right side of the road and pulling out into traffic proceed first, and bicycles, like pedestrians, should generally be yielded the right of way. Roadways are marked with a solid white line for 'do not pass', and with a broken line on the side where vehicles may pass. In mountainous areas, curves are not infrequent, dictating slower speeds and no passing. Oncoming traffic on narrow roads is required to let the uphill driver proceed. If stuck in mud or snow, gently rock the vehicle by changing from forward to reverse gears. Beware of agricultural vehicles moving more slowly than regular traffic, which will be marked with a reflector, but may scatter hay or splash snow or slush across the windscreen. Stop when a school bus lowers its red and white STOP sign or flashes its lights – and do not pass.

Fuel

Petrol (gas, gasoline) and diesel are sold at gas stations in litres. For drivers from the USA, who are used to gas sold in US gallons (3.78 litres), pump prices may be bewildering. There are several major gas companies, but prices vary only minimally, and can be higher outside of cities and major towns. Most vehicles take unleaded petrol that comes in regular, premium, and super grades. Buy regular unless the car hire company or vehicle operations manual specifies otherwise. Most stations are self-service although some offer a high-priced, full-service alternative. Pump prices include all taxes. Cash and credit cards are accepted, though for safety, most stations will not accept bills over $20. Try to keep the tank at least half-full at all times and fill up in the daytime when you can be sure stations are open.

Seat belts

The driver and all passengers must wear seat belts. A child under the age of 6 must ride in a British Columbia Motor Vehicle Act-compliant child safety restraint that has a CMVSS National Safety label as complying with Canadian Vehicle Motor Safety Standards. Infants up to 9kg must be in a rear-facing restraint seat. Toddlers from 9kg to 18kg must have a child restraint with an adult seat belt and top tether strap. Safety seats can be hired with the car or purchased for under $100 at a discount store. In an RV, passengers riding behind the driver's seat need not wear belts, but should be safely seated when the vehicle is in motion.

Information

Both Tourism British Columbia and Travel Alberta and their Visitor InfoCentres provide fine free provincial maps. The six Canadian Rockies National Parks have maps and visitor information in *The Mountain Guide*, a free brochure that is available at the parks or online at *www.pc.gc.ca/docs/v-g/guidem-mguide/index_E.asp*. Auto club maps are useful for specific areas and many area or district chambers of commerce have local maps.

Parking

Parking garages, parking lots and parkades (car parks) are indicated by a white P on a blue background. Prices are posted at the entrance and some urban parkades accept credit cards. Kerbside parking is usually limited, either by posted signs or by coin-operated parking meters, where the per-hour rate may be higher than in lots and parkades.

Kerbs may be colour-coded: red is no stopping or parking at any time; white is for passenger loading/unloading only; green is limited time parking (usually 10 minutes); yellow is a commercial loading zone; blue is special permit handicapped parking. Parking is not permitted within 5 metres of a fire hydrant; near a disabled kerb ramp; at bus stops, intersections or zebra crossings (crosswalks); blocking a driveway; on pavements (sidewalks), or on highways.

Security

Lock the vehicle when you're inside as well as when you leave it. Always park in well-lit areas at night, in the open and within view of passers-by. Check for intruders before getting in your vehicle at night – and an RV anytime. Never leave the engine running when the driver is not behind the wheel. The RCMP can always render assistance. Should you have the misfortune to become a victim of crime, your insurers will require you to report the circumstances to the police and obtain a police report that you have done so.

Speed limits

The highway speed limit is 80–100kph for cars, posted less for trucks and RVs. Slow down in towns and cities, where the speed limit is 50kph or lower. If driving conditions are poor, drivers are required to keep to a safe speed, no matter how slow. Police use radar and aircraft to track, stop and ticket (cite) speeders, but be alert – you could be stopped – even when traffic normally flows at least 10kph above the posted limit.

CANADIAN ROAD SIGNS

Yield (Give Way)

No Entry

Curve (bend)

No Left Turn

No U-turn

Divided highway
(dual carriageway)

Stop sign ahead

Signs unique to the British Columbia area

Logging trucks use
or cross the road

Deer or elk cross
the road

Moose cross
the road

This sign denotes a
severe road condition such
as a turn which requires
drivers to slow down

Freeway sign showing
distance to exit

Rural road destinations
are shown with finger
boards

B.C. Provincial

Trans-Canada
(Highway 1 and
Highway 16)

Thanks to the following website for its kind permission to reproduce the B.C. signs:
www.bchwys.ca

Getting to Vancouver and British Columbia

Unless you already live within driving distance of British Columbia, flying is the most practical way to get there, with rail a close second. **VIA Rail** operates a popular transcontinental railway service to Vancouver and Prince Rupert. Summer schedules are timed for daylight transit through the Rocky Mountains and through the Skeena River Valley to Prince Rupert.

There is also a ferry service from Seattle and other cities in Washington State to Vancouver and Victoria, as well as a rail service from the US via **AMTRAK**.

Motor coach travel is possible, though slow and cramped. Air travel is even more cramped, but travel time is counted in hours rather than days.

If your primary interest is the Rocky Mountains, consider flying into Calgary, Alberta, rather than Vancouver. Banff is two hours by car from Calgary compared to 12 to 14 hours of driving from Vancouver via Hwy 1, the TransCanada Highway. If you *are* driving from Vancouver, consider overnighting in Revelstoke, about halfway to Banff National Park.

No matter where you're flying into, don't let airline flight schedules mislead you into a full first day of touring. Vancouver may be only 10–12 air hours from much of Europe or Asia, but jet lag intensifies the effects of long distance air travel. Expect to arrive fatigued, disoriented, short-tempered and otherwise *not* ready to drive.

Night-time flights are attractive because they seem to offer an extra day of sightseeing upon arrival. Resist the temptation. Most travellers do better by timing their flights to arrive in the late afternoon or early evening, then getting a good night's sleep before tackling the sights. Since many airport-area hotels and motels offer a free shuttle service to and from the airport, you can take a shuttle to the hotel, sleep off the flight, shuttle back to the airport the next morning and pick up the rental car at no additional cost.

One of the best 'cures' for jet lag is simply spending lots of time in the outdoors and letting the sun help you

adjust to the new time zone. Drinking lots of water during the flight and going easy on the alcohol also help.

Many fly-drive programmes offer what looks like an easy first-day drive, ie Vancouver International Airport to Whistler, north of Vancouver. It's a two-hour jaunt that can stretch to half a day in weekend or holiday traffic. Better to spend the first night in an airport-area hotel and hit the road refreshed in the morning – especially if you're not accustomed to urban traffic or driving on the right side of the road.

The reverse is equally true. Don't plan a tight schedule that gets you into Vancouver or Calgary and on to the airport the requisite two or more hours before an international departure. Unexpected traffic can leave you stranded on a freeway as your plane takes off overhead. Allow a safety margin by spending your last night in Canada near the departure airport, or at least in the same city, and plan extra time to clear airport security.

Try to arrive with a few dollars in Canadian currency and coins. Luggage trolleys are free in the international arrivals area but must be paid for in some domestic airports. Some trolley stands accept credit cards, usually Visa or Access/MasterCard, but other stands require cash – and currency exchange facilities are located outside the arrivals area.

ATMs, automated teller machines, offer the best currency exchange rates and never close. Star and Cirrus are the most common international ATM networks, but check with your card issuer before leaving home to ensure that you have the proper four-digit PIN (personal identification number) for Canadian outlets. International airports have currency exchange facilities in the international terminal that are open long hours. Domestic terminals and smaller airports generally have no exchange facilities. US dollar and pound sterling traveller's cheques from Thomas Cook and other major issuers are accepted almost everywhere, but traveller's cheques in other currencies must generally be cashed at a bank. Eurocheques and personal cheques drawn on banks outside Canada are generally not accepted.

Canadian airports don't have duty-free shopping for incoming travellers, but it's no great loss. Prices for alcohol and other duty-free items are almost always lower in Liquor Stores, supermarkets and discount stores than in duty-free shops.

Some car-hire companies have cars at Vancouver Airport itself (in a car park just outside International Arrivals), others require that you take a coach to an off-airport facility to pick up your hire car – be sure to ask when making your car reservation.

If hiring an RV, ask the hire company about airport pick-up and drop-off when making your booking. Most hire companies provide free transport to and from their offices, which are usually located some distance from the airport.

Setting the scene

The land

British Columbia. It was named in the 19th century for a river, the Columbia, itself named for an 18th-century American ship that took its name from a 15th-century Italian, Christopher Columbus, who never came anywhere near his 21st-century namesake.

Like its name, BC is a hodge-podge of geography: massive glaciers and bone-dry deserts; rich alluvial plains and sheer granite canyons. Home to one of the greatest cities in North America, BC also lays claim to some of the least developed and least populated land on the continent. It's also a latecomer to the travel scene.

Above
Whistler Mountain

Early explorers

A Chinese manuscript tells of a storm-whipped voyage eastward to a land of enormous trees and red-skinned people around 220 BC, but landfall could have been among the towering redwood forests of Northern California and Oregon as easily as the red cedar and Sitka spruce stands of British Columbia. Chinese and Japanese shipwrecks along the North American coast have been dated as early as the 5th century AD, matching Asian ceramics found up and down the length of the Columbia River. Sir Francis Drake *may* have visited Vancouver Island in 1579 on his voyage to plunder Spanish possessions around the world, but any sure evidence was lost when Drake's logbook burned in an Admiralty fire.

That leaves Juan de Fuca, a Greek sailing for Spain in 1592, as the first outsider to visit BC officially. De Fuca gave his name to the strait between Vancouver Island and Washington State, due south, but neither the First Nations who lived there nor the Europeans who read of them much noticed or cared – possibly because stormy weather prevented de Fuca from landing and seeing BC first hand. It wasn't until Danish captain Vitus Bering sailed east from Russia in the early 1700s that Europe began to pay serious attention to the northwest edge of North America.

What Bering found were enormous populations of sea otters, much prized by merchants in China for their rich, silky fur. Russian hunters and merchants flocked to Alaska to trade with local Native groups for otter pelts. This sparked a race for commerce that brought Spanish, English and American traders to the coast.

Spain got there first. Juan Perez arrived from Mexico in 1774, claiming the Queen Charlotte Islands and Nootka Sound, on the western coast of Vancouver Island. Bruno de Heceta and Juan Francisco de la Bodega y Quadra sailed north in 1775, a trip most notable for what didn't happen. Heceta noted, but didn't bother to explore, 'the mouth of some great river'. It was the Columbia, the easiest way to reach the interior of British Columbia until the transcontinental railway arrived a century later.

Search for the Northwest Passage

The British had their own commercial and strategic agenda. The Admiralty as well as commercial explorers had been searching for a direct route westward across the Atlantic to Asia for nearly two centuries. Parliament had a standing offer of £20,000 to the person who discovered a northern sea route to China and Asian lands south. Innumerable navigators had failed to find the Northwest Passage from the Atlantic side, so Captain James Cook went looking for the Pacific Ocean end of the fabled passage.

The fur trade

Cook never found the passage east, but he did find safe anchorage at Nootka Sound, then controlled by Spain. His officers and men traded with the Mowachat First Nation to obtain sea otter pelts for clothing and bedding against the coming winter.

Cook eventually sailed south for Hawaii, where he was killed in 1779. Charles Clark, the expedition's second-in-command, headed for home by way of Macao. When Macanese merchants discovered the well-worn otter skins, they paid such astronomical prices that the crew threatened to mutiny if they didn't return to Nootka Sound. Clark put down the rebellion and sailed for home, where news of the voyage set off a fur rush. Ships from Boston and New York joined the fray once America's war for independence from Britain ended in 1783. The crush of traders nearly led to war between Britain and Spain, but cooler, more commercial minds prevailed. Both countries mounted expeditions to map the Northwest coast in preparation for diplomatic talks.

Spain sent Bodega y Quadra; Britain sent George Vancouver, who had sailed to Vancouver Island as midshipman under Cook. America wasn't part of the talks, but legal technicalities weren't enough to keep trader Robert Gray away. It was Gray who found and charted the mouth of the Columbia River in 1792, establishing US claims to the region. Later the same year, British and Spanish authorities signed the Nootka Accord, agreeing that the Northwest Coast should be open to traders of all nations.

The Nootka Accord was the high point of European exploration of BC by sea as war engulfed Europe and over-hunting destroyed the otter trade. Spain eventually traded its claims to the Pacific Northwest to America in return for Washington's recognition of Spanish title to California.

As far as Britain was concerned, all the important activity in Western Canada took place on land. British traders had been trading for furs across Eastern Canada for 200 years. In 1670, the Hudson's Bay Company (HBC) had wrangled rights to everything west from

Hudson Bay, a vast, unknown territory called Rupert's Land. Anthony Henday paddled up the North Saskatchewan River from Hudson Bay in 1754 and became the first known White to glimpse Canada's Rocky Mountains. He returned the next spring, canoes nearly swamped under the weight of furs, and set off an overland rush. Competitors followed, including a French-Canadian consortium, the North West Company (NWC) and numerous American companies. The race to find a way through BC to the Pacific Ocean was on.

North West Company partners Alexander Mackenzie, Simon Fraser and David Thompson grabbed an early lead. Mackenzie made his way west to the mouth of the Bella Coola River in 1793, the first White to cross the continent north of Mexico. He returned with tales of a land so filled with wild animals that it looked like a 'stall-yard'.

Americans Meriwether Lewis and William Clark explored west from American territory, reaching the mouth of the Columbia River before returning home in 1806. Fraser battled through treacherous rapids along the Fraser River to the Pacific in 1808. Thompson paddled the entire length of the Columbia in 1811, but reached the Pacific Ocean four months late. He arrived to find American traders who had sailed around Cape Horn building a fort at modern day Astoria.

American presence
That initial American presence seemed of no great import. The NWC peacefully took over Astoria when war broke out between the US and Britain in 1812. When the war ended, the 49th Parallel divided the United States and British America east of the Rockies, and the two countries jointly occupied the unmapped West. When the HBC took control of the NWC in 1821, Britain emerged triumphant with the only economic force that spanned the continent. But British power existed only on paper. On the ground, the West was beyond control.

The Americans, however, were getting restless. In 1825, Britain and the US both recognised Russian authority south to 54°40', the current boundary between Southern Alaska and Northern BC. Americans began talking of 'Manifest Destiny', the idea that they were empowered by divine right to occupy the continent from ocean to ocean. Missionaries who were moving westward to 'civilise the savages' began sending back enticing reports of rich farmland beyond the Rocky Mountains.

The HBC was just as busy, building and strengthening forts at Spokane, Okanagan, Nisqually, Langley and elsewhere to block American expansion. Company farms along the Columbia River and Puget Sound in what is now Oregon and Washington fed both inland forts and a growing export trade to Alaska, Hawaii and Asia. HBC's chief factor, Dr John McLoughlin, systematically directed American immigrants south into present-day Oregon, hoping to retain the Columbia River, the only practical route into British Columbia, the company's most profitable territory.

Opposite
Totem pole, Stanley Park,
Vancouver Island

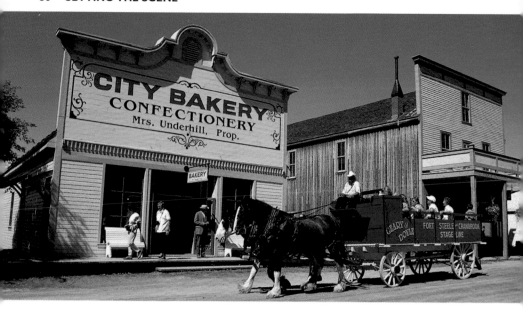

Above
Fort Steele Heritage Town

But the HBC also hedged their position. In 1841, company governor George Simpson and head trader James Douglass moved to Fort Victoria, on the southern tip of Vancouver Island. It was a foresightful move.

US Army surveyors were already mapping a wagon route westward over the Rocky Mountains by way of passes far lower and easier than any in British America. The US Navy paid a 'goodwill' visit to the Pacific Northwest, updating its charts from the Columbia River region north to Vancouver Island and noting the HBC's lack of coastal defences. In 1843, America moved.

The US Senate officially declared Oregon Territory, an enormous tract west of the Rockies, north of California and south of Alaska, to be American. Americans were told it was their patriotic duty and God-given destiny to move west. More importantly, they were given an irresistible lure: 260 hectares for every White US male and 130 hectares for his wife, free for the taking.

Fortunately for Britain, the initial settlers headed south into the Willamette River Valley, south of the Columbia River. But US–British tensions heightened in 1844 when James Polk won the presidential election on the slogan of '54°40' or Fight!', challenging Britain for control north in the West. Since neither country was anxious for a third war, diplomats simply extended the existing boundary, the 49th Parallel, to the Pacific Ocean, then west down the middle of the Strait of Juan de Fuca between Vancouver Island and Washington State.

The HBC lost the Columbia River, the only viable route from interior BC to the coast. Furs from the interior began moving eastward over the Yellowhead Pass, through the Northern Rockies and downriver through Alberta. In coastal areas, the company turned to commerce and farming.

Britain leased all of Vancouver Island to the HBC in 1849 in order to create a colony. Just months later, the Gold Rush in California sent demand for grain, timber, coal and every sort of manufactured product through the roof. Successive gold strikes in Oregon and Washington kept farming and lumbering busy even as a new Royal Navy station at Esquimalt, next to Victoria, boosted coal mining at Nanaimo. Demand for salmon kept salteries, and later canneries, busy.

Settlers, however, were in short supply. Would-be immigrants headed for Oregon and Washington in the western US, where land was less expensive and easier to get to. Until the Canadian Pacific Railway arrived in 1886, the only practicable route to BC was a brutal five-month voyage around the tip of South America. Victoria remained a prosperous but tiny town surrounded by vast forests. Gold changed history, just as it had done in California, Oregon and Washington.

The Gold Rush

HBC traders had been accepting occasional amounts of the precious metal from their First Nation trading partners for years, but the company had never revealed its discoveries, fearing further encroachment by American interests. Faced with growing piles of the stuff in Victoria vaults and rumours of gold finds on the Fraser River starting to circulate, the HBC decided to act. After enacting strict mining licence laws and laying in supplies, the company sent 20kg of raw gold to the nearest mint, San Francisco, early in 1858. The next summer, more than 30,000 miners flooded north from America.

HBC made a fortune supplying the Gold Rush. The company was also terrified that America would take control as easily as it had seized California from Mexico in 1846. Although British on the map, both Vancouver Island and New Caledonia, as the mainland was called, were effectively outside all political control.

The fears were warranted. American miners demanded immediate changes to mining regulations and government practices. A special US Commissioner sent to the Fraser River gold fields to look after American interests reported that it was only a matter of time until both Vancouver Island and the mainland became American by force of population alone. Unless, of course, Washington wanted to act sooner.

While the Americans debated, the British acted. In June 1858, the House of Commons declared the mainland a Crown Colony. Queen Victoria chose the name British Columbia and assigned key officials. A provisional government was declared at Fort Langley in November, then moved to New Westminster (now part of Greater Vancouver), a site Royal Engineers judged more defensible against an expected American invasion. Gold Commissioners and magistrates imposed strict order in the mining camps, a startling contrast to the lawlessness and self-rule that predominated in US mining communities of the time.

The new provincial government also adapted a US-style land distribution system, allowing White settlers to buy up to 65 hectares at bargain rates – the entire Lower Fraser River Valley was settled, cleared and planted within nine years. Cattle ranches sprang up across the province as drovers brought herds north from Washington and discovered fine meadows ready for the taking.

Merchants prospered, but every economic downturn prompted new calls for union with America, the land most BC residents had so recently left. Talk of a State of British Columbia increased when America purchased Alaska from Russia in 1867, bolstered by half-hearted attempts by Washington to claim BC as compensation for British support of the (defeated) Confederacy during the US Civil War.

It was an uneasy time, even as continuing gold discoveries opened the Cariboo, the Kootenays and almost every corner in between. BC's political leaders were firmly British, but business lived or died by commercial decisions made in San Francisco, not London markets. Ordinary citizens were either recent American immigrants or Canadian-born with little loyalty to any government beyond the strictly local. Talk of union with America faded after BC voted to join the new Dominion of Canada in 1870, a vote bought by promises of an all-Canadian transcontinental railway and strengthened economic ties east across the Rockies. When the rails finally arrived in 1886, an obscure lumber town called Vancouver was suddenly catapulted to fame and fortune as Western Canada's richest, most successful and most cosmopolitan city.

First Nations
The biggest losers were BC's original First Nations inhabitants. Smallpox and other European disease brought to Mexico by Spanish explorers and conquerors had been steadily moving north and west following long-established trade routes. Epidemics had begun to sweep through mainland tribes about the time Spanish and English traders first appeared off Vancouver Island. With little natural resistance to illnesses from measles and the common cold to smallpox, entire villages were wiped out. Survivors had little chance against government policies and agents intent on clearing land for White settlement. HBC agents commonly purchased tribal lands, but prices were pitiful, a few shirts in return for the entire Nanaimo waterfront, and promises to protect traditional hunting and fishing areas were routinely violated.

Colonial and Dominion officials treated tribes as well as individuals as incompetent imbeciles by policy, regularly confiscating land and resources 'for their own good'. In 1874, a BC/Canadian Indian Reserve Commission began setting aside lands for First Nations groups. The region's original inhabitants ended up with 0.34 per cent of the province. The railways alone were given 8 per cent of BC's most commercially profitable and agriculturally useful land, more than 75,600sq km.

Along the coast, First Nations' potlatches and other traditional practices were outlawed in an effort to destroy traditional culture and

make plague survivors still more dependent upon government. Generations of children were forcibly removed from their families to be raised in church- and government-run residential schools, where the use of Native languages was strictly forbidden and mercilessly punished. Claims for monetary compensation, return of traditional lands and enforcement of long-ignored treaty terms are meeting with a fair degree of success in modern courts.

The railway and the 20th century
The development boom came to an abrupt end with the Panic of 1893. Stock market failures around the world were echoed in bank and railway failures, which brought down businesses and farms dependent upon capital and transportation – which included most of BC. Recovery had to wait for the Yukon Gold Rush of 1898, which brought yet another river of miners north from America. World War I put a damper on growth, but the economy boomed again into the 1920s, as irrigation spread into the Okanagan and other areas thought too dry for successful agriculture. World War II saw the development of the chain saw and other mechanised equipment that allowed the timber industry to leap into a post-war housing boom.

But growth has come neither easily nor quietly. The last patch of virgin forest near Victoria was turned into a wasteland of splintered stumps in the 1970s, sparking furious protests. Plans to expand logging in the Queen Charlotte Islands led to the most massive campaign of civil disobedience in Canadian history – and to the formation of a new national park, Gwaii Haanas, in 1987. Similar efforts in the 1990s to log virgin forests in Clayquot Sound, off the west coast of Vancouver Island, sparked more protests.

Salmon runs, once the mainstay of BC life, have all but disappeared. Overfishing by fleets from the United States, Canada and other Pacific nations is partly to blame, but the despoliation of spawning beds by logging and other human activity is even more destructive.

The not-so-slow decline of resource industries is producing a new economic ethic by reluctant fits and starts. Although clothed in references to Mother Earth and First Nations beliefs, the new model is based in harsh economic choices: resources can be used up, as the sea otter trade, the fur trade, most fisheries, mining and a growing number of timber companies have shown. When the resource is exhausted, the industry dies. Or the resources can be preserved for some less intensive but longer-term use.

Sport fishing, for example, brings more dollars into the local economy than commercial fishing. Recreational use of forests is more profitable in the long run than clearcutting. Mountain climbers, skiers and sightseers spend more money to enjoy an undamaged mountain than mining companies pay to turn it into ore and toxic waste. The outcome of the ongoing battle between resource extraction and resource renewal will shape the face and the psyche of BC in the 21st century.

Above
Thunderbird Totem

Highlights and touring itineraries

Top ten sights

Not the top ten places visitors to BC actually *go* to, but the top ten that we recommend not to miss.

- **Barkerville Historic Town** (*page 188*)
The *real* Cariboo Gold Rush that refused to die.
- **Fort Steele Heritage Town** (*page 253*)
A frontier town that has brought the 1890s vividly back to life.
- **Fraser River Canyon & Hells Gate** (*page 193*)
The toughest terrain you're ever likely to drive.
- **Gwaii Haanas National Park, Queen Charlotte Islands** (*pages 117–8*)
Leave the car behind to see nature on the edge.
- **The Hazeltons – (Old) Hazelton, 'Ksan and Kispiox** (*pages 216–7*)
Where the heart of the First Nations beats most powerfully.
- **The Paint Pots, Kootenay National Park** (*page 261*)
The colours and the setting are magical.
- **Nelson** (*pages 246–7*)
It looks as good in person as it did on the silver screen.
- **Meadows in the Sky, Mount Revelstoke National Park** (*page 235*)
Wildflower carpets that disappear into empty summer skies.
- **Inner Harbour & Thunderbird Park, Victoria** (*pages 69–70*)
Everyone's vision of what BC *should* look like.
- **Takakkaw Falls, Yoho National Park** (*pages 265–6*)
First Nations visitors were as awe-struck as modern travellers.

The best of BC

These three circular tours start and end in Vancouver, but there's no reason not to pick up either of the last two routes from Calgary. Suggested overnight stops are shown in **bold**.

Two weeks

The Great Western BC Marathon. You'll need time at home to recover from this holiday.
Day 1 Arrive in **Vancouver** (*see page 42*).
Day 2 **Vancouver**.
Day 3 BC Ferries to **Victoria** (*see page 62*).
Day 4 The Island Highway to **Campbell River** (*see page 98*).
Day 5 The Island Highway to **Port Hardy** (*see page 101*).
Day 6 BC Ferries' **Discovery Coast** (*see page 106*) route to Bella Coola.
Day 7 Bella Coola over The Hill to **Anahim Lake/Nimpo Lake** (*see pages 198–201*).
Day 8 Hwy 20 to **Riske Creek** (*see page 201*).
Day 9 Hwy 97 to Barkerville, overnight in **Wells** or **Quesnel** (*see page 192*).
Day 10 Hwy 97 to **100 Mile House** (*see page 191*).
Day 11 Hwy 97 to **Cache Creek** (*see page 187*).
Day 12 Hwy 1 through the Fraser River Canyon to Hells Gate and **Hope** (*see page 127*).
Day 13 Hwy 1 to **Vancouver**.
Day 14 Home.

The Great Interior BC Marathon. You'll need a few days to rest up from this one, too.
Day 1 Arrive in **Vancouver** (*see page 42*).
Day 2 Hwy 1 to **Hope** (*see page 127*).
Day 3 Hwy 1 through the Fraser River Canyon and Hells Gate to **Kamloops** (*see page 138*).
Day 4 Hwy 1 through the Shuswap Lakes to **Revelstoke** (*see page 236*).
Day 5 Hwy 1 over Rodgers Pass and Glacier National Park to **Golden** (*see page 232*).
Day 6 Hwy 1 through Yoho National Park to **Lake Louise/Banff/Canmore** (*see pages 271 and 273*).
Day 7 Hwy 93 through Kootenay National Park to **Radium Hot Springs** (*see page 261*).
Day 8 Hwy 95 to Fort Steele Heritage Town

and **Cranbrook** (*see page 250*).

Day 9 Hwy 3/3A to Creston, the Kootenay Lake Ferry and **Nelson** (*see page 246*).

Day 10 Hwy 3A/3 to Castlegar and **Grand Forks** (*see page 243*).

Day 11 Hwy 3/97 to **Penticton** (*see page 153*).

Day 12 Hwy 97/3A/3 to Keremeos, Princeton and **Manning Provincial Park** (*see page 132*).

Day 13 Hwy 3 to Hope and **Vancouver**.

Day 14 Home.

Four weeks
See most of BC in a busy month.

Day 1 Arrive in **Vancouver** (*see page 42*).

Day 2 **Vancouver**.

Day 3 BC Ferries to **Victoria** (*see page 62*).

Day 4 Island Highway to Nanaimo and **Campbell River** (*see page 98*).

Day 5 Island Highway to **Port Hardy** (*see page 101*).

Day 6 BC Ferries to **Prince Rupert** (*see page 206*).

Day 7 BC Ferries/fly to **Skidegate**, Queen Charlotte Islands (*see page 120*).

Day 8 **Gwaii Haanas National Park** (*see page 117*).

Day 9 **Gwaii Haanas National Park** (*see page 117*).

Day 10 BC Ferries/fly to **Prince Rupert** (*see page 206*).

Day 11 Yellowhead Highway (Hwy 16) to the Hazeltons and **Smithers** (*see page 218*).

Day 12 Yellowhead Highway (Hwy 16) to Fort St James and **Prince George** (*see page 222*).

Day 13 Hwy 97 to Barkerville and **Wells/Quesnel** (*see page 192*).

Day 14 Hwy 97/1 to **Kamloops** (*see page 138*).

Day 15 Hwy 1 through the Shuswap Lakes to **Revelstoke** (*see page 236*).

Day 16 Hwy 1 over Rodgers Pass and Glacier National Park to **Golden** (*see page 232*).

Day 17 Hwy 1 through Yoho National Park to **Lake Louise/Banff/Canmore** (*see pages 271 and 273*).

Day 18 Hwy 93 through Kootenay National Park to **Radium Hot Springs** (*see page 261*).

Day 19 Hwy 95 to Fort Steele and **Cranbrook** (*see page 250*).

Day 20 Hwy 3 to **Creston** (*see page 243*).

Day 21 Hwy 3A to the Kootenay Lake Ferry and **Nelson** (*see page 246*).

Day 22 Hwy 3A/3 to Castlegar and **Grand Forks** (*see page 243*).

Day 23 Hwy 3/97 to **Penticton** (*see page 153*).

Day 24 Hwy 97/97C to Kelowna, Meritt, Kamloops and **Cache Creek** (*see page 187*).

Day 25 Hwy 1/99 to Hat Creek and **Lillooet** (*see page 191*).

Day 26 Hwy 12/1 to Lytton, down the Fraser River Canyon to **Hope** (*see page 127*).

Day 27 Hwy 1 to **Vancouver**.

Day 28 Home.

Vancouver

Ratings

Beaches	●●●●●
Food	●●●●●
Outdoor activities	●●●●●
Scenery	●●●●●
Children	●●●●○
History	●●●●○
Museums	●●●●○
First Nations	●●●○○

Canada's third-largest city is a small town at heart. Decades of immigration have given Vancouver more foreign-born citizens than any other North American city, yet it remains an essentially Canadian place. Yes, black is the uniform of the day, and hard-eyed attitude the public posture *du jour*, but Vancouver remains a polite, tidy town where everyone seems to know everyone else and quite prefers it that way. Harbour vistas vie with Sydney, Hong Kong and San Francisco for the world's best, while urban views stand in for big-city streetscapes from Los Angeles to London, Moscow and Shanghai. Cosmopolitan Vancouver works hard to remain an overgrown village on the edge of a vast rainforest. Serious mountains rise within sight of City Hall, while *laissez-faire* beaches are just a quick bus ride away and a young, bustling population is ready to enjoy both at the slightest excuse.

ⓘ **Tourism Vancouver/ Vancouver Tourist InfoCentre** *Plaza Level, 200 Burrard St, Vancouver, BC V6C 3L6; tel: (604) 683-2000; www.tourismvancouver.com. Open daily 0830–1800, with tourist information, bookings for accommodation and sightseeing tours, a partner travel agency for air and cruise ship reservations, and the Tickets Tonight half-price ticket service.*

Visitor Information Centre *Vancouver International Airport international and domestic arrivals level. Open daily 0730–2400.*

Arriving and departing

Most air services use Vancouver International Airport (YVR) (*www.yvr.ca*). Expect to pay an Airport Improvement Fee (AIF) on departure: $5 when travelling within BC and the Yukon; $10 for flights within North America; $15 for flights outside North America. Regional carriers offer a seaplane service from the harbour.

• **VIA Rail** *Pacific Central Station, 1150 Station St; tel: (888) 842-7245 or (604) 640-3741; www.viarail.ca*, provides national rail service.

• **Rocky Mountaineer Vacations** *1755 Cottrell St at Terminal Ave; tel: (604) 606-7245 or (800) 665-7245; www.rockymountaineer.com*, offer rail tours to the Rocky Mountains.

• **Highway access** is Hwy 1 (the TransCanada Hwy) from the east and Hwy 99 from the south and north.

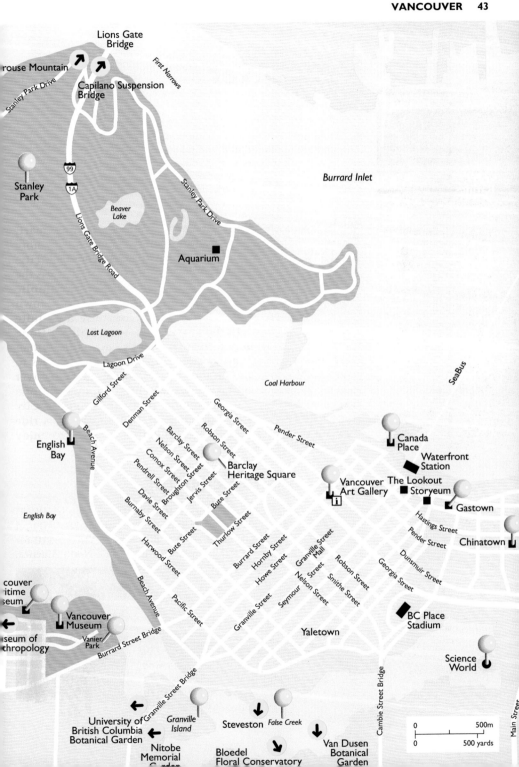

Lions Gate
Bridge

rouse Mountain

First Narrows

Stanley Park Drive

Capilano Suspension
Bridge

99

1A

Stanley
Park

Beaver
Lake

Lions Gate Bridge Road

Stanley Park Drive

Burrard Inlet

Aquarium

Lost Lagoon

Lagoon Drive

Coal Harbour

SeaBus

Gilford Street

Denman Street

Georgia Street

English
Bay

Beach Avenue

Barclay Street

Robson Street

Pender Street

Canada
Place

Waterfront
Station

Nelson Street

Comox Street

Pendrell Street

Broughton Street

Jervis Street

Barclay
Heritage Square

Bute Street

Vancouver
Art Gallery

The Lookout
Storyeum

English Bay

Davie Street

Burnaby Street

Bute Street

Thurlow Street

Gastown

Hastings Street

Pender Street

Chinatown

Harwood Street

Burrard Street

Hornby Street

Howe Street

Granville Street
Mall

Robson Street

Georgia Street

Dunsmuir Street

couver
ritime
seum

Beach Avenue

Pacific Street

Granville Street

Seymour Street

Nelson Street

Smithe Street

BC Place
Stadium

Vancouver
Museum

seum of
thropology

Vanier
Park

Burrard Street Bridge

Yaletown

Science
World

Cambie Street Bridge

Main Street

Granville Street Bridge

University of
British Columbia
Botanical Garden

Granville
Island

Steveston

False Creek

Van Dusen
Botanical
Garden

Nitobe
Memorial

Bloedel
Floral Conservatory

0		500m
0		500 yards

ⓘ **The Georgia Straight**
1770 Burrard St;
tel: (604) 730-7000;
www.straight.com, a free
weekly newspaper, has the
best listing of local events,
cultural attractions,
performances, cinemas and
other happenings.

Tickets Tonight Tourism
Vancouver Tourist Info Centre,
Plaza Level, 200 Burrard St;
tel: (604) 684-2787;
www.ticketstonight.ca; open
Tue–Sat 1000–1800, sells
half-price tickets to
performing arts, cultural
events and sports
throughout Greater
Vancouver on the day of the
event. You can also buy full-
price tickets in advance.

- BC Ferries *tel: (250) 386-3431 or (888) 223-3779; www.bcferries.com*, provide a ferry service from Tsawwassen (south of the city) to Victoria and Horseshoe Bay (northwest of the city) to Nanaimo, both on Vancouver Island.
- **Harbourlynx** *tel: (866) 206-5969 or (604) 688-5465 (Vancouver) or (250) 753-4443; www.harbourlynx.com*, operate a high-speed catamaran foot passenger ferry from the Sea Bus terminal near Canada Place to Nanaimo.

Getting around

Public transport

Translink *tel: (604) 953-3333; www.translink.bc.ca*, is Canada's largest public transport system, a combination of bus, light rail (SkyTrain) and ferry (SeaBus). All major tourist sites in the lower Mainland area are accessible by public transit, though schedules may not be convenient.
Aquabus Ferries *tel: (604) 689-5858; www.aquabus.bc.ca*, and **False Creek Ferries** *tel: (604) 684-7781; www.granvilleislandferries.bc.ca*, provide a ferry service around False Creek from Science World west to the Maritime Museum.

Driving is practical throughout Vancouver, although traffic slows during rush hours (*0730–0930 and 1600–1800*). Left turn lanes are rare and roadways can be narrow, especially in residential areas with kerbside parking. Metered parking is generally available; most car parks accept either coins or credit cards. Watch for cyclists.

Below
Vancouver cityscape

Sights

Barclay Heritage Square *Barclay, Nicola, Haro and Broughton Sts. Open daily.*

Roedde House Museum *$ 1415 Barclay St; tel: (604) 684-7040; www.roeddehouse. org. Open for guided tours.*

Bloedel Floral Conservatory & Queen Elizabeth Park *$ 33rd Ave and Cambie St; tel: (604) 257-8584; www. city.vancouver.bc.ca/parks/ parks/bloedel/index.htm. Open daily 1000–1730.*

Canada Place *Harbourside at the foot of Howe St; www.canadaplace.ca. Open daily.*

Capilano Suspension Bridge *$$ 3735 Capilano Rd, North Vancouver; tel: (604) 985-7474; www. capilanosuspensionbridge. com. Open 0800–dusk in summer, 0900–1700 in winter.*

Chinatown *Gore, Keefer, Carrall and E Hastings Sts.*

Chinese Cultural Centre *$ 50 E Pender St; tel: (604) 658-8850; www.cccvan.com, conducts daily walking tours by advance booking.*

Dr Sun Yat-Sen Classical Chinese Garden *$$ 578 Carrall St; tel: (604) 662-3207; www. vancouverchinesegarden.com. Open daily May–Oct; Tue–Sun Nov–Apr.*

English Bay *West of False Creek, between Stanley Park and Point Grey.*

Barclay Heritage Square*

Vancouver's most elegant heritage area preserves nine of the city's few remaining Victorian-era (1890–1908) homes. Most are closed to the public, but the **Roedde House****, built in 1893, has become a period museum. All nine homes are surrounded by spectacular period gardens.

Bloedel Floral Conservatory*

Perched atop Vancouver's highest hill in **Queen Elizabeth Park****, the silvery tridetic dome of Bloedel houses the city's largest tropical plant collection and 100 species of free-flying birds. A courtyard behind Bloedel is popular for *tai chi* and similar exercise activities morning and evening. Queen Elizabeth Park, 53 landscaped and wooded hectares, including a quarry next to Bloedel, has become a stunning sunken garden. Walking trails offer broad vistas of Vancouver, the harbour and the mountains beyond.

Canada Place***

The sail-like, white roofline of Canada Place marks Vancouver's cruise ship terminal, convention centre hotel and CNIMAX cinema. Look for two or three cruise ships at dock during the May–September Alaska cruise season, and vast vistas across Burrard Inlet all year.

Capilano Suspension Bridge***

This 140-m footbridge sways 70m above the Capilano River canyon to a shady forest park on the far side. The original bridge opened in 1889, creating the first tourist attraction on what was then the deserted North Shore of Burrard Inlet. Today's bridge is laced with steel cables that can carry the weight of several fully loaded Boeing 747 passenger planes, but the swaying, bouncing span feels more like a thrill ride when the spring melt turns the river below into a thundering torrent. **Treetops Adventure** is an hour's walk at the rainforest mid-storey along 250m of cable suspension bridges, suspended between eight Douglas fir trees.

Chinatown**

Vancouver's Chinatown is the third-largest Chinese community in North America after San Francisco and New York. What began as a refuge against periodic persecution has become a wealthy community infused by massive immigration from across Asia. Vegetables, fruits, fish and other goods spill from shops on to pavements that are jammed with shoppers all day. **Dr Sun Yat-Sen Classical Chinese Garden*****, the first classical Chinese garden built outside China, is an island of tranquillity.

English Bay***

The protected waters of English Bay, Captain James Vancouver's anchorage in 1792, are popular for kayaking and sailing. The

False Creek *East beneath the Burrard Bridge, past Granville Island to Science World.*

Gastown *Water St, between Columbia and E Cordova Sts; www.gastown.org*

Storyeum $$$ *142 Water St, Gastown; tel: (800) 687-8142 or (604) 687-8142; www.storyeum.ca. Open daily 0830–1900.*

Granville Island *South side of False Creek, beneath the Granville Bridge; tel: (604) 666-6655; www.granvilleisland.com/en. Open daily.*

Grouse Mountain $$$ *6400 Nancy Greene Way, North Vancouver; tel: (604) 984-0661; www.grousemountain.com. Trams depart every 15 minutes, 0900–2200.*

Lookout Tower at Harbour Centre $$ *555 W. Hastings St; tel: (604) 689-0421. Open summer 0830–2230, winter 0900–2100.*

Museum of Anthropology $$ *6393 Northwest Marine Dr (University of British Columbia); tel: (604) 822-5087; www.moa.ubc.ca. Late May–Labour Day weekend open daily 1000–1700, Tue until 2100; after Labour Day weekend–late May open Tue–Sun 1100–1700, Tue until 2100.*

shoreline, especially **Vanier♦♦♦**, **Hadden♦♦♦** and **Kitsilano Beach Parks♦♦♦** on the south and the **Seawall Promenade♦♦♦** into **Stanley Park♦♦♦** on the east, is popular for walking, cycling and rollerblading.

False Creek♦♦♦

This shallow inlet stretching east from English Bay along the south side of the inner city has become one of Vancouver's premier recreation areas. The one-time industrial slum has been reborn as a series of marinas, parks and low-rise housing developments with stunning water views, all linked by a walking and cycling trail stretching from Kitsilano Beach to Vanier Park, around False Creek to the Seawall Promenade and circling Stanley Park.

Gastown♦♦♦

Once Vancouver's red-light district, Gastown has become a less risqué, but no-less-popular, entertainment district. Many of Gastown's original brick buildings have been renovated as bars, restaurants and offices. Don't miss the **steam clock♦♦** at the corner of Water and Cambie streets, signalling the quarter hour with steam-powered chimes. **Storyeum♦♦** is a 72-minute multi-media presentation of thousands of years of BC history, combining multiple stages, narrators, living history performers, action and effects to showcase First Nations, settlers, the gold rushes, Confederation, the transcontinental railway and the province's cultural variety.

Granville Island♦♦♦

One million cubic metres of mud dredged from False Creek nearly a century ago created a metal-bashing haven called Industrial Island. Island factories produced decades-worth of rivets, chain, nails, cement and industrial pollutants. Industry was eased out in the 1960s, the site cleaned up and renamed. As Granville Island, it has become a popular refuge for boaters, artists, shoppers and entertainers. The **Public Market♦♦♦** (*open daily 0900–1800*) is Vancouver's best.

Grouse Mountain♦♦♦

Skim the slopes of 1242-m Grouse Mountain by the Skyride aerial tramway, or hike the Grouse Grind, a rugged walk that gains 850m in 2.9km. Either way, clear-weather views offer the best panorama of Vancouver ground-side of a helicopter. Peak facilities include restaurants, a cinematic exploration of lower BC from the air, kilometres of walking paths, helicopter rides, tandem paragliding, downhill mountain biking, **Refuge for Endangered Wildlife** for grizzly bear cubs and grey wolves, and **híwus♦♦♦**, a First Nations dance, song and story-telling show with traditional foods. Grouse is open for winter skiing (*snowline tel: (604) 986-6262*).

Nitobe Memorial Garden & UBC Botanical Garden $
6804 Southwest Marine Dr;
tel: (604) 822-9666;
www.ubcbotanicalgarden.org.
Open daily.

Lookout Tower at Harbour Centre◆◆

Want to get your bearings? This tower above a downtown mall has a 360-degree view of Vancouver, its waterways and mountains. Snacks and coffee are served, and a wireless Internet connection provides contact with the world from on high.

Museum of Anthropology (MOA)◆◆◆

Canada's top anthropology museum has one of the world's finest collections of First Nations artefacts and art, with modern and antique totems, feast dishes and carvings in wood, stone, gold and other media. Don't miss the outdoor totem poles, directly behind the museum.

Nitobe Memorial Garden◆◆ and University of British Columbia Botanical Garden◆◆

Nitobe is a calm Japanese tea and stroll garden 200m from MOA. The Botanical Garden has more than 400 species of rhododendrons, a 16th-century Physick Garden and thousands of other plants from around the world.

Below
Granville Island Bridge

Science World $$
*1455 Quebec St;
tel: (604) 443-7443;
www.scienceworld.bc.ca.
Open Mon–Fri 1000–1700,
Sat–Sun 1000–1800.*

Stanley Park *West end
of Georgia St; tel: (604)
299-9000 ext 4100; www.
city.vancouver.bc.ca/parks/
stanley/index.htm. Open
daily.*

**Vancouver Aquarium
Marine Science Centre**
*$$$ tel: (604) 659-3474;
www.vanaqua.org. Open late
Jun–early Sept 0930–1900,
early Sept–Jun 1000–1730.*

Steveston $ *West end of
Steveston Hwy, Richmond.*

**Gulf of Georgia
Cannery National
Historic Site $** *12138
4th Ave, Richmond; tel:
(604) 664-9009; www.
gulfofgeorgiacannery.com.
Open daily 1000–1700
(1800 Jul–Aug) Jun–Sept,
Thur–Mon 1000–1700
Apr–May, Oct.*

**Van Dusen Botanical
Garden $$** *5251 Oak St at
37th Ave; tel: (604) 878-
9274; www.vandusengarden.
org. Open 1000 daily.*

Science World✦✦

BC's largest science museum uses hands-on displays to explain the natural world for kids, who usually have to push their way through crowds of fascinated adults to reach the exhibits.

Stanley Park✦✦✦

Vancouver has one of the world's finest urban parks, 400 hectares of forest laced with 80km of walking and cycling paths. The most popular path is a 10-km shoreline loop. Highlights include totem poles, sweeping vistas across Vancouver and the North Shore, restaurants, picnic grounds, a rose garden, beaches and horse-drawn carriage tours. **Vancouver Aquarium✦✦✦**, one of the best aquaria in the region, specialises in the Pacific Northwest, with a special area for beluga whales.

Steveston✦

This former salmon cannery town at the mouth of the Fraser River is still Canada's largest commercial fishing port and a popular local getaway. The **Gulf of Georgia Cannery National Historic Site✦✦✦** is a restored fish-processing plant, all that remains of what was once the world's largest concentration of salmon canneries.

Van Dusen Botanical Garden✦✦

This one-time golf course has become one of Canada's most comprehensive collections of ornamental plants. Plantings are rotated to provide maximum colour in all seasons.

Above
Science World

Vancouver Art Gallery $$
750 Hornby St;
tel: (604) 662-4700;
www.vanartgallery.bc.ca.
Open daily 1000–1730, Thur
to 2100, closed Mon
in winter.

**Vancouver
International Airport
art** First Nations artwork is
scattered throughout the
international and domestic
terminals; tel: (604) 207-
7077; www.yvr.ca/guide/todo/
art/index.asp

**Vancouver Maritime
Museum $$** 1905 Ogden
Ave; Vanier Park; tel:
(604) 257-8300; www.
vancouvermaritimemuseum.
com. Open daily Victoria
Day–Labour Day 1000–
1700; rest of year, Tue–Sat
1000–1700, Sun
1200–1700.

Vancouver Museum $$
Vanier Park, 1100 Chestnut
St; tel: (604) 736-4431;
www.vanmuseum.bc.ca. Open
Tue–Sun 1000–1700, Thur
to 2100.

Vanier Park Chestnut St,
at English Bay; tel: (604)
257-8400. Open daily.

Vancouver Art Gallery**

This one-time courthouse showcases West Coast artists, as well as travelling exhibitions. The neo-classical exterior is often a shooting location for television and cinema productions.

Vancouver International Airport art***

Vancouver Airport (YVR) has BC's best free collection of First Nations art. Most of the monumental eye-catchers are in the International Terminal, including a trio of totems between the terminal and the car park, and *The Spirit of Haida Gwaii, The Jade Canoe*, a 6m bronze by Bill Reid, with traditional Haida themes on the departure level.

Vancouver Maritime Museum**

Canada's finest Pacific museum is filled with uniforms and memorabilia, including a weavily ship's biscuit nearly 150 years old, Captain George Vancouver's navigational instruments and Captain Cook's 1779 charts-in-progress when he was killed in Hawaii. One highlight is the **St Roch** National Historic Site, a 1928 ship built for arctic patrol by the Royal Canadian Mounted Police and docked inside the museum. The *St Roch* was the first vessel to sail the Northwest Passage from the Pacific Ocean to the Atlantic Ocean, the first to make the return voyage and the first to circumnavigate North America.

Vancouver Museum**

Canada's largest civic museum includes vast collections of local artefacts as well as a laserium and planetarium. The Orientation Gallery presents two timelines for reference: adults peruse a Timeline Wall; children have a Toy Timeline Wall.

Vanier Park***

Vanier occupies much of the headland on the west side of False Creek inlet. Lawns, marinas, a walking and cycling path and broad views across English Bay make it a popular city escape all year round. The Vancouver Maritime Museum and the Vancouver Museum are both located in the park.

First Nations art

After decades of suppression by Christian missionaries and government policy, BC's Aboriginal arts, crafts and cultures have returned to the mainstream. Academic interest at the University of British Columbia and Victoria's Royal BC Museum sparked a revival of totem-pole carving in the 1940s and 1950s. The new totems helped fuel a renaissance of cultural and artistic forms that had all but disappeared outside museum collections. Fifty years later, modern interpretations of traditionally bold, stylised First Nations motifs are everywhere.

Vancouver International Airport has a fine collection of modern First Nations art and several retail shops selling hand-made artefacts; UBC's Museum of Anthropology (MOA) has an even larger collection. MOA's gift shop is filled with affordable reproductions of display pieces. Commercial gallery prices are higher.

Accommodation and food

Hotel space can be tight and expensive in summer but prices drop once the cruise ships head south in September and October. Tourism Vancouver offer a booking service.

Fairmont Hotel Vancouver $$$ *900 W Georgia St; tel: (604) 684-3131 or (800) 257-7544; www.fairmont.com/hotelvancouver*, is the *grande dame* of Vancouver hotels, worth every penny.

Listel Vancouver $$ *1300 Robson St; tel: (604) 684-8461 or (800) 663-5491; www.listel-vancouver.com*, is a delightful hotel with art gallery décor.

Pacific Palisades Hotel $$$ *1277 Robson St; tel: (604) 688-0461 or (800) 663-1815; www.pacificpalisadeshotel.com*, combines a trendy location with Miami South Beach colours, a film production suite, and a variety of packages for families to ecotravellers.

Pan Pacific Vancouver $$$ *999 Canada Place; tel: (604) 662-8111, (800) 663-1515 or (800) 937-1515; http://vancouver.panpacific.com*, rises above Canada Place with the best harbour views in town.

Sutton Place $$$ *845 Burrard St; tel: (604) 682-5511 or (800) 961-7555; www.suttonplace.com*, is a highly successful version of traditional luxury.

Vancouverites eat out more often and drink more wine than any other city in North America. The city's young, well-travelled population, vibrant immigrant communities, fresh seafood and healthy economy have transformed food from fuel to celebration. West Coast or Northwest Cuisine is the code for fresh local ingredients (most often seafood) with a light touch on the sauces.

Bali Restaurant $ *1016 W Broadway (near Oak); tel: (604) 731-6333*, serves authentic Indonesian, Malaysian and Singaporean dishes.

Bridges Restaurant $$–$$$ *Granville Island; tel: (604) 687-4400; www.bridgesrestaurant.com*, has reliable seafood and the city's most popular patio.

CinCin $$$ *1154 Robson St (near Bute); tel: (604) 688-7338; www.cincin.net*, keeps winning awards as the top (and most expensive) Italian restaurant.

Del-Hi Darbar Restaurant $$ *2120 Main St (near 5th); tel: (604) 877-7733*, has wonderful *dhosas* and enormous portions of South Indian delights.

Dubrulle $$ *Stanley Park Dining Pavilion, 550 Pipeline Rd; tel: (604) 683-5911; www.stanleypavilion.com*, is the restaurant for the Dubrulle International Culinary Arts.

Kalamata $$ *478 W Broadway (at Cambie); tel: (604) 872-7050,* has the sparkle, bustle and sunny flavours of Greece.

Kamei Royale Japanese Restaurant $$ *1030 W. Georgia St; tel: (604) 687-8588,* has cosy booths, supreme service and marvellous sushi.

Liliget Feast House $$ *1724 Davie St (near Denman); tel: (604) 681-7044; www.liliget.com,* is Vancouver's original First Nations restaurant.

Pink Pearl $ *1132 E Hastings St (near Clark Dr.); tel: (604) 253-4316; www.pinkpearl.com,* has the best Cantonese-style seafood in Vancouver.

Raincity Grill $$$ *1193 Denman St (at Morton); tel: (604) 685-7337; www.raincitygrill.com,* pushes the edge with West Coast dishes and Canada's best selection of BC wines by the glass.

Royal Thai Seafood Restaurant $ *770 Bute St; tel: (604) 602-0603,* serves flavourful, absolutely authentic Thai dishes that go well beyond seafood.

Star Anise $$$ *1485 W 12th Ave (near Granville); tel: (604) 737-1485; www.staranise.ca,* serves the city's most successful fusion of Asian and West Coast flavours.

Shopping

Vancouver is gaining a reputation for good-value shopping. **Robson Street** is Canada's answer to Beverly Hills, with blocks of brand name and trendy shops from Burrard to Cardero streets. **Chinatown** has bargains on Asian imports. **A&B Sound** *556 Seymour St; tel: (604) 687-5837; www.absound.ca* and **Virgin Megastore** *788 Burrard St; tel: (604) 669-2289; www.virginmegamagazine.com,* are locked in perpetual competition over music CDs and tapes. **Duthie Books** *2239 W. 4th Ave; tel: (604) 732-5344; http://duthiebooks.com,* has the city's best selection of Canadiana and travel books. **Mountain Equipment Co-op** *130 W. Broadway; tel: (604) 872-7858; www.mec.ca,* is a good stop for outdoor gear. First Nations art and artefacts shops sell museum quality. Amongst the best is **Hill's Native Art** *165 Water St, Gastown; tel: (604) 685-4249; www.hillsnativeart.com*

On the water

The best way to see Vancouver is from the water. **Vancouver Harbour Cruises $** *tel: (604) 688-7246 or (800) 663-1500; www.boatcruises.com,* offer daily harbour cruises aboard the city's only authentic paddlewheeler. **Ocean West Expeditions $** *tel: (604) 898-4979 or (800) 660-0051; www.ocean-west.com,* hires kayaks from the English Bay Beach boathouse at Denman and Davie Sts. Kayaks can be taken out on your own or on a guided tour with free lessons.

Suggested tour

Total distance: 80km.

Time: Allow a half-day for driving and 2 days to see the sights. Pick up the circular tour anywhere, but try to avoid commuter traffic (*0730–0930 and 1600–1800*).

Links: The city tour links with ferry routes to Vancouver Island from **Horseshoe Bay** and the lower Fraser River valley on Hwy 1 eastbound toward **Harrison Hot Springs, Hope** and the **Okanagan Valley.**

Route: Start at **Fourth Ave**, on the western edge of Vancouver. This trendy shopping district stretches from Burrard St to Balsam St, where it becomes a residential area headed west toward **Jericho Beach Park.** Watch for cyclists as the road veers to the right and becomes NW Marine Drive towards **Locarno Park, Locarno Beach** and **Spanish Banks Beach**, all fronting on English Bay. The parks offer expansive vistas to North Vancouver and east to the inner city and Stanley Park. There is ample parking, particularly near Locarno Park, as well as picnic and recreational facilities.

Pacific Spirit Regional Park begins just west of Spanish Banks. The 770-hectare park surrounds the **University of British Columbia** campus on **Point Grey**. At the first stop sign, turn right on to Chancellor Dr and the car park for the **MUSEUM OF ANTHROPOLOGY (MOA) ❶**, on the right. The outdoor totem exhibition area is over a small rise behind the car park and behind the museum building. Walk the 200m west along Marine Dr to **NITOBE MEMORIAL GARDEN**, on the left.

Marine Dr curves south around Point Grey. Just past the **UBC Botanical Garden**, 2km beyond MOA, move into the left lane. At the first traffic signal, turn left on to 16th Ave. Follow 16th Ave east back into Vancouver and the pleasant, tree-shaded residential neighbourhoods of **Shaughnessy Heights**. The road is a broad parkway, but residential parking frequently blocks the kerb lane.

Follow 16th Ave to Arbutus St and turn north (left). Several blocks north of W 4th Ave are still paved with brick, which becomes slippery in rain. Continue downhill toward **Kitsilano Pool**, Hutton Park and Vanier Park, with English Bay behind.

Follow signs for the **VANCOUVER MARITIME MUSEUM ❷** and **VANCOUVER MUSEUM**, skirting the edge of **VANIER PARK**. Parking is extremely limited; try the Maritime Museum and the Vancouver Museum.

From the Vancouver Museum, turn south (left) on to Chestnut for one block, then go west (right) on Greer Ave, following signs for the bicycle route on to the **Burrard Bridge.**

Above
Canada Place cruise liner

After crossing the bridge, continue straight on Burrard St for 10 blocks to Georgia St. Turn east (right) for one block to Hornby St and turn south (right). **The VANCOUVER ART GALLERY ❸** is on the left. To the right is the **BC Provincial Courts** building, with an urban park and waterfalls rising above street level. Turn south (right) on to Howe St and west (right) on to Smithe St. Follow Smithe across Burrard to Thurlow and turn south (left) for two blocks to Nelson St. Turn west (right) on to Nelson for four blocks to Nicola St, then go north (right) one block to Barclay. Turn east (right) on Barclay to **BARCLAY HERITAGE SQUARE ❹** and the **Roedde House Museum.**

Take the first left turn after the museum. Continue north to Robson St and turn west (left) to Denman St. Turn north (right) on Denman, following signs for ferries to **Nanaimo** and the **Sunshine Coast.** At Georgia St, turn north (left) toward **Stanley Park.** Stay in the right-hand lane and veer right into the park.

Parking regulations are enforced all year; buy parking coupons at the yellow dispensers. The first car park on the left is convenient for visits to the **VANCOUVER AQUARIUM ❺** and **horse-drawn tours** of the park. One kilometre beyond is the main parking area and **Totem Pole Display ❻**. Just ahead and on the right are broad views back to the sail-like roofline of **CANADA PLACE.** Expect to see cruise ships docked at Canada place from May to October. Ships returning from Alaska dock around 0800 and depart 1600–1800 the same day. The **Nine O'clock Gun**, on the waterfront just past a bronze statue of a runner, is fired at 2100 each evening. The cannon originally signalled the close of commercial fishing each day.

A lay-by 1km ahead has good views across to North Vancouver. The bright yellow piles are sulphur waiting to be loaded aboard ships; the tan-coloured piles are wood pulp. The suspension bridge to the left is **Lions Gate Bridge** ❼, leading to the North Shore. Just beyond **Brockton Point** is Vancouver's answer to Copenhagen's *Little Mermaid*, **Girl in a Wetsuit**, a bronze statue of a woman diver in a wet suit. A left-hand exit 1km ahead leaves the park back to Georgia St. The entrance to **Lions Gate Bridge**, from within Stanley Park, 1km ahead, is closed 1530–1830 to minimise park traffic.

Cross the bridge and turn east (right) on to Marine Dr, following signs for **North Vancouver, Capilano Canyon** and Grouse Mountain. Turn north (left) at the first traffic signal, Capilano Road. **CAPILANO SUSPENSION BRIDGE** is 3km uphill, on the left. The swaying pedestrian bridge, built a century ago for fishing and logging access, was Vancouver's first tourist attraction. Continue 4km north on Capilano Rd, which becomes Nancy Greene Way, to **GROUSE MOUNTAIN** and the Skyride Tram.

Return downhill to Hwy 1. Take the highway eastbound to the **Second Narrows Bridge** and cross **Burrard Inlet**. Take the first exit, following signs for the bicycle route on to McGill St. Follow McGill past **Exposition Park** and along the waterfront for 3km. Turn north (right) on to Wall St and continue through residential areas above the docks for another 2km, then go north (right) on to Dundas St to Heatley St.

Turn south (left) on to Heatley to E. Pender St. Turn west (right) through the heart of **CHINATOWN** ❽, past the Chinese Cultural Centre behind the large gate on the south (left) side of the street with the Dr Sun Yat-Sen Chinese Gardens behind.

Turn north (right) on to Abbott St to E. Cordova St and turn east (right) along the edge of **GASTOWN** ❾ for two blocks to Columbia St. Go two blocks north (left) on Columbia and turn west (left) on to Alexander St. At the first stop sign, where the brick pavement begins, turn north (right) on to Water St. A flamboyant statue of **Gassy Jack** who built the first bar in Gastown is on the left. **Storyeum** is on the left as you approach the Steam Clock on the north (right) at Cambie St.

At the end of Water St, turn south (left) into Richards St, immediately west (right) on to W. Hastings St, then south (left) on to Howe St. The **Four Seasons Hotel** is on the east (left) and the **Crowne Plaza Hotel Georgia** on the west (right) at Georgia St. Cross Georgia. West (right) is the Vancouver Art Gallery. Continue south on Howe St and cross the **Granville Bridge**.

Stay in the right-hand lane and follow signs for 4th Ave W., turning on to Pine St, then north (right) following signs for **GRANVILLE ISLAND** ❿. When leaving Granville Island, follow signs for 4th Ave W. Follow 4th Ave one block back to Burrard St.

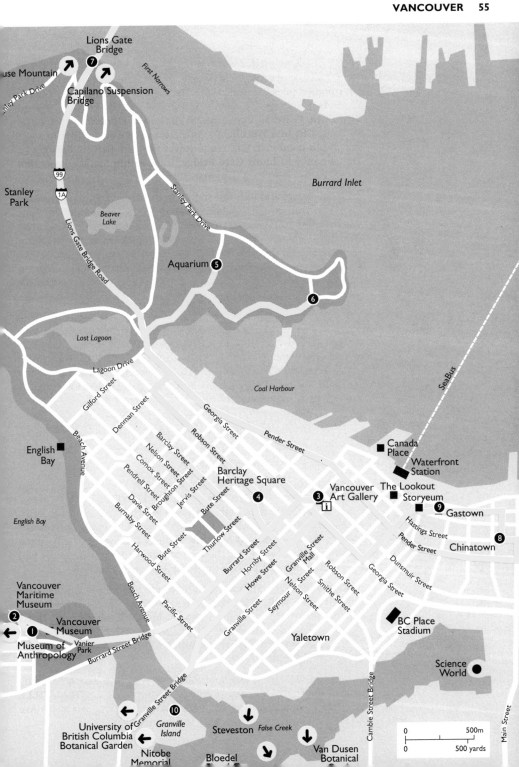

Lions Gate Bridge

use Mountain

7

First Narrows

Capilano Suspension Bridge

nley Park Drive

99

1A

Stanley Park

Lions Gate Bridge Road

Beaver Lake

Stanley Park Drive

Burrard Inlet

Aquarium **5**

6

Lost Lagoon

Lagoon Drive

Gilford Street

Coal Harbour

Sea Bus

English Bay

Beach Avenue

Denman Street

Georgia Street

Pender Street

Canada Place

Waterfront Station

Barclay Street

Robson Street

Nelson Street

Comox Street

Pendrell Street

Broughton Street

Barclay Heritage Square

4

Vancouver Art Gallery

3

The Lookout Storyeum

9 Gastown

Davie Street

Burnaby Street

Jervis Street

Bute Street

Harwood Street

Bute Street

Thurlow Street

Burrard Street

Hornby Street

Howe Street

Granville Street Mall

Robson Street

Georgia Street

Hastings Street

Pender Street

Dunsmuir Street

Chinatown **8**

English Bay

Vancouver Maritime Museum

2

Pacific Street

Granville Street

Seymour Street

Nelson Street

Smithe Street

1

Vancouver Museum

Museum of Anthropology

Vanier Park

Beach Avenue

Burrard Street Bridge

Yaletown

BC Place Stadium

Science World

Cambie Street Bridge

Main Street

Granville Street Bridge

10 *Granville Island*

University of British Columbia Botanical Garden

Nitobe Memorial

Steveston

False Creek

Van Dusen Botanical

Bloedel

0		500m
0		500 yards

The Gulf Islands

An island archipelago spans the Strait of Georgia, misnamed the Gulf of Georgia by Captain George Vancouver in 1792. Of the 200 or so Gulf Islands (the San Juans are the same group on the US side of the boundary), five of the major Gulf Islands house 12,000 permanent residents. Within a few hours' reach of Victoria or Vancouver by BC ferry, float plane or water taxi, the dry, sunny climate, small retiree and day commuter population, scenery, outdoor activities and arts communities lure visitors to posh inns and bed and breakfasts. Nostalgic vestiges of alternative lifestyles that thrived in relative island isolation in the 1960s can still be found along the rustic side routes and in crafts markets.

Rugged cliffs and smooth beaches lure sailors, kayakers and canoeists on to the water to view pods of orcas and dolphins. Panoramic views from mountaintops entice hikers and cyclists to explore island roads.

Gulf Islands National Park Reserve of Canada, *2220 Harbour Rd, Sidney, BC V8L 2P6; tel: (250) 654-4000; www.pc.gc.ca/pn-np/bc/gulf*, designated Canada's 40th national park in 2003, protects parts of 16 southern Gulf Islands, including Mayne, North and South Pender and Saturna, along with many islets in the Strait of Georgia Lowlands area.

Ratings

Art and craft	●●●●●
Nature	●●●●●
Outdoor activities	●●●●●
Parks	●●●●●
Scenery	●●●●●
Wildlife	●●●●●
Coastal villages	●●●●○
Beaches	●●●○○

GALIANO ISLAND***

ⓘ Galiano Chamber of Commerce
tel: (250) 539-2233; www.galianoisland.com

Ⓟ Go Galiano Island Shuttle $
tel: (250) 539-0202; www. moonshadowsbb.com/Go_ Galiano/Go_Galiano.html, operates from the Sturdies Bay Ferry, with some tours.

How did an island, inhabited for centuries by Coast Salish peoples, get a Spanish name? Answer: Spaniard Dionisio Alcala Galiano sailed a survey ship to the island in 1792.

Spreading 27km long over a narrow, hilly, 57sq km land area, the second-largest and northernmost main Gulf Island concentrates its thousand or so inhabitants in several population centres. Ferries call at **Sturdies Bay**. The one main route, Montague Road, goes to Montague Harbour, the other main activity centre, then becomes Porlier Pass Road, stopping short of the island's northern tip.

Many visitors choose to bring or hire bikes, take the **Go Galiano Island Shuttle**, walk, or kayak/canoe between places. Most of Galiano's parks provide views of the Strait of Georgia and vistas across to other tiny isles such as the Ballingall Islets, which shelter harbour seals and provide sanctuary for birds.

🅗 Dionisio Point Provincial Park

water access to island's northern tip; tel: (250) 539-2115; http://wlapwww. gov.bc.ca/bcparks/explore/ parkpgs/dionisio.htm

Montague Harbour Marine Provincial Park

10km northwest of Sturdies Bay at Montague Harbour; tel: (250) 539-2115; http://wlapwww. gov.bc.ca/bcparks/explore/ parkpgs/montague.htm

Galiano Bluffs Park

Bluff Rd.

Bodega Ridge *from Cook Rd on northwest of island; tel: (250) 539-2115; http://wlapwww.gov.bc.ca/ bcparks/explore/parkpgs/ bodega.htm*

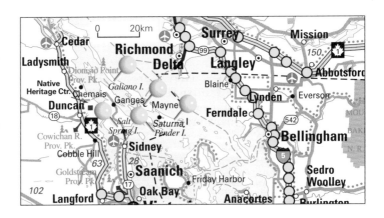

Water-access-only **Dionisio Point Provincial Park❖❖**, backed by forest, has rocky headlands looking out to Porlier Pass. **Montague Harbour Marine Provincial Park❖❖❖** offers a range of activities – walking white-shell beaches or Gray's Peninsula salt-water marsh; scuba-diving; spotting shellfish and sea stars at low tide; hiking 180m through a fir, western red cedar and arbutus forest; First Nations middens; or taking in vistas from a rocky precipice. **Galiano Bluffs Park❖❖** has fine views to Victoria and the San Juan Islands; for another awesome vista, hike up **Bodega Ridge❖❖**.

MAYNE ISLAND❖❖

ℹ Mayne Island Community Chamber of Commerce

www.mayneislandchamber.ca. In summer, get a map-brochure at the Village Bay ferry dock.

🅗 Miners Bay Gaol (Mayne Island Museum) *$ C4, Miners Bay.*

Ferries land at **Village Bay**, a transit depot for the commercial centre at **Miners Bay**, named for prospectors on their way to the Fraser and Cariboo gold rushes between 1858 and the 1860s. Look for fine late-Victorian-era houses. Since then, the 21-sq km island has fostered apple and tomato farming and remains an island getaway for Vancouverites.

Right
Bedwell Harbour

Active Pass Lighthouse *Georgina Point. Hours vary.*

Mount Parke Regional Park *off Fernhill Rd, www.crd.bc.ca/parks/mount_parke.htm. Open daily.*

Miners Bay Gaol (Mayne Island Museum)✷✷ belies its history as the 1896 Plumper Pass lockup (gaol), exhibiting wreck artefacts. **Georgina Point Heritage Park**✷ is a good picnicking and birdwatching spot, with **Active Pass Lighthouse**✷✷✷, operational since 1885. Cycle Mayne's hills, or hike 270m up **Mount Parke**✷✷✷ for a view east to Vancouver and west to Vancouver Island.

PENDER ISLANDS✷✷

Pender Island Chamber of Commerce *Pender Island; www. penderislandchamber.com*

Mount Norman Regional Park *South Pender Island, south of the causeway; www.crd.bc.ca/parks/mount_norman.htm. Open daily.*

Driftwood Centre *Bedwell Harbour Rd at Razor Point Rd has provisions and along with the Community Hall, hosts the May–Oct Saturday* **Farmers Market**.

A narrow causeway joins the 24sq km of Pender's North and South Islands. Ferries put in at **Otter Bay**, North Pender; almost all of the 2000 residents live further south near **Magic Lake**. While all the Gulf Islands have beaches, the Penders' sheltered coves are numerous and easily accessible. Try another panoramic Gulf Island hike up 217-m **Mount Norman**✷✷✷.

For a break from kayaking, horse riding, swimming and hiking from May to October, visit the (North) Island service area, **Driftwood Centre**, for a Saturday **Farmers Market**✷✷.

SALT SPRING ISLAND✷✷✷

Salt Spring Island Chamber of Commerce *121 Lower Ganges Rd, Ganges; tel: (250) 537-5252 or (866) 216-2936; www.saltspringisland. bc.ca. Open daily.*

Gulf Islands Spinning Mill *351 Rainbow Rd, Ganges; tel: (250) 537-4342; www. gulfislands.com/spinningmill. Tours by appointment (donation).*

ArtCraft *Mahon Hall, Ganges; tel: (250) 537-0899. Open daily mid-May–mid-Sept.*

Salt Spring is a 180-km² island getaway with many of the arts and amenities of a thriving metropolis without the urban angst. Sheep are reared for meat and wool, providing work for some of Salt Spring's 10,000 residents. **Gulf Islands Spinning Mill**✷✷ offer tours of its wool, mohair, llama and alpaca production.

The town of **Ganges**✷✷ is the bustling hub of this island. Local farmers rub elbows with potters and musicians at the **Salt Spring Island Saturday Market**✷✷✷ in Centennial Park each Saturday from April to Thanksgiving weekend (mid-October). In summer, **ArtCraft**✷✷✷ pulls together 200-plus island artisans' work for unique souvenir shopping from mid-May–mid-September, or visit Salt Spring's 40 or more art galleries.

Ferries call at **Long Harbour**, **Vesuvius Bay** and **Fulford Harbour**. Take time to call ahead to **Akerman Museum**✷✷, a family collection of Cowichan and First Nations artefacts, historic photographs and Akerman's memories near Fulford Harbour.

Ackerman Museum
$ 2501 Fulford-Ganges Rd, near Fulford Harbour; tel: (250) 537-9977; www.saltspringislandrealestate.com/museum.htm. Call before arrival.

Ruckle Provincial Park
via Beaver Point Rd; tel: (250) 539-2115; http://wlapwww.gov.bc.ca/bcparks/explore/parkpgs/ruckle.htm. Open daily.

Mount Maxwell Provincial Park
Southwest of Ganges, Cranberry Rd to Maxwell Rd; tel: (250) 539-2115; http://wlapwww.gov.bc.ca/bcparks/explore/parkpgs/mt_max.htm. Open daily.

Mill Farm Regional Park Reserve Southwest island section via rough Musgrave Rd; www.crd.bc.ca/parks. Open daily.

Right
Salt Spring Island

Opposite
Otter Bay

Wineries joined the attractions, with the first island-grown releases in 2003: **Salt Springs Vineyards** *151 Lee Rd at 1700 block Fulford-Ganges Rd; tel: (250) 653-9463; www.saltspringvineyards.com* and **Garry Oaks Winery** *1880 Fulford-Ganges Rd; tel: (250) 653-9463; http://garryoakswine.com*

The parks introduce what nature offers in the Gulf Islands. The shore **Ruckle Provincial Park**❖❖❖ is rocky, its 486 hectares encompassing a sheep farm, several settler homes, fields and forest walks. Hikers enjoy views towards Vancouver Island from **Mount Maxwell Provincial Park**❖❖. Rough roads access the hang-glider heaven atop 698-m **Mount Bruce** in **Mill Farm Regional Park Reserve**❖❖❖.

SATURNA ISLAND❖❖

Saturna Island; www.saturnatourism.com

East Point Regional Park East Point Rd; www.crd.bc.ca/parks/east_point.htm. Open daily.

Mount Warburton Pike
via Staples Rd, west section of the island. Open daily.

Saturna Island Vineyards 8 Quarry Trail; tel: (250) 539-5139 or (877) 918-3388; www.saturnavineyards.com. Open May–Oct 1130–1630.

Astronomy aside, the island's 350 residents proudly claim East Point's sandstone formations as the 1791 discovery site of the island by the Spanish schooner *Santa Saturnina*. Saturna's few inhabitants are spread over 96sq km, leaving most businesses close to the **Lyall Harbour** dock, where ferries connect to other Gulf Islands.

Orca-spotting is phenomenal in summer from **East Point Regional Park**❖❖❖, near an 1889 lighthouse. Salmon and raptors, including peregrine falcons, hawks, osprey and eagles, engage in preying upon the small, but numerous, offshore fish. Look for deer and racoons amid forests of fir, spruce and alder, half-hidden in ferny undergrowth.

For vista spotters, 490-m **Mount Warburton Pike**❖❖❖ can be climbed or reached via a dirt road, and island arts and crafts run the gamut from tarot readings to goldsmithing, woodworking and *raku* (lead-glazed, Japanese-style pottery), even winemaking at Saturna Island Vineyards.

Above
Canoeing in the Gulf Islands

Accommodation and food in the Gulf Islands

There is no shortage of bed and breakfasts, inns, lodges and country manors to select from, but prices can be high. Advance bookings are essential in summer and at holiday periods. Check with InfoCentres and Provincial Parks for camping; Saturna Island has no public camp pitches. Every ferry landing has a store for provisioning and most have at least one restaurant/pub nearby. Fine dining is often part of a B&B stay.

Gulf Islands Brewery on Salt Spring Island produces a number of beers for local restaurant and pub consumption, including Salt Spring Golden Ale, Mayne Sail Ale, Pender Island Porter and Saturna Island Extra Stout. Heather Beer, resembling Scottish-style fraoch ale, brews with plants from The Butchart Gardens in Victoria in place of hops, with brews served only at the gardens.

Hastings House $$$ *160 Upper Ganges Road, Salt Spring Island; tel: (250) 537-2362 or (800) 661-9255; www.hastingshouse.com,* may be the poshest collection of lodging buildings in Western Canada, including the original HBC post, secluded on 12 hectares.

**Gulf Islands
Online**
www.gulfislands.net

BC Ferries 1112 Fort St,
Victoria, BC V8V 4V2;
tel: (250) 386-3431 or
(888) 223-3779;
www.bcferries.com

BC Provincial Parks
http://wlapwww.gov.bc.ca/
bcparks

Hummingbird Pub $$ *47 Sturdies Bay Rd, Galiano Island; tel: (250) 539-5472,* is a good spot to meet local people, with live entertainment in summer. Take the pub's summertime-only red and white shuttle from Montague Bay.

Oceanwood Country Inn $$$ *630 Dinner Bay Rd, Mayne Island; tel: (250) 539-5074; www.oceanwood.com,* is a 12-room, Tudor-style waterfront inn with a solarium and fine dining room, complemented by fresh garden ingredients and one of the best wine cellars in Western Canada. *Open Mar–Oct.*

Suggested tour

Time: Via BC Ferries, distance depends on route, season and number of islands visited. In summer, June–Labour Day, from Tsawwassen, off BC Hwy 99, 45 minutes south of Vancouver, the run around four islands – but not Saturna Island – could take 5 hours; 6 hours on the direct Tsawwassen–Swartz Bay (Vancouver Island) run, with a return to one of the islands; or as little as 4 hours. Check with BC Ferries before planning a route and verify routing again on the day of travel for exact schedules.

Links: Vancouver (Tsawwassen – see page 42) is the mainland BC link to the Gulf Islands. From Salt Spring Island to Vancouver Island, sail from Vesuvius Bay to Crofton or from Fulford Harbour to **Swartz Bay** (see page 80).

Route: Ferry schedules will shape a tour, especially outside the mid-May–Sept busy season. The best strategy is to start big and work towards wilderness, ie begin with **SALT SPRING ISLAND ❶**, exploring Ganges' art and ambience, hike the trails for **Mount Maxwell Provincial Park** vistas, and work through the other islands as time and routes permit, to **GALIANO's ❷** kayak-loving shoreline and **SATURNA ISLAND's ❸** relative isolation.

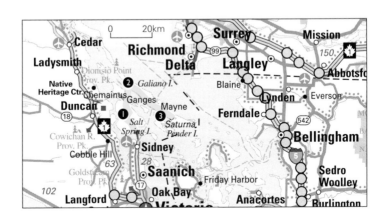

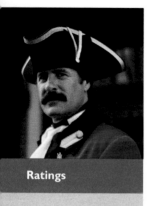

Victoria

Ratings

Architecture	●●●●●
Food and drink	●●●●●
Gardens	●●●●●
Children	●●●●○
Historical sights	●●●●○
Outdoor activities	●●●●○
Scenery	●●●●○
Shopping	●●●○○

Victoria doesn't *look* like Western Canada's oldest industrial city. British Columbia's capital has swapped the noise and the grit of old-fashioned metal bashing for cleaner, more modern technologies without sacrificing one of Canada's greatest concentration of heritage buildings. Older neighbourhoods are filled with lovingly restored storefronts, rambling mansions and social welfare programmes that city founders couldn't have imagined in their worst nightmares.

Victoria wallows in its reputation for espousing the ludicrous and the off-beat. City dwellers from Vancouver to Halifax dismiss Victorians as refugees from the *real* Canada, but these self-satisfied refugees have never forgotten the winters they left behind. Canada's mildest climate and quick access to the out-of-doors have attracted a youthful mixture of urban escapees, artists, ardent environmentalists and would-be entrepreneurs willing to meet established politicians and entrenched industrialists in a social ferment that aims to change the political and economic future.

Arriving and departing

ℹ️ **Tourism Victoria Visitor Info Centre**
812 Wharf St, Victoria, BC V8W 1T3; tel: (250) 953-2033; www.tourismvictoria. com. Open daily 0900–1700, longer in summer. Reservations, tel: (800) 663-3883.

Volunteer Downtown Victoria Ambassadors, *in green and white shirts, provide free maps and information, tel: (250) 414-6972; http://victorian ambassadors.tripod.com*

Victoria International Airport (YYJ) *tel: (250) 953-7500; www. victoriaairport.com* is 20km and 30 minutes north of downtown Victoria, near Sidney. Taxi **$$$** to downtown. **AKAL Airport Shuttle Bus $$** *tel: (250) 386-2525; www.akalairporter.travel.bc.ca.* Coach service every 30 minutes or **BC Transit $** *tel: (250) 382-2551; www.bctransit.com*

The **Inner Harbour** has seaplane and helicopter services to Vancouver, the San Juan Islands, the Gulf Islands, Nanaimo and other destinations.

By sea
Three million people visit Victoria each year, most of them by water. Advance booking is required on most routes.
• **BC Ferries** *1112 Fort St; tel: (250) 386-3431 or (888) 223-3779; www.bcferries.com,* serve Swartz Bay, at the north end of the Saanich

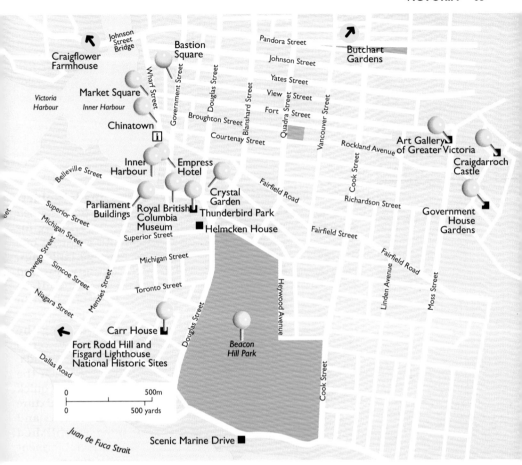

Map labels:
Johnson Street Bridge
Craigflower Farmhouse
Bastion Square
Pandora Street
Butchart Gardens
Johnson Street
Victoria Harbour
Market Square
Wharf Street
Government Street
Douglas Street
Blanshard Street
Yates Street
View Street
Vancouver Street
Quadra Street
Fort Street
Inner Harbour
Chinatown
Broughton Street
Courtenay Street
Rockland Avenue
Art Gallery of Greater Victoria
Craigdarroch Castle
Belleville Street
Inner Harbour
Empress Hotel
Crystal Garden
Fairfield Road
Cook Street
Richardson Street
Government House Gardens
Superior Street
Michigan Street
Parliament Buildings
Royal British Columbia Museum
Thunderbird Park
Helmcken House
Fairfield Street
Superior Street
Oswego Street
Simcoe Street
Menzies Street
Michigan Street
Niagara Street
Toronto Street
Fairfield Road
Linden Avenue
Moss Street
Carr House
Fort Rodd Hill and Fisgard Lighthouse National Historic Sites
Dallas Road
Douglas Street
Beacon Hill Park
Heywood Avenue
Cook Street
0   500m
0   500 yards
Juan de Fuca Strait
Scenic Marine Drive

Monday Magazine
818 Broughton St; tel: (250) 382-6188; http:// web.bcnewsgroup.com/ portals/monday, free each Friday in shops and newspaper boxes, has Victoria's best listing of current events and reviews.

Washington State Ferries
www.wsdot.wa.gov/ferries. For recorded information, tel: (800) 843-3779; to book vehicle transit between Anacortes–Sidney, tel: (888) 808-7977 or in Washington State, (206) 464-6400.

Peninsula; 45 minutes by car from downtown, with vehicle and passenger service from Vancouver and the Gulf Islands. Ferry services connect with **BC Transit** in both Victoria and Vancouver.

• **Black Ball Transport** *(MV Coho) 430 Belleville St; tel: (250) 386-2202; www.cohoferry.com*, has a car and passenger service between Victoria's Inner Harbour and Port Angeles, Washington.

• **Victoria–San Juan Cruises** *tel: (800) 443-4552 or (360) 738-8099; www.whales.com*, has passenger service between Bellingham, Washington and Victoria via Roche Harbor (San Juan Island, Washington) May–Oct.

• **Victoria Clipper** *254 Belleville, Victoria; tel: (250) 382-8100 or (800) 888-2535; www.victoriaclipper.com*, has a daily passenger catamaran service to Seattle with the fastest ships on the route.

• **Washington State Ferries** *2499 Ocean Ave, Sidney; tel: (250) 656-1831; www.wsdot.wa.gov/ferries*, has a vehicle and passenger service to Anacortes, Washington. Fares may be paid in either US or Canadian currency.

By land

• All road transport between Victoria and the mainland requires a ferry connection. **Pacific Coach Lines** *700 Douglas St; tel: (250) 385-4411 or (800) 661-1725; www.pacificcoach.com*, operate between central Victoria and central Vancouver.

• **The Malahat** *450 Pandora Ave; tel: (888) 842-7245; www.viarail.ca*, has a daily return rail service between Victoria and Courtenay via Nanaimo.

Getting around

Walking is the best way to explore touristic Victoria, a compact area around the Inner Harbour. It's also practicable to explore all but the most distant parts of the city by public transport. **BC Transit** *tel: (250) 385-2551; www.bctransit.com* and *www.busonline.ca/regions/vic/?p=1.txt*, has a dense network of bus routes throughout Greater Victoria with several discount ticket and pass schemes available at the Tourism Victoria Info Centre.

Driving

Narrow streets, busy traffic and limited street parking make it difficult to explore downtown by car. The best bet is to park and explore on foot, then drive to more distant attractions. There is ample parking off the west side of Wharf Street along the Inner Harbour, as well as parking garages east of Government Street. Parking meter time limits are strictly enforced, especially downtown.

Below
Victoria's Inner Harbour

Downtown traffic is usually heavy, but flows smoothly in other

Art Gallery of Greater Victoria $$
1040 Moss St; tel: (250) 384-4101; http://aggv.bc.ca/.
Open Mon–Sun 1000–1700, Thur 1000–2100.

Bastion Square Wharf St between Yates and Fort Sts. Open daily.

Maritime Museum of British Columbia $$ 28 Bastion Sq; tel: (250) 385-4222; http://mmbc.bc.ca/. Open daily 0930–1630, to 1700 Jun 15–Sept 15.

Afternoon tea

Every hotel, restaurant and café offers its own version of afternoon tea. **Blethering Place Tea Room and Restaurant $$** 2250 Oak Bay Ave (Oak Bay); tel: (250) 598-1413; www.blethering.com, is favoured by the Tweed Curtain set. **Fairmont Empress Hotel $$$** 721 Government St; tel: (250) 384-8111; www.fairmont.com, is overpriced and overtouristed, but it's hard to beat the city's most sumptuous setting. **James Bay Tea Room and Restaurant $$** 332 Menzies St (behind Parliament Buildings); tel: (250) 382-8282, attracts nearby residents, as well as government and legislative workers. **The White Heather Tea Room $** 1885 Oak Bay Ave; tel: (250) 595-8020, a local favourite, serves tea, Not So Wee Tea, and the Big Muckle Giant Tea for Two.

areas. Major arteries, particularly Hwy 17 and Hwy 1A, are jammed during rush hours, 0730–0900 and 1600–1800 Mon–Fri. Left turns are extremely difficult anywhere downtown, while scenic country roads on the Saanich Peninsula can be narrow, winding and slow.

Sights

Afternoon Tea**
A Victoria tradition, the Fairmont Empress Hotel serves more than 100,000 of these light meals yearly. Cups of strong tea wash down finger sandwiches, crumpets and scones arrayed on multi-tiered trays amid pots of whipped cream and conserves. An early 19th-century Duchess of Bedford gets credit for afternoon tea. Desperate to counteract 'that sinking feeling around 5pm', she tried snacking on small sandwiches and tea. The custom caught on, evolving into today's afternoon tea and the more formal version known as 'high tea'.

Art Gallery of Greater Victoria**
Victoria's city art museum concentrates on contemporary Canadian artists, as well as North American and European historical artists and notable Asian artists. The gallery shop is particularly well stocked with affordable reproductions.

Bastion Square*
The Square (actually a long rectangle) is the site of Victoria's first gaol, as well as the original Provincial Court House, used between 1889 and 1962. The Victoria Law Courts Building now houses the **Maritime Museum of British Columbia***, filled with ship models, figureheads, tools, naval uniforms and the 1860 *Tilikum*, an 11-m dugout canoe converted to a schooner that sailed from Victoria to England and back between 1901 and 1904.

Beacon Hill Park
*Juan de Fuca Strait
between Douglas and Cook
Sts; tel: (250) 381-2532.
Open daily, most attractions
open mid-Mar–mid-Oct.*

Butchart Gardens $$$
*800 Benvenetu Ave,
Brentwood Bay; tel: (250)
652-5256 or (866) 652-
4422; www.butchartgardens.
com. Open daily 0900;
closing varies with the
season. Reduced prices in
winter.*

Carr House $ *207
Government St; tel: (250)
383-5843;
www.emilycarr.com. Open
daily Victoria Day–Labour
Day 1100–1600; same
hours Tue–Sat rest of year.*

Chinatown *Between
Herald, Government,
Pandora and Store streets.*

Fan Tan Alley $
*Chinatown, between Fisgard
St and Pandora Ave. Open
daily.*

Craigdarroch Castle $$
*1050 Joan Cres;
tel: (250) 592-5323;
www.craigdarrochcastle.com.
Open Jun 15–Labour Day,
0900–1900; rest of year,
1000–1630.*

Coloured bricks set into the pavement along View Street west to Bastion Square and south along Government Street to Fort Street then west towards the harbour mark the original stockade where Victoria began.

Beacon Hill Park✦✦✦
This 62-hectare park is named for Beacon Hill, the highest seaside point in Victoria, where signal fires once burned to warn sailors off reefs guarding the harbour entrance. The park is a collection of formal gardens, small lakes and playing fields sloping down to cliffs overlooking the Strait of Juan de Fuca. Runners, dog walkers and sightseers flock to the seaside walkway with its wide vistas across the Strait to the Olympic Mountains in Washington.

Butchart Gardens✦✦✦
Originally a limestone quarry, since 1904, Butchart has become one of the most popular gardens in Canada. Its 20 manicured hectares are divided into Italian, Japanese, rose and sunken gardens, plus other landscape creations. The gardens are colourful all year and spectacular in summer – as are the crowds. The crush lessens after tour coaches depart at 1530.

Carr House✦
The cream-coloured Victorian building is the birthplace of Emily Carr, one of Canada's most famed artists and authors. She took the country by storm in the 1930s with wild, haunting images of forests and totem poles before turning to books that re-created late 19th-century Victoria. A description of Carr's father, 'more English than the English', became an unofficial goal for three generations of Victorians. The house is open for tours.

Chinatown✦✦
The oldest Chinese community in Canada began in the 1840s when Victoria was BC's only serious settlement. Don't miss **Fan Tan Alley✦✦✦**, the width of an adult armspan in places. Small shops set into the walls sell everything from haircuts and antique jewellery to New Age crystals and incense in what were once brothels, opium dens and gambling parlours.

Craigdarroch Castle✦✦✦
The castle was the grandest home atop the grandest hill in Victoria, a 39-room rough stone castle built by Nanaimo coal baron Robert Dunsmuir. The house was completed in 1889, months after Dunsmuir's death, but his family lived there until 1909. The intricately ornamented mansion is resplendent in carved wood, polished marble and fine paintings, elegantly restored after decades' service as a hospital, music academy, offices and decaying derelict.

Opposite
*Bastion Square's Law Courts
Building now houses the
Maritime Museum*

Craigflower Farmhouse $ 110
Island Hwy (Hwy 1A and Admiral Rd); tel: (250) 479-8053; www.heritage.gov.bc.ca/craig/craig.htm. Grounds open daily, call for hours.

Fairmont Empress Hotel $ 721 Government St; tel: (250) 384-8111 or (800) 257-7544; www.fairmont.com/empress

Craigflower Farmhouse◆◆◆

This 1856 farmhouse was the command centre for one of the Hudson's Bay Company's most successful farms. Most of the furnishings came to BC with Scottish families brought by the HBC to colonise the area. Guides in period costume conduct tours of the interior as well as heritage gardens, orchards, oatfields and the Kosapsom (First Nation) village site.

Fairmont Empress Hotel◆◆◆

Opened in 1908 by the same architect who built Parliament House, the ivy-covered Empress sits surrounded by gardens on what was once a garbage-filled tidal flat. The posh Edwardian décor in The Fairmont Empress's original lobby (south end of the building) is worth visiting, if only for a drink, but beware of Tea Time in summer, when the hotel is swamped with tourists. Corridors in The Fairmont Empress's first underground level are lined with photographs showing the world's upper crust at play around Victoria during the first half of the 20th century.

Fort Rodd Hill and Fisgard Lighthouse National Historic Sites◆◆◆

The massive seaside fortress protected the naval base and coaling station at Esquimalt, just west of Vancouver, between 1878 and 1956, when missiles replaced coastal defence guns. White Fisgard Lighthouse, atop a rocky islet connected to the mainland by modern

Fort Rodd Hill and Fisgard Lighthouse National Historic Sites
603 Fort Rodd Hill Rd, west of Esquimalt off Hwy 1A; tel: (250) 478-5849; www.pc.gc.ca/lhn-nhs/bc/fortroddhill/index_e.asp; www.pc.gc.ca/lhn-nhs/bc/fisgard/index_e.asp. Open daily Mar–Oct, 1000–1730; Nov–Feb 0900–1630.

Government House Gardens *1401 Rockland Ave; www.ltgov.bc.ca/gardens. Open daily dawn–dusk.*

Inner Harbour *Between Parliament Buildings, the Fairmont Empress Hotel, Johnson Street Bridge and West Victoria.*

Market Square *560 Johnson St; tel: (250) 386-2441; www.marketsquare.ca. Open daily.*

Parliament Buildings *South end of Inner Harbour; www.legis.gov.bc.ca/info/2-9.htm. Open during business hours.*

Royal British Columbia Museum *$$ 675 Belleville St; tel: (250) 356-7226 or (888) 447-7977; http://rbcm1.rbcm.gov.bc.ca/. Open daily 0900–1700, shorter hours in winter.*

walkway, is the oldest lighthouse on the west coast of Canada. The lightkeeper's house has become an excellent lighthouse and shipping museum with broad ocean views.

Government House Gardens✦✦✦
You can't tour the official residence of BC's Lieutenant Governor, but the 14 hectares of azaleas, blossoming shrubs, formal flowerbeds, heather, ivy, lawns and rhododendrons are open to the public – unless the British royal family happens to be in residence.

Inner Harbour✦✦✦
Nearly all of touristic Victoria is packed into a 10-block area along the south and east sides of the Inner Harbour, where the city began about 160 years ago. Ferries from the US dock inside the harbour, as do seaplanes from Vancouver and the rest of Vancouver Island, whale-watching boats, sea kayakers and dozens of pleasure boaters, while tiny ferries dart from shore to shore like water bugs. The best views are from the harbour side of Government Street, across from The Fairmont Empress Hotel, and from the waterside pedestrian promenade.

Market Square✦✦✦
The collection of nine red-brick heritage buildings, now an open shopping arcade, were originally shops and storehouses for the docks and industrial areas built to supply successive waves of gold miners, fishing fleets, seal hunters, coal ships and general cargo vessels that sailed into Victoria.

Parliament Buildings✦✦✦
The imposing buildings at the south end of the Inner Harbour were built by British architect Francis Mawson Rattenbury. Ratz, as he preferred to be called, arrived in Victoria in 1892 and promptly won an Empire-wide competition to build the province's new Parliament House at the age of 25.

He also built the opulent Edwardian Empress Hotel, the now closed Crystal Garden and other ornate edifices in Victoria, before a lurid divorce and lusty remarriage to a woman 30 years younger. Stuffy Victoria ostracised both the avant-garde wife, who dared to smoke cigarettes in public, and her new husband. Ratz was murdered by his wife's young lover in 1934, after fleeing to England to escape Victoria's withering disdain.

Royal British Columbia Museum✦✦✦
Centrepiece of this sprawling museum is a First Nations collection. Enter through the full-sized Kwaktuil chief's house with displays of totems, carvings and chiefly regalia. Even more striking are artefacts, including story-telling masks, from the apex of First Nations arts and handicrafts in the lucrative decades after first contact with White fur traders and merchants. Many tribes disappeared as smallpox and other

Thunderbird Park
*Belleville and Douglas
Sts; tel: (250) 356-7226.
Open daily.*

Victoria Bug Zoo $$
*631 Courtney St;
tel: (250) 384-2847;
www.bugzoo.bc.ca.
Open Sept–mid-June
Mon–Sat 0930–1730,
Sun 1100–1730, longer
hours in summer.*

diseases decimated BC's Native population between 1843 and 1885. One outbreak of smallpox alone that spread from Victoria in 1862 killed 20,000, a third of the Province's non-White population.

Thunderbird Park✦✦✦

Next to the museum is Thunderbird Park, created to display totem poles in the 1940s. As the outdoor poles began to crumble from the effects of weather and time, museum curators sought out carvers to create replacements. Mungo Martin, Chief of the Kwagiulth band near Fort Rupert, organised a carving group in the 1950s that successfully recreated what had already become a lost art. Many of the poles towering above the park are replicas of Martin's original creations, while the originals stand protected inside the museum.

Victoria Bug Zoo✦✦

The City of Victoria hangs 1500 flower baskets from downtown lampposts from June to September in an ever-so-civilised bow to summer, colour, and a city symbol. For a feel of the wilderside, this bug zone is home to an astounding variety of insects and spiders. Bug guides help with holding a tickling 400-leg millipede. The bug haven is Canada's largest ant farm and the spot to see leaf-cutter ants in action if a jungle is not on your itinerary. Check the white-eyed assassin bugs, giant stag and giant rhinoceros beetles, walking sticks, or glow-in-the-dark scorpions. For the brave who can make a home for one, the Bug Zoo has an Arthropod Sales division, offering, if available, Mexican red-legged or Indian ornamental tarantulas, giant whip scorpions, or Oriental praying Mantis. The gift shop is wacky, including cricket-infused lollipops. When sated with the natural world's oddities, The Fairmont Empress Tea is only a block away.

Right
Thunderbird Park

Accommodation and food

Hotel space is tight in summer. Budget–moderate motels line Hwy 1/1A (Douglas Street) north of downtown. Most rooms can be booked through **Tourism Victoria** *tel: (800) 663-3883; www.tourismvictoria.com*.

Days Inn on the Harbour $$ *427 Belleville St; tel: (250) 386-3451 or (800) 329-7466; www.daysinn.com*, is across the street from the Inner Harbour ferry docks, a 10-minute walk from The Fairmont Empress.

Executive House Hotel $$ *777 Douglas St; tel: (250) 388-5111 or (800) 663-7001; www.executivehouse.com*, rises directly behind The Fairmont Empress with sweeping harbour views from the upper floors.

The Fairmont Empress Hotel $$$ *721 Government St; tel: (250) 384-8111 or (800) 257-7544; www.fairmont.com/empress*, is the most prestigious and most central address in town.

Laurel Point Inn $$$ *680 Montreal St; tel: (250) 386-8721 or (800) 663-7667; www.laurelpoint.com*, overlooks the Inner Harbour entrance with modern luxury in contrast to The Fairmont Empress's Edwardian gloss.

Quality Inn Downtown $$ *850 Blanshard St; tel: (250) 385-6787 or (800) 661-4115; www.victoriaqualityinn.com*, is within easy walking distance of the Inner Harbour.

The Victoria population demands and gets the kind of variety, quality and value you'll find in Vancouver. Booking essential in summer.

The Bay Centre $ *Government St, Fort–View Sts, 4th floor; tel: (250) 952-5680; www.victoriaeatoncentre.ca*, caters for a quick lunch or dinner.

Chandlers Seafood House $$ *1250 Wharf St; tel: (250) 385-3474*, has served some of the best seafood in town since 1862.

Deep Cove Chalet $$$ *11190 Chalet Rd, Sidney, along Saanich Inlet; tel: (250) 656-3541; www.deepcovechalet.com*, is the best French restaurant on Vancouver Island with one of the largest wine cellars in the province.

Herald Street Caffe $$ *546 Herald St; tel: (250) 381-1441*, is Victoria's other top seafood choice.

Sticky Wicket Pub $ *Strathcona Hotel, 919 Douglas St; tel: (250) 383-7137; www.strathconahotel.com*, is a sports bar for families, complete with a pair of rooftop volleyball courts.

Swan's Hotel $$ *506 Pandora St; tel: (250) 361-3310 or (800) 668-7926; www.swanshotel.com*, has one of BC's best breweries, **Buckerfield's Brewery**, on the premises, plus fine Northwest cuisine in a restored heritage building.

Wharfside Eatery $$ *1208 Wharf St; tel: (250) 360-1808; www.wharfsideeatery.com*, offers great harbour views with tasty fish and pizza.

Suggested tour

Total distance: 60km, or 110km with all detours.

Time: Allow a half-day for driving and 2 days to see all the sights, starting from the southwest corner of Beacon Hill Park, Douglas Street and Dallas Road. Pick up the circular tour anywhere, but avoid rush hours (*0730–0900 and 1600–1800*), especially downtown.

Links: Victoria connects with the **Gulf Islands** (*see page 56*) and with routes to **Southern Vancouver Island** (*see page 76*) or **Central Vancouver Island** (*see page 86*).

Route: Follow Dallas Road east through BEACON HILL PARK ❶ along the **Juan de Fuca Strait** separating the US and Canada. The wooden sign marking Mile 0 of the TransCanada Highway is scenic, but the highway now extends west to **Tofino**.

A shoreline walking and cycling path is as popular with runners as it is with photographers entranced by the **Olympic Mountains** across the strait.

Detour 1: Dallas Road continues past **Ross Bay Cemetery**, where most early Victoria citizens can be found. Dallas Road changes names to Hollywood Crescent just beyond the cemetery, then becomes Hollywood Road as it curves around **Gonzales Bay**, usually called **Foul Bay** for the leavings of its sea birds.

Take King George Terrace to the right, following green Scenic Drive signs. The **King George Lookout**, part of **Trafalgar Park**, has Victoria's best sea-level view across the Strait to **Port Angeles**, Washington, 37km due south.

King George Terrace ends at Beach Drive. Go right (east) on Beach Drive along the shores of **McNeil Bay** to the **Municipality of Oak Bay**. Tudor motifs are so popular that the municipal limit is half seriously called the 'Tweed Curtain'. Beach Drive swings north through the **Victoria Golf Club**, favoured by strollers. Visitors occasionally meet Doris Gravlin, the resident ghost, usually wearing a long white dress. Gravlin's body was found in a sand trap in the 1930s. Her husband was suspected of murder, but he drowned before the investigation was completed.

Just north are **Haynes Park** and the **Oak Bay Marina**. The **Oak Bay Rose Garden** and more than 500 plants from the private estate that once occupied the area fill the southeast corner of **Windsor Park**, west on Currie Road opposite the breakwater.

Continue north past **Willows Park** and through the massive stone gates of **Uplands**. The posh 1912 housing estate was designed by the Olmsted brothers, who designed New York's Central Park. The 30-hectare **Uplands Park**, part of the original estate plan, is the largest

Above
Butchart Gardens

tract of undeveloped Garry oak habitat in Victoria. Known as Oregon white oak in the US and British Columbia's only native oak, immense groves of Garry oaks once flourished in the drier meadows of Victoria. Many of the graceful trees became furniture or house beams. Most of the park is undeveloped. Continue 5km north to **Loon Bay**, the **Royal Victoria Yacht Club** and another massive stone gate marking the northern boundary of Uplands. Beach Drive becomes Cadboro Bay Road at Sinclair Road (end of detour).

Detour 2: Follow Cadboro Bay Road to Arbutus Road. Turn left (north) on to Arbutus and keep to the main roads headed north and west through **Mount Douglas Park** to Royal Oak Drive. Take Royal Oak Drive to Hwy 17 northbound. Go left (west) at Keating Cross Road, following signs to **Butchart Gardens**. Return to Victoria via Hwy 17A, passing the **Dominion Astrophysical Observatory** on the way to Hwy 17.

Above
Fisgard Lighthouse, Fort Rodd Hill

Go right (west) on Sinclair Road through the **University of Victoria** and across the Saanich Peninsula to Hwy 17. Turn left (south) on Hwy 17 to Victoria. At the end of the dual carriageway, make a sharp left turn on to Douglas Street at the **Town and Country Centre**. Turn right 1km later on to Cloverdale Road, following signs and lane markings for 'Victoria by way of Douglas St'. At the second traffic signal, turn left on to Douglas to pass **Mayfair Shopping Centre**, one of the largest shopping malls on Vancouver Island, and a strip of motels.

The bright pink and grey brick **Victoria City Hall** is on the west side of Douglas at Pandora Street.

Continue five blocks to Broughton Street and turn right (west) at the red brick **St Peter's Presbyterian Church**, right again at Broad Street and again on to Fort Street, one-way eastbound. Follow Fort Street 2km past **Antique Row** to Moss Street. Turn right (south), following green signs for the Art Gallery of Greater Vancouver (*end of detour*).

Head east to skirt Beacon Hill Park, then north up Cook Street, right in Richardson Street and left in Moss Street to reach the **ART GALLERY OF GREATER VICTORIA ❷**. From the Gallery, turn right on to Will Spencer Place, left on to Moss and right on to Fort Street. Turn right into Joan Crescent to **CRAIGDARROCH CASTLE ❸**.

Exit right into Joan Crescent. Continue to Rockland Avenue, turn right and then immediately left into **GOVERNMENT HOUSE GARDENS ❹**. Leave Government House to the left (west) on Rockland. Continue across Moss Street, Cook and Vancouver Streets, where Rockland becomes Courtney Street, to Quadra Street and **Christ Church Anglican Cathedral**, built in 13th-century Gothic style. Turn left (south) on to Quadra, which becomes Arbutus Way in **BEACON HILL PARK**. Continue on to Circular Drive, or follow Park Way to the top of Beacon Hill for views across Victoria and Juan de Fuca Strait and return to Circular Drive. Follow the circle left to Douglas Street and go left. Go right (west) on to Niagara Street two blocks to Government Street and turn right (north). **CARR HOUSE ❺** is ahead on the right (east).

Continue north past the **James Bay Inn** toward Belleville Street, with the **PARLIAMENT BUILDINGS ❻** on the left and the **ROYAL BRITISH COLUMBIA MUSEUM ❼** on the right. Across Belleville, the **INNER**

HARBOUR **8** is on the left and **THE FAIRMONT EMPRESS HOTEL 9** on the right. Move to the right lane following Government Street north, passing the **Tourism Victoria Visitor Info Centre** on the left.

Continue past Fort Street with **The Bay Centre** on the right and **Munro's Books** on the left. At View Street, **BASTION SQUARE 10** and the **Maritime Museum** are to the left.

Detour: Turn left (west) on to Yates Street, then right (north) on to Wharf Street one block later, and move into the left or middle lane. Turn left (west) and cross the sky-blue **Johnson St Bridge** over **Victoria Harbour** to **Esquimalt**. Follow Esquimalt Road west to Admirals Road and turn right (north) to Hwy 1A at **CRAIGFLOWER HOUSE**. Turn left (west) on to Hwy 1A. Go straight to Ocean Boulevard, the first traffic signal beyond the **Juan de Fuca Recreation Centre** (on the south side), following signs for **FORT RODD HILL** and **FISGARD LIGHTHOUSE**. Return via Hwy 1A, which becomes Douglas Street.

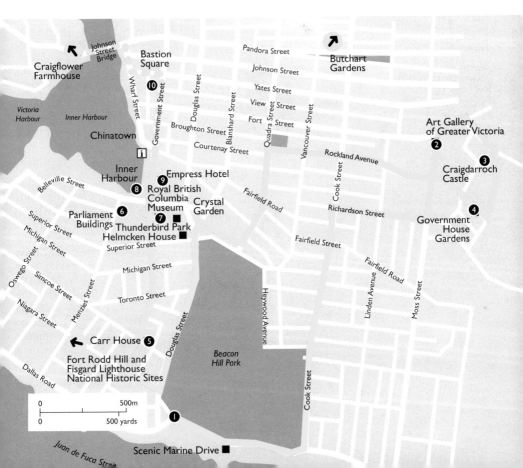

South Vancouver Island

Ratings

Beaches	●●●●○
Nature	●●●●○
Parks	●●●●○
Scenery	●●●●○
Walking	●●●●○
Children	●●●○○
Food	●●●○○
History	●●●○○

Don't expect to visit Victoria without exploring South Vancouver Island. Routes from Victoria's airport and major ferry terminals include a scenic drive through peaceful farming country north of the city. To the west lie increasingly wild stretches of forest and storm-wracked beach as the Strait of Juan de Fuca opens into the Pacific Ocean. Much of the oceanfront is protected in a series of parks linked by a rugged walking trail.

Inland forests have long since been logged, regrown and logged again in a seemingly endless cycle that despoils land and streams. It isn't until Port Renfrew and the roadless areas north that timber companies relinquish their hold. The variety of outdoor leisure activities, from boating and birding to strolling the lush glades of Butchart Gardens, mountain biking former railway lines and wilderness hiking, have made South Vancouver Island a playground for Victorians of all persuasions.

BOTANICAL BEACH PROVINCIAL PARK❖❖❖

Botanical Beach Provincial Park
3.5km south from Port Renfrew on gravel road;
http://wlapwww.gov.bc.ca/bcparks/explore/parkspgs/juanfuca.htm. Open daily.

Botanical Beach, at the mouth of the Juan de Fuca Strait, is one of BC's best known, if seldom seen, beaches. Sandstone cliffs drop to a cobble beach and rich tide pools that have been studied by generations of marine biologists from around the globe. At low tide, the pools are filled with green sea urchins, purple sea stars, scuttling red crabs, the waving green tentacles of anemones and swarms of silvery fish. The best and safest time to visit is near the end of a falling tide (use tide tables for Tofino) just before slack water. Rising tides sweep in rapidly, with massive rogue waves scouring what had been dry land an eyeblink earlier.

Rough tides and massive winter storms have eroded cliffs and headlands into swirling stone sculptures topped with Sitka spruce and shore pine. Several easy trails, including Mill Bay, Botany Bay and Shoreline, offer fine views even at high tide. All three trails converge on the Juan de Fuca Marine Trail, which leads 47km to China Beach.

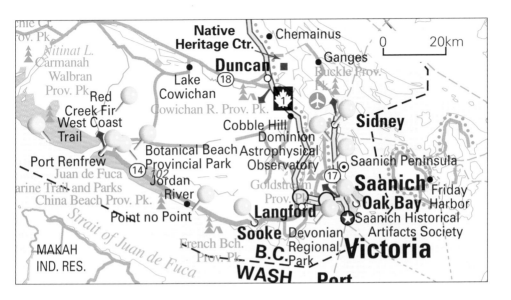

DEVONIAN REGIONAL PARK✦✦✦

Devonian Regional Park *William Head Road, 1km west of My-Chosen Café; tel: (250) 478-3344; www.crd.bc.ca/parks/devonian.htm. Open daily dawn–dusk.*

My-Chosen Café $$ *4492 Happy Valley Road; tel: (250) 474-2333, is a local favourite, especially at weekends.*

An easy 1-km nature trail on this former farm leads from the car park past **Sherwood Pond✦** (once used to water cattle) to the beach at **Perry Bay✦✦✦**, a favourite spot to watch for seals, sea lions and whales. A 5-km trail leads east to **Witty's Lagoon✦✦✦**, but the trail is walkable only at low tide.

Right
Devonian Regional Park

DOMINION ASTROPHYSICAL OBSERVATORY❖❖

Dominion Astrophysical Observatory Observatory Hill, 5071 W. Saanich Rd; tel: (250) 363-8262; www.hia-iha.nrccnrc.gc.ca/dao/index_e.html. Open daily, call for hours and programmes.

The 1.82-m reflecting telescope inside the white dome atop Observatory Hill was the world's largest when it opened in 1918 and is still in active use. A scenic access road spirals around the hill to a car park just outside the observatory dome. The observatory interpretive centre calls itself 'The Centre of the Universe'. A planetarium and multimedia shows like *Falling Asteroid Blues* further engage visitors.

EAST SOOKE REGIONAL PARK❖❖❖

East Sooke Regional Park Off Rocky Point Rd; tel: (250) 478-3344; www.crd.bc.ca/parks/east_sooke.htm. Open daily dawn–dusk.

South Vancouver Island's prime park has 1436 hectares of semi-wild shore and forest laced with walking trails. The foreshore is framed by twisted arbutus and stunted pines, backed by Sitka spruce, red cedar, hemlock and Douglas fir. Look for bald eagles perched at the edge of the forest, river otters and mink scurrying through piles of tangled driftwood and cormorants diving offshore. Sea lions are common from September to May. Walking routes range from pre-picnic walks to an all-day, 10-km trek along the park shoreline. Tiny spits and offshore islands protect dozens of pocket-sized beaches and picnic spots.

GALLOPING GOOSE REGIONAL TRAIL❖❖❖

Galloping Goose Regional Trail $ Multiple entry points between Victoria and Leechtown; tel: (250) 478-3344; www.crd.bc.ca/parks/galloping_goose.htm. Open daily dawn–dusk.

This linear park (70km long by 10m wide) follows the railbed of the *Galloping Goose*, a 1920s passenger railway that once ran from Victoria to Leechtown, an abandoned mining camp north of Sooke. The almost-level trail meanders through a variety of landscapes from urban streets to dense forest. Popular stretches for walking or cycling are Roche Cove Regional Park (off Gillespie Road in Metchosin) to Matheson Lake Regional Park, about 4km, and through Sooke Potholes Provincial Park (*see page 82*).

JUAN DE FUCA MARINE TRAIL❖❖❖

Juan de Fuca Marine Trail Between China Beach, west of Jordan River (near Port Renfrew), BC Parks; tel: (250) 474-1336; http://wlapwww.gov.bc.ca/bcparks/explore/parkpgs/juanfuca.htm

Park and trail cover 47km of spectacular beaches, dazzling marine views, lush coastal forest and rich wildlife habitat. Experienced hikers should allow four days to walk the entire trail, but shorter sections make easy day hikes. **China Beach**❖, just west of Jordan River, has crashing surf 20 minutes from the trail head. **Botanical Beach**❖❖❖, the west end of the trail, is famed for its tide pools and easy walks along the **Mill Bay**❖❖❖, **Botany Bay**❖❖❖ and **Shoreline**❖❖❖ trails. Other trail access points include **Sombrio Beach**❖❖ and **Parkinson Beach**❖.

LOCHSIDE REGIONAL TRAIL❖❖❖

Lochside Regional Trail *Lochside Dr and Beacon Ave to Quadra St in Victoria; tel: (250) 476-3344; www.crd.bc.ca/bcparks/lochside.htm*

Scrap the railway but keep the right of way. That's the idea behind the **Lochside Regional Trail**, named after its starting point. By either name, the walking and cycling trail connects with the Galloping Goose trail at Quadra Street near Greenridge Circle in Victoria. Much of the trail is gravel, passing through forest, fields, hobby farms with pig and turkey pens, open-air museums, and even a field for flying model aeroplanes. Allow three hours one way to cycle the 30km to or from Victoria.

POINT NO POINT❖❖❖

Point No Point Resort $$ *1505 West Coast Rd (21km west of Sooke); tel: (250) 646-2020; www.pointnopoint.com*

The point of Point No Point (named by early chartmakers who either saw or didn't see the point, depending on their position) is a 400-m rock pile pounded by ferocious waves. The inn of the same name is a traditional stopping point for modern Victorians on the way to or from Port Renfrew. Afternoon tea is a local classic.

PORT RENFREW❖❖

Port Renfrew Chamber of Commerce *1 Parkinson Rd., Port Renfrew; tel: (250) 647-5557; www. portrenfrew.com/renfrew.html*

This tiny village at the mouth of the San Juan River is the end of the road on South Vancouver Island. It's also the terminus (or the beginning) of the Juan de Fuca Marine Trail south and east to China Beach, the West Coast Trail north to Bamfield and a maze of logging roads that converge on Cowichan Bay and Duncan (*see page 89*). Expect at least a smattering of hikers, paddlers, beachcombers, fishers and hunters all year, though traffic is heaviest from June to mid-September when hundreds of West Coast Trail walkers pour through town.

Right
Port Renfrew's Botanical Beach

Accommodation and food in Port Renfrew

Don't expect big-city cuisine in this frontier town that caters to outdoor recreationists.

Lighthouse Pub $$ *Parkinson Rd; tel: (250) 647-5505; www.portrenfrew.com/lighthouse,* is a good alternative restaurant.

Port Renfrew Hotel & Pub $$ *Foot of Government Pier; tel: (250) 647-5541,* is a rustic hotel/pub for backpackers and the hunting crowd.

RED CREEK FIR❖

Red Creek Fir *12km from Port Renfrew; http://portrenfrew.com/redfir. htm. Ask for directions and (especially) road conditions; in 2004 it was accessible only with 4-wheel drive.*

Thought to be the largest Douglas fir in Canada, this 73m-high tree was probably closer to 90m tall before the top blew off in a windstorm sometime in the past 900 or so years. Its 349sq-m of wood were left when loggers clearcut the area in 1987. Another record holder is a Douglas fir in the upper Coquitlam watershed that was measured at 94m tall in 1996.

SAANICH PENINSULA❖❖

Saanich Peninsula Chamber of Commerce *West side Hwy 17, half-way between Swartz Bay Ferry Terminal and Sidney; 2480 Beacon Ave, Sidney; tel: (250) 656-3616; www.spcoc.org. Open daily.*

BC Aviation Museum $$ *1910 Norseman Rd (at Victoria International Airport), Sidney; tel: (250) 655-3300; www.bcam.net. Open daily summer 1000–1600; rest of year 1100–1500.*

Pointing north from Victoria like a thumb, the Saanich Peninsula is largely open, rolling country. Much of the peninsula is protected from future development within regional parks or agricultural preserves, but Victoria's expanding population has led to traffic congestion and pollution problems. Hwy 17, which leads from the BC Ferries landing at Swartz Bay to central Victoria, is the main traffic artery. Hwy 17A, W. Saanich Road, is a more scenic alternative, but considerably slower.

At the tip of the peninsula and Hwy 17 are **Swartz Bay❖❖❖** and the **BC Ferries terminal**. Just south is **Victoria International Airport** and the **BC Aviation Museum❖**, which showcases the history of flight in Canada. The emotional highlight is a replica of the Gibson Twin built by Victorian William Gibson in 1910 – the craft flew 60m before crashing into a Garry oak tree, beating the American Wright brothers' 1903 flight record of 36m.

Right
Vintage seaplane

SAANICH HISTORICAL ARTIFACTS SOCIETY*

Saanich Historical Artifacts Society $
7321 Lochside Rd, Saanichton;
tel: (250) 652-5522;
www.horizon.bc.ca/~shas.
Open 0930–1630 Jun–early
Sept, 0930–1200 early
Sept–May.

The 12-hectare site looks like a junk yard from the highway, but the antique farming equipment, model railway, sawmill and almost everything else are maintained in perfect working order. Facilities include a small lake, forest hiking trails, a nature pond and picnic facilities.

Accommodation on the Saanich Peninsula

Brentwood Bay Lodge & Spa $$$ *849 Verdier Ave, Brentwood Bay; tel: (250) 544.2079 or (888) 544-2079; www.brentwoodbaylodge.com*, has luxury ocean view suites with outside balconies and fireplaces, a wood-fire grill restaurant, art gallery, 65-slip marina and a scuba-diving centre.

SIDNEY*

The Marine Ecology Station *Port Sidney Marina, 9835 Seaport Place; tel: (250) 655-1555; www.mareco.org/home/default.asp. Open daily 1200–1700.*

Sidney Spit (Provincial) Marine Park *Sidney Island, 3km from Sidney.*

Princess Margaret (Provincial) Marine Park *Portland Island, 8km from Sidney. Both former provincial marine parks are in* **Gulf Islands National Park Reserve***, Gulf Islands National Park Reserve, 2220 Harbour Rd, Sidney, BC, V8L 2P6; tel: (250) 654-4000; www.pc.gc.ca/pn-np/bc/gulf/index_e.asp*

The town was built in the 1890s at the terminus of the Victoria and Sidney Railway. The railway is long gone, but the high street, Beacon Avenue, is a pleasant place to wander. Look for bookshops along Beacon Avenue and Third Street, as well as a variety of speciality shops. The waterfront includes several restaurants with pleasant outdoor decks, pubs, parks, a marina and a popular fish market.

The Marine Ecology Station** is a combination aquarium and marine research station dedicated to local marine life. Volunteers are usually on hand to explain exhibits in the touch tanks and aquaria as well beneath a battery of microscopes. Exhibits are designed for children, but there are details and information enough to keep professional researchers entranced.

Just offshore are the former **Sidney Spit Provincial Marine Park***** and **Princess Margaret Provincial Marine Park*****, now included in Gulf Islands National Park Reserve. Both are accessible by private boat or by ferry from the marina at the end of Beacon Avenue. The parks offer calm, sandy beaches, open lagoons, meadows and forests teeming with birds, deer and other wildlife, and camping.

SOOKE**

Sooke Region InfoCentre *Sooke Region Museum, see overleaf.*

Sooke is the southernmost harbour in Western Canada, a bustling fishing, logging and tourist town. The harbour is protected by **Whiffen Spit*****, a narrow strip of sand, gravel and driftwood nearly 5km long. Both Sooke Harbour and Sooke Basin, a large sheltered backwater, are popular with kayakers.

Sooke Region Museum $
2070 Phillips Rd, Sooke;
tel: (250) 642-6351;
www.sooke.museum.bc.ca.
Open daily 0900–1700.

Moss Cottage $ 2070
Phillips Rd, Sooke; tel: (250)
642-6351. Moss Cottage is
part of Sooke Region
Museum (see above).

Sooke was the site of Vancouver Island's first successful steam-powered sawmill and one of BC's last commercial fish traps. **Sooke Region Museum❖❖❖** tells both stories in lavish detail, as well as recounting a short-lived gold rush at Leechtown and the large First Nations villages that once dominated the area. **Moss Cottage❖❖❖** is the oldest structure in Sooke, built in 1870 with lumber from the original Muir Mill, itself built around a boiler salvaged from a shipwreck in 1849. The cottage, furnished as a working-class home from 1902, is open all year. Guides explain the displays in summer.

Accommodation and food in Sooke

Mom's Café $$ 2036 Shields Rd; tel: (250) 642-3314; www.momscafe.net, is a busy local eatery, known for beer batter halibut.

Sooke Harbour House $$$ 1528 Whiffen Spit Rd; tel: (250) 642-3421 or (800) 889-9688; www.sookeharbourhouse.com, is one of the most acclaimed restaurant-hotels in Western Canada, specialising in all-local products: scallops, shrimp, geoducks, whelks, salmon, squid, two dozen types of crab, duck, rabbit and vegetables fresh from the kitchen garden.

SOOKE POTHOLES PROVINCIAL PARK❖❖

Sooke Potholes Provincial Park
Sooke River Rd, 5km north of
Sooke; tel: (250) 474-1336;
http://wlapwww.gov.bc.ca/
bcparks/explore/parkpgs/
sooke.htm. Open daily.

The potholes, natural holes in the Sooke River filled with cool, clear water, have been a popular summer swimming destination since the 1860s. It is also a place where people come to ride bikes and watch spawning salmon. Expect crowds on hot summer days, but winter visitors are rare.

WEST COAST TRAIL❖❖❖

West Coast Trail
Pacific Rim National
Park Reserve, 2185 Ocean
Terrace Rd, Box 280, Ucluelet
or Parks Canada West Coast
Trail InfoCentre, Hwy 14,
16km west of Sombrio Beach;
tel: (250) 726-7721;
http://parkscan.harbour.com/
pacrim/wctu.htm

Port Renfrew is the end or the beginning of the rugged 6-day, 75km trek through bogs, beaches, forests, rivers, rain and sun along the western edge of Vancouver Island. Created as a life-saving route for sailors shipwrecked on the treacherous coast in the 19th century, the Trail has become one of the most popular hikes in Canada. Sixty hikers are allowed to start each day, with groups leaving from Port Renfrew or Pachena Bay (3km from Bamfield) and Nitinat, the midway point. Most permits are booked up months in advance, but a handful are available, especially in shoulder seasons, on a first come, first served basis each day at 1300. The trail is part of Pacific Rim National Park Reserve.

WITTY'S LAGOON REGIONAL PARK✦✦✦

Witty's Lagoon Regional Park
Metchosin Rd; tel: (250) 478-3344;
www.crd.bc.ca/parks/wittys_lagoon.htm

Witty's perfectly encapsulates the West Coast with luxuriant forests, clear creeks, a waterfall, long sandy beaches backed by wracks of driftwood, bald eagles, blue herons, 158 other bird species, seals and passing whales. A 5-km trail leads to **Devonian Regional Park** (*see page 77*) at low tide.

Suggested tour

Total distance: 260km.

Time: Allow a half-day to drive east from Victoria and a full day to drive west, or 2–4 days to explore.

Links: Combine the south end of Vancouver Island with a visit to Victoria or island routes north.

Route: The south island tour has two sections, east up the Saanich Peninsula (70km return) and west to Port Renfrew (190km return). Drive each section as a day trip from Victoria, or allow at least one overnight in Sooke or Port Renfrew.

Below
Dusk on Vancouver Island

From downtown Victoria, follow Hwy 17 north along the Saanich Peninsula towards the **Victoria Airport** and the BC Ferries landing at **Swartz Bay**. The rolling countryside becomes increasingly agricultural

Above
A popular pastime on
Vancouver Island

beyond Victoria. Follow exit signs to **SIDNEY** ❶, a lively seaside town
and terminus for Washington State Ferries from the US. Return
southbound on Hwy 17 to Keating Cross Road and turn right (west) to
Butchart Gardens (*see page 66*).

From Butchart Gardens, return southbound to W Saanich Road and
turn right (south). The country road winds through 6km of scenic
hills, farms and townships to **Observatory Hill** and the **DOMINION
ASTROPHYSICAL OBSERVATORY** ❷. Continue on W Saanich Road
and follow signs for Hwy 17. Take Hwy 17 into central Victoria or
follow Hwy 1A (Gorge Road) westbound (right) to avoid the central
city and continue the south island tour.

For the western tour, continue along Hwy 1A or the Victoria City Tour Detour to Fort Rodd Hill and Fisgard Lighthouse (*see page 69*) to **Craigflower Farmhouse** (*see page 68*) and **Fort Rodd Hill/Fisgard Lighthouse**. From the Ford Rodd Hill car park, continue straight for 2km to Esquimalt Lagoon. Just offshore is **Royal Roads**, a protected anchorage first charted by Spanish sailors in 1790. At the west end of the lagoon, turn right on to Lagoon Road. At the top of the hill, turn left on to Metchosin Road. Pass Albert Head Lagoon Park and **WITTY'S LAGOON REGIONAL PARK ❸**, 3km to **My-Chosen Café** and veer right on to William Head Road. Turn right up the narrow avenue of **Lombard Poplars** just past **DEVONIAN REGIONAL PARK ❹**. Turn left on to Rocky Point Rd and right 3km later on to Matheson Lake Park Road. Pass East Sooke Regional Park to Gillespie Road. Turn right (north) on to Hwy 14 and turn west (left).

Pass Sooke River Road and the **SOOKE POTHOLES ❺**, the **Sooke River Hotel**, the Sooke Region Museum and continue into Sooke, a small fishing and resort town. Hwy 14 continues west into increasingly mountainous country past the **Shearingham Light** and **Shirley, POINT NO POINT ❻**, the lumber town of **Jordan**, and into **PORT RENFREW ❼**.

Take Hwy 14 back to **Victoria**.

Detour: In good weather, you can follow unpaved logging roads from Port Renfrew to **Lake Cowichan** and **Douglas**, then south along the Island Highway to **Victoria**. Allow half a day for the return trip. Ask about logging road closures and driving conditions in Port Renfrew before setting out.

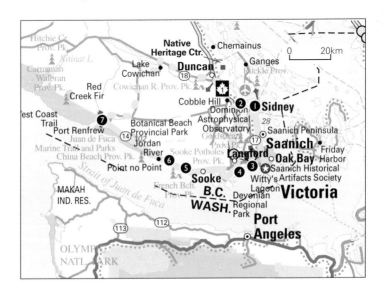

Central Vancouver Island

Ratings

First Nations art	●●●●●
Historical sights	●●●●●
History	●●●●●
National parks	●●●●●
Nature	●●●●●
Beaches	●●●●○
Children	●●●●○
Outdoor activities	●●●●○

Rolling hills, lush valleys, mossy forests, protected harbours, tranquil lakes, art from several First Nations bands and trackless beaches define the central section of Vancouver Island. So do clearcuts, tree plantations, slag heaps and abandoned mining towns. The coal mines that once made Nanaimo one of the richest cities in Canada are long closed, the grimy, sooty waterfronts transformed into sparkling marinas and busy bayside walking paths. Chemainus, Duncan and similar towns once dependent on forest industries have been reborn as tourist centres with museums, murals, totem poles and other artistic productions. Across Vancouver Island, great swaths of beach, island and forest have been preserved within Pacific Rim National Park, much of it unreachable except by foot or by boat. In between lies an irregular chequerboard of natural forest, farmed forest, burgeoning dormitory communities and quiet villages. The area is also becoming BC's second wine region.

CHEMAINUS✧✧

ⓘ Chemainus & District Chamber of Commerce *9796 Willow St (across from Waterwheel Park);* tel: *(250) 246-3944;* www.chemainus.bc.ca. *Open Mon–Fri.*

Chemainus calls itself 'The Little Town that Did' in memory of its successful transition from timber to tourism. When its mainstay mill closed in the early 1980s, the city paid local artists to paint **murals✧✧✧** on the buildings to lure coach tours. The ploy worked, sparking a business boom and nearly three dozen murals.

Centre of the boom is **Waterwheel Park✧** and the **Chemainus Valley Museum✧**, with local artefacts from the past century. Pick up a Mural Map at the museum or from most local businesses. The 30-plus paintings depict local history from the original First Nations inhabitants of the area to the arrival of Europeans and the development of local timber and agricultural industries. A new sawmill has reopened, but lumber plays second fiddle to a growing arts community.

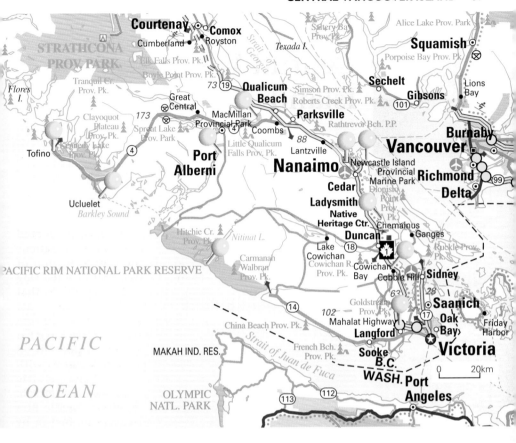

Chemainus Valley Museum $
Waterwheel Park; tel: (250) 246-2445. Open daily mid-Feb–mid-Dec 1000–1600.

Waterwheel Park
Willow St. Open daily.

Accommodation and food in Chemainus

Fuller Lake Motel $$ *9300 Smiley Rd, Canada Hwy; tel: (250) 246-3282 or (888) 246-3255; www.chemainus-fullerlakemotel.com,* is the largest motel in the area.

Hummingbird Tea House & Restaurant $$ *9893 Maple St; tel: (250) 246-2290,* is a convenient stop.

Pacific Shores Inn $$ *Tel: (250) 246-4987* is near ferries and the beach.

COWICHAN BAY❖ & DUNCAN❖❖

Tourism Cowichan
175 Ingram St, Duncan, BC, V9L 1N8; tel: (250) 746-1099 or (888) 303-3337; http://cowichan.net/ visit/contact.htm

This tiny bayside town was once the heart of the entire Cowichan region, stretching from the Malahat Hills north nearly to Nanaimo and west to the Pacific Ocean. Meaning 'warm land' in the Cowichan First Nations language, Cowichan Bay was a major timber and farm port until railway builders opened a station in Duncan in the late 19th century.

Bluenose Steak & Seafood Restaurant $$ *north end of the village; 1765 Cowichan Bay Rd; tel: (250) 748-2841,* is a popular local coffee shop and steakhouse.

Rock Cod Café $$ *1759 Cowichan Bay Rd; tel: (250) 746-1550,* is the local favourite for fresh seafood.

Cowichan Bay Maritime Centre $ *1761 Cowichan Bay Rd; tel: (250) 746-4955; www.classicboats.org. Open daily Apr–Oct 0900–dusk.*

Duncan Cowichan Visitor InfoCentre *381 TransCanada Hwy; tel: (250) 746-4636 or (888) 303-3337. Open daily 0900–1800.*

Quw'utsun' Cultural & Conference Centre *200 Cowichan Way; tel: (250) 746-8119 or (877) 746-8119; www.quwutsun.ca. Open daily May–Sept 0900–1800, Oct–Apr 1000–1700.*

British Columbia Forest Discovery Centre *2892 Drinkwater Rd, Hwy 1, just north of Duncan; tel: (250) 715-1113; www.bcforestmuseum.com. Open daily Apr–Oct.*

Most buildings in this one-road town have their front doors on Cowichan Bay Road and their back doors on Cowichan Bay. The **Cowichan Bay Maritime Centre**✦✦✦ is a combination museum and wooden-boat-building centre. Best views of the town are from the Centre's 100m pier. Pavilions along the pier display historic photographs and boat-related memorabilia.

Duncan✦✦✦ became the Cowichan's main town when the railway arrived in the 1880s. A busy commercial and agricultural centre, it is best known for the 40 or so totem poles scattered around town and the **Quw'utsun' Cultural and Conference Centre**✦✦. Don't miss the multimedia programmes and exhibits on local First Nations history. In summer, a daily **Salmon BBQ**✦✦✦ includes dances and story-telling with an excellent meal.

British Columbia Forest Discovery Centre✦ is the forest industry's own vision of BC history. Exhibits include a working lumber mill and steam train, as well as forest machinery and easy-to-understand displays of how trees are cut, sorted and processed.

Right
Logging boats

Cowichan Valley Museum $ *120 Canada Ave; tel: (250) 746-6612; www.cowichanvalley.museum. bc.ca. Open Jun–Sept, Mon–Sat 1000–1600; Oct–May, Wed–Fri 1100–1600, Sat 1300–1600.*

Freshwater Ecocentre *1080 Wharncliffe Rd; tel: (250) 746-6722; www.islandtrout.org. Open Mon–Fri 0930–1600.*

Somenos Marsh Wildlife Refuge *East side of Hwy 1, north of Duncan.*

Cowichan Valley Museum** offers domestic and industrial artefacts in period settings in a 1912 railway station. The photographic collection is one of BC's best local archives. Park at the museum and follow the yellow footsteps around town to see the entire totem collection.

Freshwater Ecocentre* has interactive exhibits on local freshwater habitats and tours of the trout hatchery next door, while **Somenos Marsh Wildlife Refuge***** is good for summer and winter birdwatching.

Food in Duncan

Gossips $$ *161 Kenneth St; tel: (250) 746-6466; www.gossipscafe.ca,* uses local ingredients in outstanding Italian-inspired dishes.

Vigneti Zanatta & Vinoteca Restaurant $$ *5039 Marshall Rd; tel: (250) 709-2279; www.zanatta.ca,* focuses on local food and wines, most grown on the property.

GABRIOLA ISLAND*

Gabriola Island Chamber of Commerce and Visitor InfoCentre *#3–575 North Rd, Gabriola, BC V0R 1X0; tel: (250) 247-9332 or (888) 284-9332; www.gabriolaisland.org*

Gabriola Island, reached by ferry from Nanaimo, is the northernmost Gulf Island, with 4500 permanent residents, an artists' colony, tide pools, beaches, petroglyphs and the **Malaspina Galleries***, cavernous sandstone formations on the northwest side. Activities include fishing, diving in clear cold waters, kayaking, beachcombing, hiking, biking, or golf.

MacMILLAN PROVINCIAL PARK***

MacMillan Provincial Park *Cameron Lake; tel: (250) 248-9460; http://wlap-www.gov.bc.ca/bcparks/ explore/parkpgs/macmillan. htm. Open daily.*

This roadside park includes **Cathedral Grove*****, one of BC's only surviving stands of virgin forest accessible by highway. The park is named for Harvey MacMillan, BC's first Chief Forester and later head of what is now MacMillan Bloedel, one of BC's largest timber companies. The virgin grove stands in stark contrast to MacMillan Bloedel clearcuts and plantation projects nearby.

MALAHAT HIGHWAY***

Malahat Highway winds through the Malahat Hills separating the Saanich Peninsula from the Cowichan region. Views eastward to the mainland are stunning in clear weather.

Nanaimo*

Tourism Nanaimo
*2290 Bowen Rd;
tel: (800) 663-7337 or
(250) 756-0106; www.
tourismnanaimo.com. Open
daily in summer 0800–1900;
in winter Mon–Fri 0900–
1700, Sat 1000–1600.*

Nanaimo has two **BC
Ferries terminals,**
*tel: (888) 223-3779 or (250)
386-3431.*

The Bastion *www.
nanaimo.museum.bc.ca/
bastionpage.htm. Open daily
Jul–Sept.*

**Nanaimo District
Museum** *$ 100 Cameron Rd;
tel: (250) 753-1821; www.
nanaimo.museum.bc.ca. Open
daily May–Sept 1000–1700;
Tue–Sat Oct–Apr 1000–1700.*

Petroglyph Provincial Park
*Hwy 1; tel: (250) 248-9460;
http://wlapww.gov.bc.ca/bcparks/
explore/parkpgs/petrogly.htm*

The town developed as a coal centre and remains Vancouver Island's major export centre. The coal docks, foundries and other industries that once lined the harbour have been replaced by marinas, parks and the 4-km **Harbourfront Walkway***. Ask for self-guiding walking maps of historic areas and buildings at the Tourist InfoCentre. **The Bastion*** is the sole surviving Hudson's Bay Company bastion, or fortress, in BC. The white wooden redoubt houses a small museum. Guardsmen in 1850s naval uniforms parade and fire a cannon at noon each day in summer. **Nanaimo District Museum*** uses local artefacts to reproduce a coal mine, pioneer town and Chinatown. **Petroglyph Provincial Park,** *on Hwy 1* just south of Nanaimo, has thousand-year-old petroglyphs and is a chance for petroglyph rubbing as a souvenir.

Accommodation and food in Nanaimo

Best Western Dorchester $$ *70 Church St; tel: (250) 754-6835 or (800) 661-2449; www.dorchesternanaimo.com,* is a heritage building across the street from the Harbour Seawalk and one block from the museum.

Blackbear Pub $ *6201 Dumont Rd; tel: (250) 390-4800,* is a comfortable local pub.

Coast Bastion Inn $$ *11 Bastion St; tel: (250) 753-6601 or (800) 663-1144; www.coasthotels.com,* is just up the street from The Bastion.

Newcastle Island Provincial Marine Park***

**Newcastle Island
Provincial Marine
Park** *Just off Nanaimo;
tel: (250) 754-78793; http://
wlapww.gov.bc.ca/bcparks/
explore/parkpgs/newcastl.htm*

This 306-hectare island sheltering Nanaimo Harbour has been home to Snuneymuxw First Nations villages, coal mines, fish processing plants and resorts. Accessible by ferry from Nanaimo, it has become a favourite getaway for picnicking, walking, swimming and camping.

Pacific Rim National Park Reserve***

**Park Information
Centre** *Hwy 4, 3km
north of Ucluelet–Tofino
junction; tel: (250) 726-4212.
Open mid-Mar–mid-Oct, daily.*

**Pacific Rim National
Park Reserve** *west
coast of Vancouver Island;
tel: (250) 726-7721;
www.pc.gc.ca/pn-np/bc/
pacificrim/index_e.asp*

This is three parks in one – the **West Coast Trail***, stretching north from Port Renfrew, the **Broken Group Islands***, more than 100 islands in Barkley Sound, and **Long Beach***, between Ucluelet and Tofino – the only section accessible by road. The 30km of sandy beaches, rocky headlands, forests and bogs are busy in summer and deserted from November to April, except for seagulls, sea lions and crabs hiding in the tangled driftwood.

Wickaninnish Centre* (*Long Beach; tel: (250) 726-7333. Open mid-Mar–mid-Oct, daily 1030–1800*) is the main interpretive centre, with a museum, restaurant and elevated walkways with expansive views. The surf-swept sand of Long Beach stretches 10km north.

PORT ALBERNI❖❖

Alberni Valley Chamber of Commerce *2533 Redford St; tel: (250) 724-6535 or (866) 576-3662; www.avcoc.com. Open Mon–Fri 0900–1700, Sat–Sun 1000–1400.*

Alberni Pacific Railway $$ *Kingsway Ave at Argyle St near Harbour Quay; tel: (250) 723-1376; www.alberniheritage.com/rail.shtml. Operates Thur–Mon late Jun–early Sept.*

Alberni Valley Museum $ *Echo Centre, 4255 Wallace St; tel: (250) 723-1376; www.alberniheritage.com/museum.shtml. Open Mon–Sat 1000–1700, Thur to 2000.*

Lady Rose and Frances Barkley $$ *5425 Argyle St, Alberni Harbour Quay; tel: (250) 723-8313 or (800) 663-7192; www.ladyrosemarine.com*

McLean Mill National Historic Site *Smith Road; tel: (250) 723-1376; www.alberniheritage.com/mill.shtml. Open daily late Jun–early Sept 1030–1630.*

Choo Kwa Ventures $$ *5323 River Rd; tel: (250) 724-4006 or (866) 294-8687; www.chookwa.com/tours.html*

Forty kilometres from the Pacific Ocean at the head of a fjord-like inlet, Port Alberni is shifting from mining and timber to tourism, although logging tours remain popular attractions.

Alberni Pacific Railway❖❖ provides steam train service to the McLean Mill National Historic Site in summer. The restored 1929 2-8-2 Baldwin Locomotive No 7 spent its working life in island logging.

Alberni Valley Museum❖ has a major collection of local Nuu Chah Nulth First Nations artefacts, as well as an operating steam engine, water wheel and similar practical items.

The ships **Lady Rose**❖❖❖ and **Frances Barkley**❖❖❖ provide freight, passenger and sightseeing services to Ucluelet via Bamfield and the Broken Group. Expect to see marine life all year and hikers, kayakers and boaters coming and going to one of BC's most popular marine parks in summer.

McLean Mill National Historic Site❖❖ is the only remaining steam-powered mill in British Columbia. The mill has been restored to its operating condition in 1965 when it was typical of the remote lumber camps and sawmills that dotted Vancouver Island.

First Nation Hupacasath **Choo Kwa Ventures** narrator-guides paddle bright red and white canoes around Sproat Lake or on the Somass River. A cedar-flavoured barbeque salmon lunch is an option before departure.

Accommodation and food in Port Alberni

Best Western Barclay $$$ *4277 Stamp Ave; tel: (250) 724-7171 or (800) 563-6590; www.bestwesternbarclay.com*, is the largest hotel in town.

Coast Hospitality Inn $$$ *3835 Redford St; tel: (250) 723-8111 or (800) 663-1144; www.coasthotels.com*, has big-city facilities.

Right
Pacific Rim National Park Reserve

Little Bavaria $$ *3035 4th Ave; tel: (250) 724-4242; www. littlebavariarestaurant.com*, is the only German restaurant in town.

Paradise Restaurant & Bistro $$ *4505 Gertrude St; tel: (250) 724-5050*, specialises in seafood and steaks.

Swale Rock Café $$ *5328 Argyle St; tel: (250) 723-0777*, serves seafood to a largely local crowd.

TOFINO✦✦✦

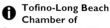

Tofino-Long Beach Chamber of Commerce *Campbell St; tel: (250) 725-3414; www.island.net/~tofino. Open daily Jul–Aug; May–Jun and Sept, weekends. Call in advance.*

Eagle Aerie Gallery *350 Campbell St; tel: (250) 725-3235; www.royhenryvickers.com*

House of Himwitsa *300 Main St; tel: (250) 725-2902 or (800) 899-1947; www.himwitsa.com*

Whale Centre & Museum $$ *411 Campbell St; tel: (250) 725-2132 or (888) 474-2288. Whale watching daily Mar–mid-Oct.*

This one-time timber town has become a busy tourist centre for Pacific Rim National Park Reserve and **Clayoquot Sound✦✦✦**, a UNESCO Biosphere Reserve. Tofino has also become a centre for First Nations artists and galleries. **Eagle Aerie Gallery✦✦✦** exhibits works by Roy Vickers, one Canada's most commercially successful First Nations artists. **House of Himwitsa✦✦✦** is a combination First Nations gallery, restaurant and motel.

The **Whale Centre & Museum✦✦✦** sponsors whale-watching excursions to supplement displayed artefacts from local shipwrecks and First Nations history.

Accommodation and food in Tofino

Best Western Tin Wis Resort $$ *1119 Pacific Rim Hwy; tel: (250) 725-4445 or (800) 661-9995; www.tinwis.com*, overlooks a calm cove that was a traditional launching point for First Nations whalers.

Common Loaf Bake Shop $ *180 First St; tel: (250) 725-3915*, is the town's best bakery and café.

Pacific Sands Beach Resort $$$ *Cox Bay; tel: (250) 725-3322 or (800) 565-2322; www.pacificsands.com*, has beachfront villas just north of Pacific Rim National Park.

Weigh West $$$ *634 Campbell St; tel: (250) 725-3277 or (800) 665-8922; www.weighwest.com*, is a waterfront hotel and restaurant popular with visiting fishermen.

Wickaninnish Inn $$$ *Chesterman Beach; tel: (250) 725-3100 or (800) 333-4604; www.wickinn.com*, gets international attention as one of BC's finest restaurants and most luxurious inns.

UCLUELET✦✦

The logging and fishing village of Ucluelet is trying to switch to tourism, but Tofino gets most of the traffic. Ucluelet is smaller, quieter and more focused on outdoor activities such as kayaking, fishing, whale-watching and boating. **Amphitrite Point Lighthouse✦✦✦** has

**ⓘ Ucluelet Chamber
of Commerce**
*Government Wharf (foot of
Main St); tel: (250) 726-
4641; www.uclueletinfo.com.
Open daily in summer;
Mon–Fri autumn–spring. Call
in advance.*

**ⓘ Amphitrite Point
Lighthouse** *south of
downtown. Open daily.*

He-Tin-Kis Park *1km
south of downtown. Open
daily.*

Government Wharf
Foot of Main St.

stunning views of Barkley Sound. Look for migrating grey whales between March and April, raging storms in winter and spectacular sunsets all year.

He-Tin-Kis Park◆◆◆ boardwalk trails wander through old-growth cedar and spruce forests to open shoreline vistas, while **Government Wharf**◆◆◆ is a convenient spot to watch bald eagles, seals and sea lions.

Accommodation and food in Ucluelet

Canadian Princess Resort $$$ *Harbourfront; tel: (250) 598-3366 or (800) 663-7090; www.canadianprincess.com,* is a historic steamship turned resort, restaurant and mothership for salmon and halibut fishing and nature trips into Barkley Sound.

Snug Harbour Inn $$$ *460 Marine Dr; tel: (250) 726-2686 or (888) 936-5222; www.asnugharbourinn.com/600/index.asp,* offers plush cliffside suites overlooking a private beach.

Suggested tour

Total distance: 320km.

Time: Allow a full day to drive from Victoria to Tofino; up to a week for sightseeing.

Links: Continue north to **Port Hardy** and **ferry routes** to the mainland (*see page 108*), take the ferry from **Nanaimo** back to **Vancouver** (*see page 42*), or return to Victoria.

Below
Chemainus mural

Rainforest archipelago

Clayoquot Sound⁺⁺⁺, a UNESCO Biosphere Reserve, is the largest surviving temperate rainforest in North America, thanks to Canada's largest-ever civil protest. A provincial decision to allow logging in 1993 sparked hundreds of arrests, road blockades and world-wide boycotts of BC products before most logging permits were rescinded. The 65km-long sound includes 3000sq km of islands, rivers and forests accessible only by air or boat. **Meares, Vargas** and **Flores** are the largest and most popular islands. **Hot Springs Cove**, the only natural hot springs on Vancouver Island, is another popular destination. Sea and air operators in Tofino and Ucluelet offer daily trips, weather permitting.

Route: Follow signs for Hwy 1 north from Victoria past **Portage Inlet** and **Thetis Lake Park**. The road swings north at **Goldstream Provincial Park** to become the **MALAHAT HIGHWAY ❶**. Broad vistas across the **Saanich Peninsula** to the mainland and the **Cascade Range** are stunning in clear weather, but lay-bys at the 352-m summit are accessible only from the northbound lanes. The Malahat Hwy becomes the Island Hwy as it runs north through the rolling agricultural lands from Duncan to Nanaimo.

Detour: The scenic route follows the direct route 50km north to Cowichan Bay Road and a rest area 18km north of the **Malahat Summit**. Turn west (left) through 6km of rolling farmland and forests dotted with tiny lakes to **COWICHAN BAY ❷** and continue north. The road becomes Tzouhalem Road at a T-junction just north of the roadside historical marker lauding the landing of the first shipload of English settlers in 1862. A second marker is dedicated to poet Robert W Service, who worked and wrote locally in the early 1900s.

Continue north, then west, to **Maple Bay**. Take Maple Bay Road northeast (right) through 6km of exclusive housing estates to Genoa Bay Road and turn right (east). The narrow road climbs through a range of granite hills to emerge at tiny **Genoa Bay**.

Return to Maple Bay, with **Salt Spring Island** (*see pages 58–9*) just offshore. Take Herd Road north and west to Osborne Bay Road and turn north (right) to Champlain Street. Go east (right) into **Crofton**. Go back up Champlain Street to Crofton Road and turn north (right) to Chemainus Road, 2km beyond the Fletcher Challenge pulp and paper mill. Continue north to **CHEMAINUS ❸**.

Chemainus Road runs 10km to the Island Hwy. Turn right (north) towards Nanaimo. At Cedar Point Road, turn right (east) through pastoral farmland to Yellowpoint Road and go east (right). Continue past **Roberts Memorial Provincial Park**, a popular summer swimming spot, and back on to Cedar Point Road. At MacMillan Road, turn right to visit the **Harmac Pulp Mill** or continue on to the Island Hwy and **NANAIMO ❹**.

Hwy 1 becomes Hwy 19 at Nanaimo, but keeps the Island Hwy name. Continue north along a narrowing strip of flat land along the coast. Just before **Parksville**, take Hwy 4 west towards Port Alberni. The settlement just south of the highway with goats grazing on the roof is **Coombs**, a convenient rest and ice cream stop. The highway climbs past **MACMILLAN PROVINCIAL PARK ❺**, one of the rare bits of virgin forest left along any highway in BC, then drops down to **PORT ALBERNI ❻**, the island's most interior Pacific port.

The road continues past **Sproat Lake**, home to the world's largest water bombers (used to fight forest fires), and twists through the increasingly rugged **MacKenzie Range** and **Hydro Hill**, an 18 per cent grade. At the T-junction, go left to **UCLUELET ❼** or right to **PACIFIC RIM NATIONAL PARK** and the end of the road at **TOFINO ❽**.

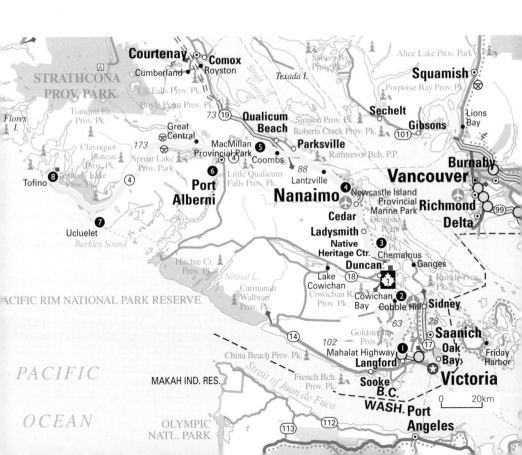

North Vancouver Island

Ratings

Beaches	●●●●●
Children	●●●●●
First Nations art	●●●●○
Mountains	●●●●●
Nature	●●●●○
Outdoor activities	●●●●○
Scenery	●●●●●
Wildlife	●●●●●

The northern portion of Vancouver Island stretches from warm, gentle beaches hundreds of metres wide and kilometres long to treacherous cliffs rising sheer from the turbulent ocean. Logging trucks and heavy equipment share the few northern roads and infrequent hamlets with hunters, fishers, RVs and long-distance cyclists, all of them outnumbered by bear, deer and bald eagles.

Just offshore, the Inside Passage between Vancouver Island and the mainland narrows from a broad marine highway at Parksville to a narrow, twisting channel dotted with jagged rocks and turbulent eddies from Campbell River northward.

Pods of orcas patrol the cold, fish-rich waters, dodging fleets of cruise ships, humpback whales and sea kayakers. On shore, look for the ornate, richly coloured totem poles created by the First Nations bands which have emerged from generations of repression and cultural twilight to become a major social and economic force once again.

ALERT BAY✦✦✦

ⓘ Alert Bay Information Centre *118 Fir St; tel: (250) 974-5024. Open daily Jul–Aug, Sept–Jun Mon–Fri.*

⇄ BC Ferry *tel: (888) 223-3779 or (250) 386-3431; www.ferries.bc.ca, from Port McNeill.*

🏛 'Namgis Burial Ground *Fir St, south of the ferry landing; roadside viewing.*

Alert Bay was a hotbed of First Nations resistance to discriminatory laws in the 19th and early 20th centuries. The fishing and tourist community on Cormorant Island is an ethnic mix today, but the look and feel are solidly Kwakwaka'wakw; Kwaguilth and Kwakiutl are other spellings for the band of kwak'wala-speaking people of Vancouver Island and the adjacent mainland inlets. Don't miss the **'Namgis Burial Ground✦✦✦** with its stunning totem poles (the cemetery is closed to the public, but clearly visible from the street), and the **U'mista Cultural Centre✦✦✦**, a model Big House built to display half of a potlatch (*see box, page 101*) collection that was confiscated by government agents in 1922 and returned in 1978 after decades of wrangling. The rest of the collection is in the (closed at press time) **Kwagiulth Museum and Cultural Centre** on Quadra Island (*see page 102*). U'mista also has an excellent selection of prints, lithographs, photographs, masks and other works by First Nations artists.

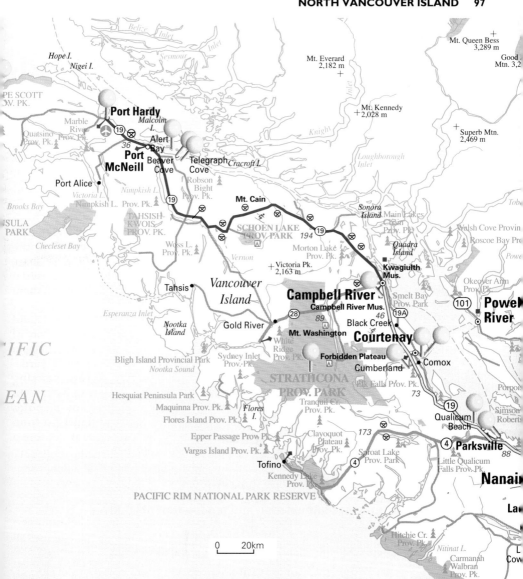

U'mista Cultural Centre Front St, north of the ferry landing; tel: (250) 974-5403; www.umista.org. Open daily May–Sept; Oct–Apr Mon–Fri.

Accommodation and food in Alert Bay

Nimpkish Hotel $$ *318 Fir St; tel: (888) 646-7547 or (250) 974-5716; www.nimpkishhotel.com*, is the largest hotel and restaurant on the island.

BEAVER COVE***

Beaver Cove $
12km off Hwy 19 from the North Island Discovery Centre; tel: (250) 956-3844; www.island.net/~nifetour for summer tours.

Beaver Cove handles 1.4 million cubic metres of logs annually, Canada's largest dryland sort where logs are separated by species, grade and intended use. The sorted logs are dumped in huge ponds or 'booming grounds' in the cove to be chained together, or 'stowed up' into rafts 21m wide by 121m long. The rafts are then towed to pulp and lumber mills for processing.

CAMPBELL RIVER*

Campbell River Visitor Information Centre *1235 Shoppers Row, Tyee Plaza; tel: (250) 298-4636 or (866) 830-1113; http://visitorinfo. incampbellriver.com. Open Jun–Aug daily 0900–1900, Sept–Apr Mon–Fri 0900–1700 Sat 1000–1600, May Mon–Sat 0900–1800.*

Campbell River & District Public Art Gallery *1235 Shoppers Row; tel: (250) 287-2261; http://crartgal.ca. Open Sept–May Tue–Sat 1200–1700, Jun–Aug Mon–Sat 1000–1700.*

The Museum at Campbell River $ *470 Island Hwy; tel: (250) 287-3103; www.crmuseum.ca. Open daily May–Sept; Oct–Apr Tue–Sun.*

Beaver Aquatics $$ *760 Island Hwy; tel: (250) 287-7652; www.connected.bc. ca/~baquatics/beaver.htm*

Timber is the main industry, but Campbell River is better known for fishing and scuba diving. The town has become the gateway for North Island hiking and trekking, fishing charters, sea kayaking, dive trips and other outdoor activities, with a cruise ship terminal in 2004.

Campbell River & District Public Art Gallery* features local artists and representations of the local area by outside artists. **The Museum at Campbell River**** looks across Discovery Passage to Cape Mudge on Quadra Island. Exhibits cover local First Nations history, European exploration and exploitation, and local natural history. Museum field trips to nearby historic sites are particularly interesting but must be booked in advance.

Scuba diving* is stunning all year, with protected waters for beginners, racing tidal currents for thrill seekers and some of North America's richest marine environments. Several ships have been scuttled nearby to serve as artificial reefs and scuba dive destinations. During the spring–autumn salmon runs, look for snorkelling trips that put even non-divers face-to-face with salmon migrating upstream to spawn. Don't even dream about diving the tricky tidal waters without a local guide; **Beaver Aquatics*** is one of the best operators.

Accommodation and food in Campbell River

Seafood is always a good choice in a town that has fancied itself the Salmon Capital of BC for most of the past century.

BeeHive Seafood Grill & Café $$ *921 Island Hwy; tel: (250) 286-6812*, has had views of Discovery Passage since the 1920s and now provides high-speed Internet access.

Harbour Grill $$$ *#112 1334 Island Hwy; tel: (250) 287-4143; www.harbourgrill.com*, overlooks Discovery Harbour and the restaurant website links to the summertime Alaska cruise ship schedule, to better time dining to cruiser viewing.

Ramada Hotel & Suites Campbell River $$$ *261 Island Hwy; tel: (250) 286-1131 or (800) 663-7227; www.ramadacr.ca/index.php*, offers water views and an African-themed Safari Suite.

Royal Coachman Pub $$ *84 Dogwood St; tel: (250) 286-0231*, is a Tudor-style pub with a full menu and the slogan, 'haggard and thin they stagger in, fat and stout they waddle out'.

Town Centre Inn $ *1500 Dogwood St; tel: (250) 287-8866 or (800) 287-7107; www.towncentreinn.com*, is a basic, good value choice with full breakfast.

CAPE SCOTT PROVINCIAL PARK✦✦✦

Cape Scott, the northernmost tip of Vancouver Island, is a tough two-day 27-km return trek from the trailhead. An easy 45-minute trail leads to the sandy shores of San Josef Bay. The 46-km North Coast Trail goes from Nissen Bight to Shushartie Bay. (**Cape Scott Provincial Park** *63km from Port Hardy by logging road; tel: (250) 954-4600; http://wlapwww.gov.bc.ca/bcparks/explore/parkpgs/cape.htm*.) Watch for bears, cougars, Roosevelt elk, and for river otters and mink near San Josef Bay. Be prepared for dramatic weather changes.

COURTENAY AND THE COMOX VALLEY✦✦✦

ℹ **Tourism Comox Valley** *2040 Cliffe Ave, Courtenay, BC, V9N 2L3; tel: (250) 334-3234 or 888-357-4471; www.tourism-comox-valley.bc.ca. Open daily.*

🏛 **Courtenay and District Museum $**
207 Fourth St; tel: (250) 334-0686; www.courtenaymuseum.ca. Call for days and hours.

Mt Washington Alpine Resort $$
1 Strathcona Parkway; tel: (250) 338-1386 or (888) 231-1499; www.mountwashington.ca. Open year-round.

Courtenay and the Comox Valley are amongst the sunniest parts of Vancouver Island, sheltered behind the highest peaks on the island. **Courtenay and District Museum**✦✦✦ occupies the Native Sons Hall, Canada's largest free-span log structure. Highlight is a 14m, 80-million-year-old elasmosaur fossil, the largest marine dinosaur ever found in Canada west of the Rockies.

Mt Washington Alpine Resort✦✦ has the highest vertical ski drop on the island. Views of the surrounding mountains are breathtaking in any season. Resort facilities and chairlift are open all summer, and alpine hiking, mountain biking and horse riding are easy ways to get to nature.

CUMBERLAND***

ⓘ Cumberland District Chamber of Commerce *2755 Dunsmuir Ave; tel: (250) 336-8313; www.cumberland bc.org. Open Jul–Aug Mon–Sat 0900–1700, Sept–Jun Mon–Fri 1000–1400.*

ⓜ Cumberland Museum Archives *$ 2680 Dunsmuir Ave; tel: (250) 336-2445; www.cumberlandmuseum.ca. Open daily.*

Cumberland was the heart of a massive coal field opened by Nanaimo coal baron Robert Dunsmuir, who built Craigdarroch Castle in Victoria (*see page 66*). Dunsmuir encouraged ethnic strife amongst British, Chinese, Italian, Japanese, Mexican and other workers to minimise union activities. The last mines closed in the 1960s, but slag heaps, derelict buildings, abandoned mine sites and a downtown mural showing a once-active Chinese community remain. **Cumberland Museum Archives***** explores the dramatic history of the region, including fatal mine accidents, bitter strikes, martial law and an awe-inspiring collection of period photographs.

PARKSVILLE** AND QUALICUM BEACH**

ⓘ Parksville and District Chamber of Commerce *Hwy 19; tel: (250) 248-3613; www. chamber.parksville.bc.ca. Open Mon–Fri 0900–1700.*

Qualicum Beach Chamber of Commerce *2711 W. Island Hwy; tel: (250) 752-9532; www. qualicum.bc.ca. Open daily.*

ⓜ Craig Heritage Park Museum $ *1245 E Island Hwy (at the InfoCentre), Parksville; tel: (250) 248-6966; www.macn. bc.ca/~d69hist/parkwelc.html. Open daily Jun–Labour Day 1000–1600.*

Qualicum Beach Historical Museum & Power House Museum *$ 587 Beach Rd; tel: (250) 752-5533. Open mid-May– mid-Sept, Tue–Sat 1100– 1600. Open daily in summer.*

Englishman River Falls Provincial Park *Errington Rd; tel: (250) 948-9460; http://wlapwww.gov.bc.ca/ bcparks/explore/parkpgs/ english.htm*

Parksville and Qualicum Beach are a burgeoning holiday destination backed by kilometres of broad, sandy beach. Each receding tide leaves hundreds of shallow pools that warm to tropical temperatures in the summer sun. Anonymous strip malls line much of Hwy 19A, but the twinned towns are worth a visit.

Craig Heritage Park Museum*** offers local history and artefacts in heritage buildings moved to the site.

Qualicum Beach adjoins Parksville but has more open beachfront. **Qualicum Beach Historical Museum & Power House Museum***** explores local history and the history of electrical power in BC in the town's original brick powerhouse.

Englishman River Falls Provincial Park*** has a scenic waterfall as well as easy forest walks, picnicking and swimming.

Potlatch

The potlatch ceremony, for naming of children, memorialising the dead, transferring rights and privileges, marriages, or the raising of memorial totem poles, was a central feature of First Nations life among coastal bands. Usually held in the quiet winter months, potlatch reinforced traditional chiefly authority through performances of sacred rituals and cemented political power by redistributing prodigious quantities of food, trade goods, clothing and household items in front of witnesses. The more wealth a leader could give away, the greater his power and influence.

The practice was banned in 1884 as sinful, wasteful and supportive of what Christian missionaries termed a 'decrepit' culture. A few First Nations communities complied, others continued to hold potlatches in secret. In more remote areas, the ban was simply ignored. In 1918, a government agent complained that 'During these gatherings, they lose months of time, waste their substance, contract all kinds of diseases and generally unfit themselves for being British subjects in the proper sense of the word'.

In 1922, federal officials raided potlatch ceremonies and confiscated an enormous collection of ceremonial and sacred objects. The potlatch ban was quietly dropped in the 1950s, along with prohibitions against other traditional First Nations practices, but the 1922 hoard of masks, headdresses, blankets, baskets, boxes and other regalia wasn't returned until the 1970s. The collection was divided between the U'mista Cultural Centre at Alert Bay and the (closed at press time) Kwakiutl (Kwagiulth) Museum at Cape Mudge, Quadra Island. Potlatch ceremonies are again being held publicly, especially in the Queen Charlotte Islands (see page 116), and Alert Bay (see page 96).

PORT HARDY*

Port Hardy & District Chamber of Commerce 7250 Market St; tel: (250) 949-7622; www.ph-chamber. bc.ca. Open daily Jun–Sept; Oct–May Mon–Fri 0830–1700.

Port Hardy Museum and Archives $ 7110 Market St; tel: (250) 949-8143. Open daily.

Port Hardy is the end of the road on North Vancouver Island and a centre for North Island outdoor adventures. The walkway along **Hardy Bay**◆◆◆ is a favourite gathering spot for bald eagles and other birds. BC Ferries' terminal is just south at **Bear Cove**.

    Port Hardy Museum and Archives◆◆ concentrates on local Kwakwaka'wakw First Nations history and later White arrivals.

Accommodation and food in Port Hardy

Ferry traffic is extremely heavy in summer. Book accommodation well in advance or expect to sleep in the back seat.

Pioneer Inn $$ 4965 Byng Rd; tel: (250) 949-7271 or (800) 663-8744; www.vancouverisland.com/pioneerinn, is a quiet choice outside of town.

Port Hardy Inn $$ 9040 Granville St; tel: (250) 949-8525, is a central, if busy, hotel and restaurant.

Sportman's Steak House $$ 8700 Market Street; tel: (250) 949-7811, offers Greek dishes plus steaks and seafood.

Left
Port Hardy thunderbird

STRATHCONA PROVINCIAL PARK✦✦✦

Strathcona Provincial Park
Tel: (250) 248-9460;
http://wlapwww.gov.bc.ca/
bcparks/explore/parkpgs/
strathco.htm

Strathcona Park Lodge $ Strathcona
Provincial Park; tel: (250)
286-3122;
www.strathcona.bc.ca

Strathcona Provincial Park stretches nearly across Vancouver Island to include the tallest mountain on the island (Mt Golden Hinde, 2200m) and the tallest waterfall in Canada (Della Falls, 440m). The **Strathcona Park Lodge✦✦✦** is the best-developed accommodation and activity centre in the largely wilderness park. Visiting in winter? Cross-country skiing and snowshoeing are popular in Paradise Meadows and Mount Washington Alpine Resort (*see page 99*), adjacent to **Strathcona Provincial Park**, is known for downhill skiing.

TELEGRAPH COVE✧✧✧

Telegraph Cove Resort $$$
Telegraph Cove;
tel: (250) 928-3131 or
(800) 200-4665; www.
telegraphcoveresort.com

Telegraph Cove was named for a telegraph line at the turn of the 20th century. Surviving buildings, most on stilts above the water, are either museum pieces or part of a busy resort and ecotravel centre with whale-watching trips by boat or kayak.

Suggested tour

Total distance: 360km.

Time: Allow 6 hours to drive from Parksville to Port Hardy; 2–3 days to enjoy the sights. In a hurry to get north? Take the 4-lane Inland Route, Hwy 19, from Nanaimo to Campbell River and continue north to Port Hardy. The scenic Seashore Route along the Strait of Georgia, now Hwy 19A, will take longer, but will visit every interesting hamlet along the water.

Links: From Port Hardy, ferry routes lead north to Bella Coola and Prince Rupert (*see page 206*) or retrace Vancouver Island routes south.

Route: Follow Hwy 19 or 19A from Nanaimo to the adjoining beach towns of **PARKSVILLE ❶** and **QUALICUM BEACH ❷**. Hwy 19 continues inland, bypassing the beach and cutting at least an hour off the drive to Campbell River, but Hwy 19A along the **Strait of Georgia** is far more interesting.

Detour: From Hwy 19 in **COURTENAY ❸**, go east (right) on to 17th Ave towards **COMOX ❹**, and right again on Comox Road, passing a wildlife viewing area on the Comox River. To visit **Comox Spit** and expansive good-weather views back along the coast, turn right into Balmoral Avenue and right again on to Croteau Road.

Return to Comox Road and turn right on to Lazo Road to **Lazo**, following the blue and white 'scenic drive' signs – watch out for deer grazing along the verges. The road curves around the Canadian Forces Base Comox, with a golf course (open to the public) and the Comox Valley Regional Air Terminal. Ryan Road leads directly back to Hwy 19, or follow back roads to **Little River** and BC Ferries routes to the mainland at **Powell River**, then back to Hwy 19 by way of the **Seal Bay Nature Park**.

Take Hwy 19 north from **CAMPBELL RIVER ❺** past the turn for **STRATHCONA PROVINCIAL PARK ❻** to the **Norske Skog Elk Falls Pulp and Paper Mill**, *tel: (250) 287-5594*, with free tours in summer. Signs in the large lay-by overlooking a mill and barge terminal explain plant operations. Continue north 7km to **Seymour Narrows**, one of the most perilous passages between Vancouver and Prince Rupert. Swift currents churn the Narrows into a boiling mass of white water at flood tide. There's a convenient overlook on the north side of Hwy 19.

Left
Telegraph Cove

Above
Port Hardy totem pole

ⓘ **Schoen Lake
Provincial Park**
tel: (250) 248-9460;
http://wlapwww.gov.bc.ca/
bcparks/explore/parkpgs/
schoen.htm

With strong coastal currents such as those in Johnstone Strait, and much of Vancouver Island and mainland BC's coast accessible only by water, booking an adventure tour is usually the only way to see nature at close range. In addition to whale-watching boat tours from major towns, guided kayaking with established operators like **Northern Lights Expeditions** *tel: (800) 754-7402; www.seakayaking.com* and **Sea Kayak Adventures** *tel: (800) 616-1943; www.seakayakadventures.com*, ensures safety and naturalist and cultural interpretation.

Detour: Turn north (right) 29km north of **McNair Lake**, following signs for **Sayward**, one of the few remaining company-owned towns in BC. The road passes clearcuts, tree farms and isolated towns on the way to Sayward, then continues to **Kelsey Bay**. The bay, protected by the rusting hulks of sunken barges, was once the terminus for the BC Ferries route to Prince Rupert that now departs from Port Hardy. Return to Hwy 19 and turn north (right).

Hwy 19 continues north past **Schoen Lake Provincial Park**, a wilderness park best visited by high-clearance vehicles. **Hoomac Lake**, 4km north, is a more convenient rest break. A few hectares of old growth forest have been left around the lake shore as habitat for elk and other animals that don't take well to tree farms. One of the few gas stations and restaurants between Campbell River and Port McNeill is in the town of **Woss**, 7km north of the lake and 2km west. The highway skirts **Nimpkish Lake** for 20-plus km beyond the Woss turn-off.

Detour: Turn south (right) off Hwy 19 at the **North Island Discovery Centre**; *tel: (250) 956-3844; www.island.net/~nifctour*. Book summer forest and mill tours by phone in advance. Continue past the centre to a T-junction at the end of the paved road. Turn left, following signs for the Telegraph Cove Resort. Just beyond is **BEAVER COVE** ❼ and a massive dryland sort. Watch the action from a lay-by near the top of the hill just beyond the dryland sort entrance.

Continue another kilometre to a second T-junction. Turn left for **TELEGRAPH COVE** ❽. Return to Hwy 19 and turn north (right).

The highway passes the **Nimpkish Fish Hatchery**, *tel: (250) 974-9556*, with excellent explanations of how poor logging practices and overfishing have blighted salmon runs in recent decades.

An imposing totem pole just across the Nimpkish River was carved in 1966 to commemorate the 1866 political union of Vancouver Island and mainland BC. Six kilometres north is the turn for **Port McNeill** and the ferry to **ALERT BAY 9**. Continue north past the turn-off for **Bear Cove** and the BC Ferries terminal, and into **PORT HARDY 10**.

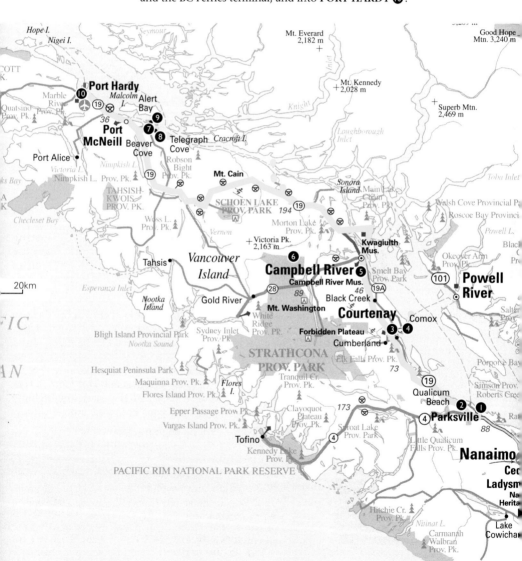

Ferry voyages

Ratings

Children	●●●●●
History	●●●●●
Mountains	●●●●●
Nature	●●●●●
Scenery	●●●●●
Villages	●●●●●
Wildlife	●●●●●
Food and drink	●●●○○

BC Ferries are the most popular cruise company in Canada. Strictly speaking, the privately-owned ferries are simply transportation for vehicles and foot passengers, but even the most prosaic ferry run from Vancouver to Vancouver Island can take on the air of a cruise when the summer sun shines bright and temperatures climb.

On the north coast, a ferry trip is more adventure than transportation. Plying the waters of the Inside Passage between Port Hardy and Bella Coola or Port Hardy and Prince Rupert, a ferry voyage is the best way, and most often the only way, to enjoy some of North America's most dramatic coastal vistas in a region where roads are all but unknown. Expect to see snow-capped peaks dropping steeply into icy blue fjords lined with dark green forests – and don't be surprised to see nothing at all if a storm blows through.

DISCOVERY COAST: PORT HARDY TO BELLA COOLA❖❖❖

Below
Bella Coola harbour

Unlike most BC Ferries runs that cater to commuters, commercial traffic and local residents, the Discovery Coast route was created for tourists. This summer-only service aboard the *Queen of Chilliwack* was named 'Discovery' for Alexander Mackenzie, who, in 1793, was the first European to cross North America north of Mexico. Mackenzie emerged from the mountains at Bella Coola to discover that he had finally found the Pacific Ocean.

There are more ghost towns – reminders of the days when timber and fishing ruled the BC Coast – than modern settlements along the route, but the often-narrow, always-scenic channels are seldom empty. Cruise ships and fishing boats make regular runs between Alaska, to the north, and Canadian ports to the south. Pleasure craft throng the protected inlets and passages of the **Hakai Recreation Area**❖❖❖, one of the more popular areas in BC for sea kayaking.

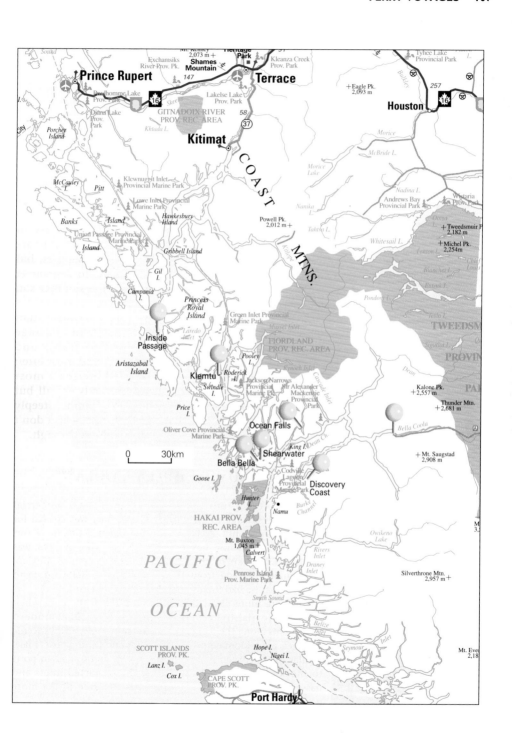

Hakai Luxvbalis Conservancy Area

The Heiltsuk First Nation has inhabited the coast and islands of what is now known as the Hakai Recreation Area for 10,000 years, believed to be the oldest continuously inhabited area of Western North America's coastline. In 2003, the Heiltsuk and the BC provincial government settled differences and agreed to co-manage the 122,998 hectares of environmentally precious land and marine areas, technically, the Hakai Luxvbalis Conservancy Area. Hakai ('wide passage') is BC's largest marine park.

Wolves and deer swim between islands and one hundred bird species fish the waters. Premier human activities are fishing for salmon, halibut, and rockfish and scuba diving.

Discovery Coast, Port Hardy–Bella Coola $$$
www.discoverycoast.bcferries.bc.ca. The summer-only route operates late May–early Jun and late Sept.

BC Ferries 1112 Fort Street, Victoria BC V8V 4V2; tel: (250) 386-3431 or (888) 223-3779; www.bcferries.bc.ca

Hakai Recreation Area http://wlapwww.gov.bc.ca/bcparks/explore/parkpgs/hakaicsa.htm

The entire voyage takes between 15 and 33 hours, depending on how many of four potential port calls the *Queen* makes. Allow about 50 hours for a return voyage from either Port Hardy or Bella Coola. The ship stays reasonably close to schedule, but don't expect slavish devotion to the timetable. The 114m car ferry also carries kayaks and other small craft that can be dropped off and picked up at irregular stops along the trip. There may be detours when the captain spots a pod of orcas or a humpback whale nearby.

For the best sightseeing, sail the Discovery Coast southbound, Bella Coola–Port Hardy, to enjoy the panorama of mountains surrounding North Bentinck Arm (near Bella Coola) in daylight. For easier driving, take a northbound sailing, Port Hardy–Bella Coola. The trip *up* The Hill, a steep gravel section of Hwy 20 just east of Bella Coola, is considerably less thrilling than twisting down the unpaved hairpin curves.

In Port Hardy (*see page 101*), passengers and vehicles board at the Bear Cove ferry dock. In Bella Coola, foot passengers board at the ferry dock, but vehicles must check in at the Co-op Parking lot or Tweedsmuir Travel, not at the ferry terminal, to pick up a boarding pass before driving to the dock. Check current procedures with BC Ferries when making your booking.

Boarding starts 60 minutes before sailing at both ports, but it's better to board early than late – early arrivals get the coveted seats next to the *Queen's* oversized view windows. Seating is first-come, first-served, so passengers in the know race aboard to drop a jacket or a backpack on their preferred window seat, usually in the forward lounge. Hotels, motels and bed and breakfasts at either end of the route can arrange transport to and from the dock for foot passengers.

Reservations are required for vehicles and are *highly* recommended for foot passengers – space is limited and the season short. There may be space on the first few and last few sailings at the last moment, but book four to six months in advance for June to August trips. Reservations can be changed (if space is available on the new date), but each change costs

$30 per segment. You can check availability, make reservations and buy tickets by credit card on-line or by telephone.

Summer weather is usually good, but the coastal climate is fickle. Rain, fog and wind are at least as common as sunshine, which comes and goes almost without warning. Stick to comfortable, layered clothing and flat shoes for walking about on deck, up and down outside stairways and on shore. Long trousers, long sleeves, closed shoes and a warm jacket with a hood are likely to be as useful as sunglasses and sun block, even if the weather forecast predicts nothing but sunshine.

Seas will likely be calm no matter what the weather. Except for a short stretch of open water in the Queen Charlotte Sound just north of Port Hardy, a maze of islands protects the entire route from ocean swells and large wind waves.

The Discovery Coast is a tourist cruise, but the *Queen* is no cruise ship: no disco, no casino, no swimming pool, no sauna, no beauty parlour, no dressy dinners. There is a gym, a couple of stationary bicycles on the solarium deck, as well as a full-service cafeteria, bar, lounge, laundry, showers, video arcade and gift shop. There is also plenty of outside deck space to enjoy the passing scenery while looking for orcas, humpback whales, eagles, seals, dolphins and passing vessels of all sizes. Binoculars and telephoto camera lenses are a must.

The *Queen* has no passenger cabins, but the reclining seats are extremely comfortable for night-long napping. Blankets, sheets and pillows can be hired on board, or bring your own. You can also pitch your own tent on the outer decks (or perhaps indoors, depending on the weather). A popular option is to overnight in Klemtu, Ocean Falls or Shearwater and pick up the ship on a later sailing, but rooms on shore are extremely limited. Book shoreside accommodation first (and explain that you're arriving aboard the *Queen*), then book passage to match your dates ashore.

BC Ferries has named its routes. The same-day Port Hardy to Bella Coola service on Thursday is an *Orca Voyage*. The SS *Beaver Voyage* Tuesday departure is named for the coast's first steamship, and lays over at McLoughlin Bay and Shearwater. The *Chartmaker's Voyage*, a nod to Captain George Vancouver's heroic coastal charting two centuries ago, stops at Klemtu, McLoughlin Bay, Shearwater and Ocean Falls. It is designed for weekend tourists, with departures on Friday, Saturday and Sunday.

Port calls stretch from 30 minutes to half a day, depending on the port and day of the week. Arrival and departure times are posted near the Purser's Office, forward of the cafeteria. There are shore excursions in most ports, usually walking tours, traditional dancing, salmon feasts or paddle trips. Buy shore tours as soon as possible after boarding. The better the weather, the earlier excursions sell out.

You can also explore ashore on your own, but watch the time. The *Queen* doesn't wait for late returners. The only departure warning is a long whistle blast 15 minutes before pulling away from the dock.

BELLA BELLA/McLOUGHLIN BAY*

Bella Bella/McLoughlin Bay Heiltsuk Band Administration; tel: (250) 957-2381; www.heiltsuk.com

The Heiltsuk Band, based at Bella Bella, is opening the door to tourism slowly and cautiously. For now, tourists are generally restricted to McLoughlin Bay, 3km south of the village. The Purser may say that Bella Bella is too far to walk during the short port call, but it's not too far for several local artists to set up shop at the dock when the *Queen* calls, including famed silversmith Peter Gladstone. McLoughlin Bay is also a popular stop for kayakers setting off for or returning from camping trips through the Hakai Recreation Area (*see page 106*).

If the weather is reasonable, that is, blowing anything less than a full gale, walk a few hundred metres down the crushed shell beach to the traditional-style longhouse. Built by Heiltsuk carvers Frank and Kathy Brown, the longhouse is a combination local history museum, First Nations art gallery and simple restaurant specialising in salmon roasted on cedar planks over an open fire.

Brown also takes passengers on a one-hour paddle in the *Glwa*, a traditional Heiltsuk canoe carved from a single cedar log. The trip passes old totem poles, deserted fish canneries, ravens, eagles, orcas, herons, dolphins and often bear and deer before rejoining the *Queen* in the next port, Shearwater.

On ferry trips that stop at Shearwater but not McLoughlin Bay, Brown brings his authentically carved canoe out to meet the ship and take on paddlers. Seats on the canoe are limited and extremely popular with repeat passengers, so sign up immediately after boarding the *Queen*.

KLEMTU✧✧✧

Klemtu *Kitasoo Band Council; tel: (250) 839-1255; www.kitasoo.org*

Klemtu Tourism Ltd
tel: (877) 644-2346 or (25) 839-2346; www.klemtutourism.com

This is one of the most popular overnight stops on the Discovery Coast, thanks to a bed and breakfast operated by the Kitasoo Band – book accommodation first, then the Discovery Coast sailing that matches your stay and a number of well-organised ecotours✧✧✧.

Most of Klemtu's 300 or so residents turn out to welcome the *Queen*. Main Street is among the longest boardwalks in Canada, skirting two sides of a bay that is alive with bald eagles, dolphins and orcas on the hunt for salmon and other fish. The most popular activity is a three-hour walking tour of town with stops at a busy carving shed and a traditional First Nations feast guaranteed to finish before the ship sails. Bring your own kayak, rent one, or charter boats from band operators for fishing, sightseeing, hiking and camping on nearby islands.

OCEAN FALLS✧✧✧

Ocean Falls
BC Ferries; tel: (250) 386-3431 or (888) 223-3779; www.bcferries.bc.ca

Named for Link Falls, a waterfall that thunders directly into the sea, Ocean Falls was once a thriving pulp mill town at the head of Cousins Inlet. Three thousand people lived here in the mid-20th century, enough to fill a hospital, high school, hotel and Olympic-sized swimming pool. When the mill closed in 1980 and jobs evaporated, so did most of the people. A few families remain at the original town site, which spreads uphill from the ferry dock, a few more in nearby Martin Valley, but the population more than doubles when *Queen* passengers hit the streets on walking tours. Fishing and sightseeing boat charters are also available, as are a few bed-and-breakfast rooms – book onshore accommodation first, then matching sailing dates.

There's home-made soup, ice cream and espresso at the one café in town, a fire hall, a modern school and the mouldering remains of a long-closed hotel, but most of Ocean Falls is vanishing beneath a creeping carpet of blackberry bushes, alders and seedling pines. It's hard to miss the occasional splash of colour, usually a bright blue hydrangea in what was once a carefully tended front garden.

Today's residents wouldn't change much about their town. A hydroelectric dam built for the mill still churns out power, but with no logging and no toxic pulp waste pouring into the ocean, salmon, halibut, eagles, dolphins and other wildlife have returned.

SHEARWATER/DENNY ISLAND✧✧

Shearwater/Denny Island *Shearwater Marine Resort; tel: (604) 270-6204 or (800) 663-2370; www.shearwater.ca*

Flying boats based at Denny Island, opposite Bella Bella, once patrolled the Queen Charlotte Channel for World War II submarine invaders. The base is long gone (so is an early 20th-century fish-packing plant), but with the newer name of Shearwater, the sheltered bay has become a base for tourism, sport fishing and maritime traffic. The Shearwater Resort includes a small hotel, fishing charters, restaurant, pub, marina and bed-and-breakfast accommodation.

Look for commercial fishing boats, sailboats and luxury motor yachts tied up to the dock. Crew and passengers are most likely tied up to the bar inside, the only full-service stop between Port Hardy and Bella Coola. The *Queen* ties up long enough for a meal or a drink at the resort. The alternative is to spend several days cycling and hiking the island or boating nearby waters.

INSIDE PASSAGE: PORT HARDY TO PRINCE RUPERT✦✦✦

ⓘ Inside Passage, Port Hardy–Prince Rupert $$$ *1112 Fort Street, Victoria BC V8V 4V2; tel: (250) 386-3431 or (888) 223-3779; www.bcferries.bc.ca*

Eagles, whales and mouth-dropping scenery on all sides make this all-year car-ferry route the most popular 15-hour cruise in Canada. Look for sheer mountains cloaked with red cedar and Sitka spruce rising from glacier-carved channels, low islands swept clean by winter storms and lighthouses marking channels less than 250m wide.

The entire trip takes place during daylight hours from mid-May to the end of September, when most sailings leave at 0730 and arrive at 2230 the same day. There are twice-weekly departures in early May and one return trip weekly from October to April; check with BC Ferries for off-season schedules.

Vehicle spaces *must* be reserved in advance. Foot passengers should also book space, especially June to August when tour groups flock to north-coast ferry trips. A 60-seat restricted access reserved seating lounge guarantees a seat for the voyage. Last-minute vehicle space *may* be available mid-September to mid-May, but make reservations four to six months in advance for summer travel.

In Port Hardy, board at Bear Cove, just south of town. In Prince Rupert, follow Second Avenue (Hwy 16) to the ferry dock. Boarding starts one hour before sailing. There's no rush to be first on board in winter, when there are few passengers. In summer, be prepared to scramble for window seats in the forward cabins with the best views or opt for an outdoor seat.

Weather is usually warm and clear (but not always sunny) in summer, while storms are common in winter. The Inside Passage route is calm and well protected by dozens of islands off the BC coast, but rain, wind, fog and snow blast down from the Arctic in winter.

In any season, most passengers opt to spend the trip in comfortable reclining chairs or in the many lounge areas set with tables and chairs. Private cabins are available at an additional charge. There's also a fine dining room, complete with silver and white linen tablecloths. Most passengers go for the less expensive cafeteria that serves everything from snacks to full meals. Pre-paid buffet dining room packages for breakfast and dinner or for all three meals may be

Above
Port Hardy welcome sign

purchased when booking a ferry reservation. Ferries also have a licensed lounge, video arcade, games, free videos in public rooms and a well-stocked gift shop.

The Inside Passage

Fewer than 5000 people live on BC's central and northern coast, half of them in Bella Coola (*see page 200*) and another quarter in Queen Charlotte City, in the Queen Charlotte Islands (*see page 116*). Two hundred years ago, the waters and islands between Port Hardy and Prince Rupert were the realm of First Nations bands who lived well from the bounty of temperate coastal forests and the rich sea. A century ago, the same waters teemed with floating logging camps, pulp mills and fish canneries. Changing economic conditions closed most of those outside industries, leaving the Inside Passage once again a largely First Nations area where humans are vastly outnumbered by the wildlife and the scenery draws visitors from around the globe.

Suggested tours

Time: Allow up to 33 hours to travel the **Discovery Coast** between **Port Hardy** ❶ and **Bella Coola** ❷ or 15 hours along the **Inside Passage** between **Port Hardy** and **Prince Rupert** ❸.

Links: Both ferry routes meet at **Port Hardy** (*see page 101*), at the north end of Vancouver Island, for the drive south toward **Victoria** (*see page 62*). From **Bella Coola** (*see page 200*), it's possible to drive the **Cariboo-Chilcotin** to **Williams Lake** (*see page 202*) and either north to **Prince Rupert** (*see page 206*) or south towards **Vancouver** (*see page 206*). **Prince Rupert** is the mainland terminus of the **Yellowhead Highway** (*see page 214*), which continues westwards in the **Queen Charlotte Islands** (*see page 116*) or eastwards to the **Rocky Mountains** and **Jasper National Park** (*see page 275*).

Route: Both ferry trips fit into a circular driving tour from **Vancouver** to **Victoria** by ferry, up **Vancouver Island** to **Port Hardy** by highway, ferry to the mainland at **Bella Coola** or **Prince Rupert**, then south by road to **Vancouver**. Allow 7–10 days for the entire route. It's also possible to combine both ferry voyages by driving to either Port Hardy or Bella Coola, taking one ferry route into **Port Hardy** and then taking the second route back to the mainland. Allow 10–14 days for the two ferry trips, plus long-distance driving on the mainland and any excursions on Vancouver Island.

Both routes are served by car ferries, but don't take *car* too literally. If it's street-legal in BC, BC Ferries will carry it: cars, vans, RVs, motor coaches, motorcycles, bicycles, trucks and foot passengers. Both tours can be taken in either direction and both can be made with a combination of train, coach and air connections to avoid driving altogether.

Below
McLoughlin Bay (Bella Bella)

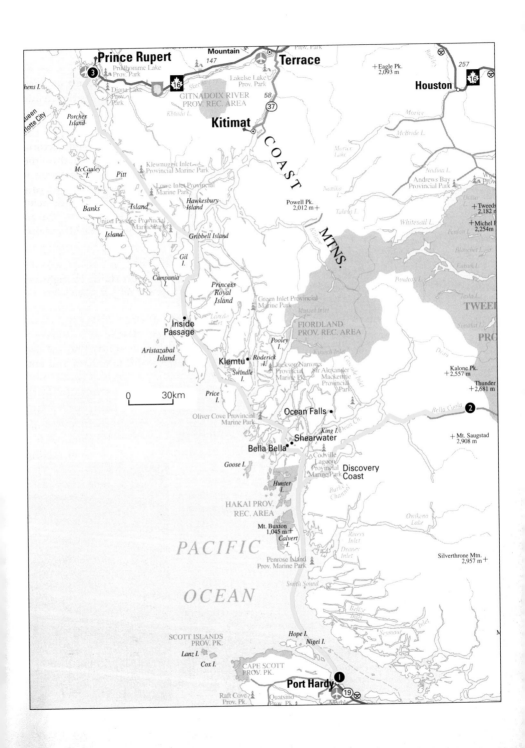

Queen Charlotte Islands

Ratings

First Nations	●●●●●
History	●●●●●
Nature	●●●●●
Outdoor activities	●●●●●
Parks	●●●●●
Beaches	●●●●○
Children	●●●●○
Walking	●●●●○

Also known as *Haida Gwaii*, Home of the People, the Queen Charlottes are BC's most remote islands. By any name, this isolated, storm-swept, rain-forested archipelago 100km west of Prince Rupert is the best-known corner of Canada that almost nobody has ever seen. There are fewer than 150km of paved roads, more black bears and eagles than humans and barely enough vehicles to fill a small car park in downtown Vancouver.

Home to the Haida, proud, artistic warriors who once ruled the Pacific Northwest coast from cedar canoes, the Charlottes are an ecological wonder snatched from the jaws of timber cutters. Nearly overwhelmed by epidemics, discrimination and logging, the Haida rebounded as a vibrant traditional culture and artistic tradition. Gwaii Haanas National Park preserves links to 10,000 years of Haida history in a wilderness of moss-covered forests and village sites dotted with totem poles slowly crumbling back to earth.

Getting there

ⓘ **Queen Charlotte City Visitor Information Centre**
3220 Wharf St; tel: (250) 559-8316; www.qcinfo.com. Open daily May–mid-Sept.

Ⓩ **Sandspit Airport (YZP)** tel: (250) 637-5313. A visitor information centre is open daily, May–mid-Sept.

Principal access is by air from Vancouver to Sandspit or **BC Ferries**, *tel: 888-223-3779; www.bcferries.bc.ca*, 6 hours from Prince Rupert to Skidegate Landing.

Getting around

There is no public transport. Hire a car from the Sandspit Airport or Queen Charlotte City, or bring your own vehicle by ferry. Weather is highly variable – rain, fog and sun alternating with blustery winds and dead calm, even in summer.

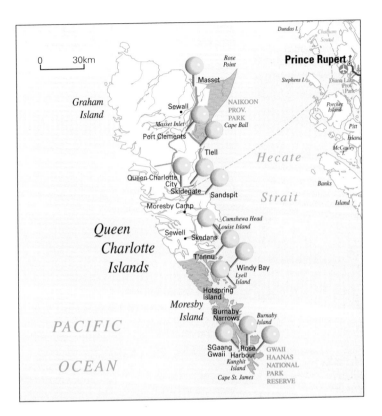

GWAII HAANAS NATIONAL PARK RESERVE/HAIDA HERITAGE SITE❖❖❖

One of North America's most spectacular natural areas became a park in 1987 following a stand-off between the Haida and logging companies on Lyell Island. The 1500-sq km park protects rich marine environments, as well as trackless areas of old growth cedar and spruce forest carpeted with moss and orchids, deep fjords, sandy scimitars of beach, enormous colonies of puffins and sea lions, some of the world's largest nesting populations of falcons and bald eagles, and over 500 Haida sites.

Credit isolation for the park's splendour. The only access is by water or air, and only when weather, currents and 7m tides allow. Parks Canada approves operators for day-trips as well as multi-day boat trips and guided or self-guided kayak trips.

On the water, expect to see orcas, humpbacks and other whales, dolphins, porpoises and clouds of seabirds. Black bears roam the intertidal areas, black-tailed deer the meadows and open forests. Bald eagles are common.

**⊕ Gwaii Haanas
National Park
Preserve/Haida
Heritage Site $$**
*Above city centre grocery
store, Queen Charlotte City;
tel: (250) 559-8818; http://
parkscan.harbour.com/gwaii.
Open Mon–Fri 0800–1200,
1300–1630. Entry by
commercial tour or individual
permit. For permit
reservations tel: (250) 387-
1642 or (800) 435-5622. All
visitors must attend a park
and Haida Gwaii heritage
orientation session before
entering the park.*

**⊖ Rose Harbour
Guest House $$**
*Rose Harbour, Gwaii Haanas
National Park; tel: (250) 559-
2326; www.roseharbour.com,
has bed-and-breakfast
accommodation with hot
water.*

**Gwaii Haanas Guest
House $$** *Rose Harbour,
Gwaii Haanas National Park;
tel: (250) 559-8638;
www.gwaiihaanas.com, has
similar bed-and-breakfast
accommodation.*

Most Haida village sites have been reclaimed by the forest, but a few remain visible. All were once marked by forests of totem poles, most removed to museums as smallpox and other epidemics swept Haida Gwaii in the 19th century and villages were abandoned. A few poles remain, decaying, weather-beaten and returning to the earth in keeping with Haida tradition. Haida Gwaii watchmen (guardians) live at major village sites to discourage vandals and over-eager collectors.

Burnaby Narrows✦✦✦ This twisting passage is navigable by small boats at high tide and dry at low tide. Walking is banned to protect the profusion of sea stars, urchins, mussels and other species.

Hotspring Island✦✦ The only natural hot spring in the Charlottes was a traditional Haida healing place. Several soaking pools overlook the waters of Ramsay Passage.

Rose Harbour✦✦✦ The tiny community of Rose Harbour is a convenient stop-over for quick trips: fly in from Queen Charlotte City, visit SGaang Gwaii by speedboat and fly out. Rose is also a convenient base for kayak trips.

SGaang Gwaii (Ninstints, Anthony Island)✦✦✦ This abandoned village at the south end of Haida Gwaii was named a UNESCO World Heritage Site in 1981. The world's largest collection of totem poles in their original location still stands along the beach.

Skedans✦✦✦ Skedans is the most accessible village site for day-trips.

T'annu✦✦✦ There are no standing totem poles, but many visible house sites draped with moss. The ashes of famed Haida artist Bill Reid are buried in his ancestral village.

Windy Bay✦✦✦ A modern longhouse here was the focus of Haida battles with logging companies in the 1980s.

Gwaii Haanas under sail

Expert kayakers rate Gwaii Haanas National Park amongst the best water on earth – as famous for swirling currents, racing tides and blasting storms as for protected shores, stunning scenery and rich wildlife. For the rest of us, there's the *Duen*.

Michael Hobbis has been sailing his 22-m, eight-passenger ketch around the Charlottes for more than a decade, exploring remote inlets that larger boats will never see. Inflatable zodiacs take passengers ashore for daily forest hikes with kayaks available for calm waters. The *Duen* visits several Haida sites during her week-long trips, but the route depends on wind, tides and passenger preferences. **Duen Sailing Adventures $$$**, *Box 398, Brentwood Bay, BC, Canada V8M 1R3; tel: (250) 652-8227 or (888) 922-8822; www.duenadventures.com*

MASSET✧✧

ⓘ Masset Travel InfoCentre *400m from the 'Welcome to Masset' sign, east side of Hwy 16; tel: (250) 626-3982. Open daily Jun–late Aug. Find Masset Village information at www.island.net/~masset/index.html*

Old Masset Village Council *Eagle Rd; tel: (250) 626-5115.*

ⓟ Naikoon Provincial Park *tel: (250) 625-5115; http://wlapwww.gov.bc.ca/bcparks/explore/parkpgs/naikoon.htm*

ⓧ Sandpiper $$$ *Collison Ave; tel: (250) 626-3672, specialises in seafood.*

Villager Cafe $$ *Orr St; tel: (250) 626-3694, has Chinese dishes.*

ⓒ Copper Beech House $$ *1590 Delkatla; tel: (250) 626-5441; www.copperbeechhouse.com, is Masset's most comfortable bed and breakfast.*

Right
Masset welcome sign

Masset is a fishing and tourist town at the north end of Graham Island. **Old Masset**✧✧✧, 2km west, is Canada's largest Haida community with modern totem poles, artist workshops and galleries. To the east is **Naikoon Provincial Park**✧✧✧, stretching to **Rose Spit**✧✧✧, where Haida legend says humans appeared, and south to Tlell. Don't miss **Tow Hill**✧✧✧, a 100-m outcrop of basalt columns with active tidal blowholes at the base. Sandy beaches backed by mossy forest and bog stretch nearly 100km from Tow Hill to Rose Spit and south. **Delkatla Wildlife Sanctuary**✧✧✧ east of Masset, is a premier spot for viewing trumpeter swans, sandhill cranes, great blue herons, and many other species pausing on the Pacific Flyway.

PORT CLEMENTS✧

ⓘ The Village of Port Clements *tel: (250) 557-4295.*

ⓜ Port Clements Museum $ *45 Bayview Dr; tel: (250) 557-4576; wwwportclements.com/museum.htm. Open Tues–Sun Jun–Sept; call for winter hours.*

Port Clements is a tiny logging supply centre. The top attraction is the **Port Clements Museum**✧, an eclectic collection of early logging paraphernalia and household items.

The pleasant **Golden Spruce Trail**✧✧✧, 5km south on the gravel logging road, leads in 10 minutes to the site of a unique golden spruce tree destroyed by a vandal in 1997. Eight kilometres south is the **Haida Canoe**✧✧✧, a partially carved wooden canoe abandoned in the forest over a century ago.

QUEEN CHARLOTTE CITY❖❖

ℹ Queen Charlotte Visitor Information Centre *3220 Wharf St; tel: (250) 559-8316. Open May–mid-Sept.*

The administrative centre for the Charlottes is also the archipelago's largest town. Serious people live here, trying to pursue the area's traditional fishing and lumbering, while Haida arts and crafts are for sale in local galleries.

Accommodation and food in Queen Charlotte

Hecate Inn $$ *321 3rd Ave; tel: (250) 559-4543 or 800-665-3350; www.qcislands.net/hecateinn*, is the most modern motel in the islands.

Howler's Pub & Bistro $$ *tel: (250) 559-8600*, has Charlotte's best beer selection and restaurant views.

Premier Creek Lodging $–$$ *3101 3rd Ave; tel: (250) 559-8415 or (888) 322-3388*, is a 1910 heritage building with a garden that overlooks the ocean.

Sea Raven Restaurant $$ *3301 3rd Ave, Sea Raven Motel; tel: (250) 559-4423*, has the town's best seafood selection.

SKIDEGATE❖❖

🏛 Haida Gwaii Museum $
Qay'llnagaay, east off Hwy 16, 1km north of Skidegate Landing; tel: (250) 559-4643. Open Jun–Sept, Mon–Fri 1000–1700, and weekend afternoons all year. Call in advance to verify hours.

Pronounced 'skid-e-git', this one-time mission settlement is a Haida village. The **Band Longhouse❖❖** has a fine Bill Reid-carved **totem pole❖❖❖** overlooking the water. Just south of town is the **Haida Gwaii Museum❖❖❖**, with a collection of local totem poles and the world's largest collection of carvings in argillite, a type of slate. Just off Hwy 16 is the **Spirit Lake Trail❖❖❖**, a moderate 3km, 90-minute hike through second-growth and old-growth forest around two small lakes.

TLELL❖

🏛 Naikoon Provincial Park $ *tel: (250) 625-5115; http://wlapwww. gov.bc.ca/bcparks/explore/ parkpgs/naikoon.htm. Open daily.*

This one-time ranching town has become an artistic centre, where roadside signs announce galleries. Tlell is also the southern entry for **Naikoon Provincial Park❖❖❖** with camping, hiking, and the 1928 wreck of the timber ship *Pesuta*.

◐ Cacilia's Bed & Breakfast $$
tel: (250) 557-4664; www. qcislands.net/ceebysea, is a log home behind beach dunes.

Tlell River House $$$
tel: (250) 789-9494; www.tlellriverhouse.com, is Tlell's only hotel.

Suggested tour

Total distance: 300km.

Time: 2–4 days by road; 7–10 days by water.

Links: BC Ferries to Prince Rupert (*see page 206*) or air to Vancouver (*see page 42*).

Sandspit*

This scattered village has the Charlottes' major airport.

Sandspit/North Moresby Chamber of Commerce *P.O. Box 148, Sandspit, B.C. V0T 1T0; tel: (250) 637-2466; www.sandspitqci.com*

Accommodation in Sandspit

Sandspit Inn $$$ *tel: (250) 637-5334 or 800-666-1107, is next to the airport.*

Route: From the airport at **Sandspit** ❶, drive east along **Shingle Bay** to the ferry at **Alliford Bay**. If time allows, take an hour to walk the **Dover Trail**, just west of **Haans Creek**, through dense thickets of alders, red cedar and Sitka spruce. The Haida peeled strips of bark from cedars to make rope, baskets, clothing and other items, leaving long, triangular scars on the trees. The ferry to **Skidegate Landing** is free, the return ferry is $$.

From the landing, follow traffic uphill and around to Hwy 16, the Yellowhead Hwy. Queen Charlotte City is 4km to the right (west); Skidegate, Tlell, Port Clements and Masset to the left (east).

North of **SKIDEGATE** ❷, the highway passes **Balanced Rock**, beyond a small sign east of the highway. Continue north along **Jungle Beach**, a tangle of driftwood stretching nearly 10km. The road follows the shoreline to **TLELL** ❸, near **Naikoon Provincial Park**.

From Tlell, Hwy 16 turns inland to **PORT CLEMENTS** ❹, a tiny logging supply centre. The Golden Spruce Trail and the Haida Canoe are off the logging road just south of town. Return to Port Clements and continue 38km to **MASSET** ❺, at the north end of Graham Island.

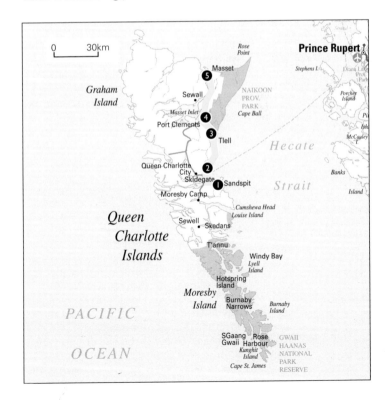

Lower Fraser Valley

Ratings

Children	●●●●●
Gardens	●●●●●
History	●●●●●
Scenery	●●●●●
Museums	●●●●○
Outdoor activities	●●●●○
Parks	●●●●○
Beaches	●●●○○

The lower section of the Fraser River Valley is the heart of BC, and not just for the flat, rich farmlands that keep Vancouver well supplied with milk and vegetables. BC began along the Fraser with the creation of the Hudson's Bay Company post at Fort Langley in 1827. The Fraser River gold rush in the 1850s opened the interior to the outside world and transformed BC into a Crown Colony in 1858 to thwart American expansion from the south.

The Lower Fraser is a microcosm of BC. It was the first section of the mainland to be explored by Whites, the first to be settled and the first to feel the impact of over-development. Half of BC's population lives, works and plays in the Lower Fraser River Valley, yet despite population and pollution, the Fraser remains the most productive salmon stream in the world.

FORT LANGLEY❖❖❖

ⓘ **Greater Langley Chamber of Commerce** #1, 5761 Glover Rd, Langley, BC V3A 8M8; tel: (604) 530-6656; www.langleychamber.com

This small rural town began as a Hudson's Bay Company trading fort in 1827. The original site was about 4km downstream, but the fort was moved a decade later to be closer to HBC's rich grain fields and pastures. When word of gold deposits on the Fraser finally leaked out in the 1850s (HBC had tried to downplay earlier reports in order to retain control), Fort Langley was promptly overrun by 30,000 goldseekers, most of them Americans. With only a handful of HBC men on the scene, the company worried that their mainland holdings would be annexed by the US. On a rainy November day in 1858, BC was declared a Crown Colony at the fort's 'Big House' and the British government took control.

The gold rushes eventually declined and HBC closed its fort, but the town thrived as an agricultural and residential centre. Today, a rebuilt Fort Langley National Historic Park is the centrepiece of a thriving tourism trade. The 4.6-km **Fort to Fort Trail** connects the 1827 HBC

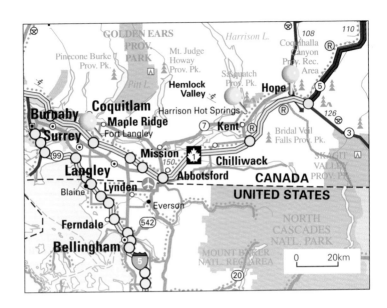

BC Farm Machinery and Agricultural Museum $ 9131 Kings St; tel: (604) 888-2273. Open daily Apr–early Oct 1000–1630.

Domaine de Chaberton Estates $ 1064 216 St, Langley; tel: (604) 530-1736 or (888) 332-9463; www. domainedechaberton.com

Fort Langley National Historic Site $ 23433 Mavis St; tel: (604) 513-4777; www.pc.gc.ca/lhn-nhs/bc/langley/index_e.asp. Open daily Mar–Oct 1000–1700; Nov–Feb by advance appointment 1000–1630.

Langley Centennial Museum $ Mavis St at 9135 King St; tel: (604) 888-3922; www.langleymuseum.org. Open Mon–Sat 1000–1645, Sun 1300–1645.

site in present-day Derby Reach Regional Park with the Fort Langley National Historic Site.

The collection at the **BC Farm Machinery and Agricultural Museum*** emphasises 20th-century farm machinery, most of it used locally and much of it displayed outdoors. Inside displays concentrate on household items and logging equipment.

Domaine de Chaberton Estates***, an estate winery in the Fraser Valley, concentrates on French and some German varietals.

Fort Langley National Historic Site*** was established by the Hudson's Bay Company as a fur-trading centre, but the local fur supply was quickly trapped out and the fort was moved to its present location in a lush agricultural region adjacent to a traditional First Nations trading site. With help from local Sto:lo bands, HBC created the salmon-packing industry, shipping 300-kg barrels of salted salmon to markets across the Pacific and creating BC's first major export trade. HBC farmers fed customers from Hawaii and Alaska to California and the Company's own inland settlements.

News of gold deposits along the Fraser changed BC forever. American miners flooded north from California, some of them stopping in Victoria to obtain the required mining permits, others simply sailing up the Fraser River to the head of navigation at Fort Langley. The HBC found itself in a quandary: as the only source of food, supplies and transport, the Company was profiting hugely. But the influx of Americans threatened annexation by the US.

The HBC's solution was to turn its mainland holdings into a Crown Colony and let London deal with the American problem. British

Columbia was declared in November 1858, at a ceremony in the Chief Trader's house, the 'Big House', at Fort Langley.

Colonial status was the death of Fort Langley. Competitors moved into fishing, farming and commerce. Navigation was extended to Hope, then to Yale, destroying the fort's role in shipping. BC's capital moved to New Westminster, then Victoria, eclipsing the fort's political power. The fort finally went out of business in 1886 and fell into ruin.

The site became a National Historic Park in 1955 and was reconstructed for BC's centenary in 1958. Most of the storehouse is original (the building was used as a barn for decades), but the rest of today's Fort Langley, from the log palisade to the imposing white Big House and Blacksmith's shop, is modern reconstruction. Living-history volunteers conduct tours year-round, with regular demonstrations of barrel-making, blacksmithing, cooking, clerking and trading. A small Visitor Centre museum just outside the palisade covers the history of the fort.

Langley Centennial Museum✧✧ offers more complete explanations of Sto:lo First Nations settlements in the lower Fraser Valley and later agricultural expansion than the Fort Langley visitor centre, as well as a look at local agricultural history. Don't skip the recreated general store, Victorian parlour and homesteader's kitchen.

Below
Trading beaver pelts at Fort Langley

Accommodation and food in Fort Langley

Bedford House Restaurant $$ *9272 Glover Rd; tel: (604) 888-2333* is a restored lumber baron's home set in expansive gardens.

Fort Langley Sandman Hotel $$ *8855 202nd St, Langley; tel: (604) 888-7263; www.sandmanhotels.com/hotels/bc/langley.asp*, is a reliable chain choice in the neighbouring town of Langley.

The Marr House $$$ *9090 Glover Rd; tel: (604) 888-6455*, is Fort Langley's most elegant restaurant.

Wendel's Bookstore & Café $ *103-9233 Glover Rd; tel: (604) 513-2238; www.wendelsonline.com*, has Fort Langley's best selection of local-interest books as well as a popular all-day café.

HARRISON HOT SPRINGS**

Harrison Hot Springs Chamber of Commerce *499 Hot Springs Rd; tel: (604) 796-1133; www.harrison.ca*

Sasquatch Provincial Park $ *Rockwell Dr; tel: 795-6169; http://wlapwww.gov.bc.ca/bcparks/explore/parkpgs/sasquatc.htm. Open daily except for periodic closure for heavy snowfall.*

Harrison Public Hot Pool $ *Hot Springs Rd and Esplanade Ave; tel: (604) 796-2244. Open daily 0900–2100.*

There's been a hotel and mineral baths at Harrison Lake since the 1880s, but the hot springs themselves are out of sight along the western lakeside, a 10-minute walk from the Harrison Hot Springs Hotel. The lake has a broad sandy beach, boating and fishing, with camping and hiking along the water and up nearby mountainsides. A small tourist town sits on the south shore. Surrounding forests are the haunt of Sasquatch, a legendary hairy forest giant that has been reported as far south as the Trinity Alps in Northern California. Hikers are more likely to spot deer, squirrels, Canada geese and the occasional beaver.

Although named for the shy, oversized creature of the northern forests, **Sasquatch Provincial Park*** is actually one of the more popular spots for camping, hiking and boating on the lower mainland. Attractions include four lakes surrounded by rugged mountains. Look for mountain goats on the **Slollicum Bluffs*** just north of **Deer Lake***.

Harrison Lake is 60km long and favoured by windsurfers and sailors for the heavy winds blowing southward most afternoons. Lake tour boats depart daily from the dock in front of the Harrison Hot Springs Hotel in summer. There's a wide swimming beach directly in front of the town as well as marina facilities.

The actual hot springs supplying **Harrison Public Hot Pool*** are about 2km away, but the sulphur- and potassium-rich water is too hot to touch. The indoor soaking and swimming pool is cooled to 38°C.

Accommodation and food in Harrison Hot Springs

Executive Hotel $$ *190 Lillooet Ave; tel: (604) 796-5555 or (888) 265-1155; www.harrisonhotsprings.com*, is the best value in town, across the street from the lake.

Above
Harrison Hot Springs

Harrison Hot Springs Resort $$$ *Hot Springs Rd; tel:(604) 796-2244 or (800) 663-2266; www.harrisonresort.com*, is a full-service resort and spa on the shores of Harrison Lake.

Jorg's Cafe $ *105-196 Esplanade; tel: (604) 796-8424*, lures locals for simple but filling meals.

Kitami Restaurant $$ *318 Hot Springs Rd; tel: (604) 796-2728,* serves great Japanese food, including sushi, and gets plenty of visiting Vancouverites who want a taste of home.

Rustica's Ristorante $$ *310 Hot Springs Rd; tel: (604) 796-8422,* serves Italian for lunch and dinner.

HOPE❖❖

ⓘ Hope & District Chamber of Commerce *tel: (604) 869-3111; www.hopechamber.bc.ca*

ⓗ Hope Museum $ *919 Water St; tel: (604) 869-7322. Open daily June–Sept 0900–1700.*

Japanese Friendship Gardens *Memorial Park, Third and Park streets. Free.*

Minter Gardens $$ *52892 Bunker Rd, Rosedale (exit 135 off Hwy 1); tel: (604) 794-7191 or (888) 646-8377; www.mintergardens.com. Open daily Apr and Oct 1000–1700, May and Sept 0900–1730, Jun 0900–1800, Jul–Aug 0900–1900.*

Coquihalla Canyon Provincial Park and Othello Tunnels $ *10km east from Kawkawa Lake; tel: (604) 795-6169; http://wlapwww.gov.bc.ca/bcparks/explore/parkpgs/coquih_can.htm. Open daily; tunnels closed in winter due to ice.*

Sitting at the head of the lower Fraser River Valley, Hope was long the head of navigation upriver and an important transfer point for goods and gold moving between the interior and coast. Navigation eventually moved upstream to Yale, but railway traffic revitalised the town, which has developed into a centre for hiking, rafting, cycling, fishing, soaring, mountain biking and other outdoor activities. Hollywood and Vancouver camera crews regularly use Hope for film shoots.

Highlight of **Hope Museum**❖❖ is a restored ball mill from a nearby mine. Other displays cover Sto:lo life in the area, early White settlers and Canada's treatment of its Japanese citizens during World War II. The calm meditation garden in the **Japanese Friendship Gardens**❖❖❖ is dedicated to the 2300 Japanese-Canadians who were interned in barns at Tashme, 24km east, during World War II.

Minter Gardens❖❖❖ doesn't have quite the advertising budget or the formality of Victoria's Butchart Gardens (*see page 66*), but Butchart can't begin to match Minter's setting against the Cascade Range. Eleven themed areas include rose gardens, the largest collection of Penjing rock bonsai outside China, a maze and Canada's largest floral flag.

Coquihalla Canyon Provincial Park & Othello Tunnels❖❖❖ This is the canyon where Rambo blazed his name in *First Blood.* It's also one of the most famous sets of railway tunnels in Canada, carved through solid granite for the Kettle Valley Railway to the Kootenay region between 1910 and 1916. The almost flat 2.8-km return stroll includes four tunnels and pleasant views of the rushing Coquihalla River.

The KVR ran between Hope and Nelson (*see page 246*), but was plagued by snow, washouts and rock slides. A 130m washout just north of the Othello Tunnels closed the railway permanently in 1959. Most of today's Coquihalla Highway (*see page 144*) follows the old KVR railbed, including one section which cost $300,000 per mile to build in 1914.

Accommodation and food in Hope

Dee's Riverview Café $ *875 Water St; tel: (604) 869-5534,* has Hope's best espresso, cookies, soups and quick meals.

New Golden Star Restaurant $ *377 Hope-Princeton Hwy; tel: (604) 869-9588,* is Hope's best Chinese choice.

Above
Minter Gardens

Quality Inn $ *350 Hope-Princeton Hwy; tel: (604) 869-9951 or (877) 424-6423; www.qualityinn.com,* is on the outskirts of Hope.

Skagit Motor Inn $$ *655 3rd Ave; tel: (604) 869-5220 or (888) 869-5228; www.skagit-motor-inn.com,* is quiet and central.

Suggested tour

Total distance: 130km, or 260km as a long day trip from Vancouver.

Time: Allow 2 hours to drive to Hope, plus at least 2 hours each for Fort Langley and Minter Gardens and time to soak in Harrison Hot Springs.

Links: This route links with **Vancouver** (*see page 42*) to the west and the **Cascade Mountains** (*see page 130*) or the **Gold Rush Trail** (*see page 186*) to the east.

Route: From Central **Vancouver**, take either Broadway or Hwy 7A east to Hwy 1, the TransCanada Highway, eastbound towards Hope. Once across the **Fraser River**, the freeway runs through a mixture of rural farmland and small towns in the **Lower Fraser Valley**.

The flat plain stretching from the river to the base of the Cascades is one of BC's prime agricultural areas. Dairy herds alternate with fields of raspberries, blueberries, strawberries and grain, with the occasional horse farm and llama pasture. Try to resist the temptation to speed along the freeway – the RCMP set up frequent radar speed traps in both directions. Drivers who keep within 8–10kph of the posted speed limit may get a stern warning, but seldom a speeding ticket. Many Vancouver radio stations include speed trap locations in their traffic reports.

Albion Ferry/
Fraser River
Marine Transportation
www.translink.bc.ca/Service_
Info_and_Fares/Albion_Ferry.
asp, has ferry schedules.

Much of the farming land east of **Langley** has gone into agricultural preserve that gives owners tax incentives to continue farming rather than selling out to the suburban sprawl of Greater Vancouver. *Farm Fresh Guide (www.bcfarmfresh.com/default.asp)*, available at tourist infocentres, petrol stations and tourist stops throughout the valley and in Vancouver, maps farms in the Langley area selling produce to the public. *The Harvest Guide*, with similar free distribution, covers the valley from **Abbotsford** east towards Hope.

The town of **Langley** is a busy farming and commercial. Follow freeway signs to **FORT LANGLEY ❶**, its older, smaller and more sedate cousin.

Detour: From Fort Langley, drive north to the **Fraser River** and the free ferry to **Albion**, on the north side of the river. Take Hwy 7 to the east (right), following signs to Harrison Hot Springs to rejoin the route.

From Fort Langley, return to Hwy 1 and continue eastward. **Abbotsford** calls itself the Raspberry Capital of the World. It's hard to wax ecstatic about neat rows of raspberry plants, but Minter Gardens draws raves and visitors from around the world – exit north on to Hwy 9 and follow signs to the left (west) just after crossing the Fraser River.

Return to Hwy 9 and turn left (north) through maize fields and dairy pastures toward **Agassiz**, which fancies itself the 'Corn Capital of BC'. Follow signs towards Hwy 7 and **HARRISON HOT SPRINGS ❷**, then return to Hwy 1 and continue east to **HOPE ❸**.

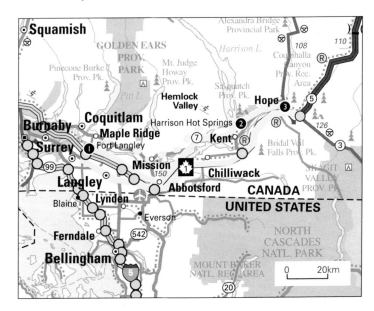

The Cascade Mountains

Ratings

History	●●●●●
Mountains	●●●●●
Scenery	●●●●●
Children	●●●●○
Nature	●●●●○
Outdoor activities	●●●●○
Walking	●●●○○
Wildlife	●●●○○

The Cascades aren't the tallest mountains in BC, nor the highest, but they're far and away the most scenic, the most rugged and the most inaccessible by road. Only one highway crosses the range east–west, the Crowsnest, which follows a gold rush trail built for pack mules in the 1860s. The modern roadway is wider, smoother and not nearly as steep as the early track, but the snow-capped peaks, rushing rivers and dense forests that gradually give way to cacti and desert sand are as memorable today as they were to early surveyors.

The Cascades also form one of BC's most obvious political and economic barriers. Nearly the entire population of the province lives west of the mountains. With a few exceptions, such as the Okanagan Valley and isolated towns on major highways, the countryside from Hope eastwards becomes increasingly wild, rugged and invitingly empty.

APEX ALPINE MOUNTAIN RESORT✦✦✦

Apex Alpine Mountain Resort
$$$ Green Mountain Rd, Apex Mountain Provincial Recreation Area; tel: (250) 292-8222 or (877) 777-2739; www. apexresort.com. Open all year.

With a reputation as the sunniest of Canada's Cascade ski resorts, Apex also has some of the best alpine skiing near the Okanagan Valley. The main lift is open in summer to carry walkers, mountain bikers and sightseers up to alpine meadows. Camping, horse riding and back-country trail trips are also available in summer.

HEDLEY✦✦

Hedley Heritage Museum 712 Daly Ave, Hedley, BC V0X 1K0; tel: (250) 292-8787; www. hedleybc.ca. Open summer 1000–1700 daily; winter Wed–Sun 1000–1700.

This is one of the best preserved of BC's Cascades boom towns. Hedley has dwindled to less than a tenth of its pre-World-War-I population of 5000, but many of its old buildings remain. So does the **Mascot Mine✦✦✦**, perched on a mountain slope 1000m above the town. A 3-km aerial tramway hauled a bonanza in gold, silver and copper down to mills in Hedley, but the good times were cut short by falling commodity prices and World War I labour shortages. Surviving Mascot Mine buildings

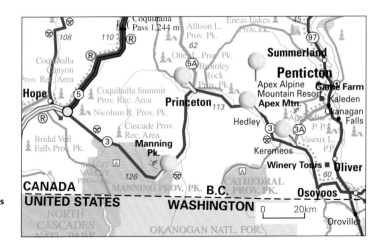

Mascot Mine Tours
$$ Tel: (250) 292-
8733; via shuttle bus up
Nickel Plate Rd from Old
Hedley School.

**Wild Goat Gift
Shop** Hedley Heritage
Museum, tel: (250) 292-
8422, has snacks and
small meals when the
museum is open.

looming far above Hedley have been restored and are open for guided tours in summer. Tours depart from the **Hedley Heritage Museum✦✦✦**, which has a fine collection of local mining artefacts and period photographs. Gold panning is still allowed in the Similkameen River just south of town, but trout fishing is likely to be more productive.

KEREMEOS✦✦✦

**Similkameen
Country** 427 7th
Ave, Keremeos; tel: (250)
499-5225; http://
similkameencountry.org.
Information centre open in
Memorial Park in summer.

**Crowsnest
Vineyards** $ Surprise
Dr, just east of Cawston;
tel: (250) 499-5129;
www.crowsnestvineyards.com
Open daily.

**The Grist Mill at
Keremeos** $ Upper Bench
Rd; tel: (250) 499-2888;
www.heritage.gov.bc.ca/grist_
mill.htm. Open daily.

Perched on a bench above the Similkameen River, Keremeos still looks and feels like the frontier town it once was. Orchards and pastures stretch nearly to the main street, which is lined with false-front wooden buildings and well-used pick-up trucks. The village began as a First Nations town big enough to convince the Hudson's Bay Company to build a trading post, and slowly grew as settlers started cattle ranches, fruit orchards and, more recently, vineyards. **Crowsnest Vineyards✦** offers broad mountain vistas from the tasting room.

The **Grist Mill at Keremeos✦✦✦**, an 1877 water-powered mill, is BC's only surviving 19th-century mill with the original machinery intact and working. Built next to Keremeos Creek, the grounds have been turned into a heritage garden surrounded by more modern orchards. The BC Heritage Trust site is open all year, but costumed interpreters operate the mill and demonstrate period farming and household tasks in summer. The tea room is an excellent summer lunch stop.

South Similkameen Museum✦ fills the former Provincial Police building and gaol with its pioneer artefacts and antique police uniforms.

Cliffs of basalt columns (geologically like Wyoming's Devil's Tower or Northern Ireland's Giant Causeway) soar 30m in the blazing sun at **Keremeos Columns Provincial Park✦**. A survey error in the 1930s left the columns on private land outside park boundaries; ask permission to hike the 8-km trail from the house at the end of the paved road.

South Similkameen Museum $ *604 6th Ave St; tel: (250) 499-5445; http://keremeos.net/museum. Call for hours.*

Keremeos Columns Provincial Park *North on Hwy 3A, east at the cemetery, a 16-km return hike from the end of the pavement; http://wlapwww.gov.bc. ca/bcparks/explore/parkpgs/ keremeos.htm*

The Red Bridge *Just west of Keremeos and south of Hwy 3; http:// keremeos.net/redbridge.html*

St Laszlo Estate Winery $ *Hwy 3 East, Upper Bench Rd; tel: (250) 499-2856. Open daily.*

The faded **Red Bridge⁺** over the Similkameen River was built as a railway bridge around 1907. When the line was abandoned, the bridge was converted to highway use. Deep pools just below the bridge are popular local swimming holes during the blazing days of summer.

St Laszlo Estate Winery⁺ spreads across the upper bench above the Similkameen River providing expansive views of Cascade peaks in every direction. The wines are largely Hungarian- and German-inspired.

Right
Keremeos Mill

MANNING PROVINCIAL PARK⁺⁺⁺

Manning Provincial Park Visitor Centre *Hwy 3, 1km east from Manning Park Resort. Open daily Jun–Labour Day 0900–1430.*

Manning Provincial Park $ *Hwy 3; tel: (604) 795-6169; http://wlapwww.gov.bc.ca/ bcparks/explore/parkpgs/ manning.htm*

Originally created as a game preserve, Manning displays jagged, snow-capped peaks, alpine meadows, deep valleys, teal-blue lakes and dense forests. Vegetation and wildlife are as varied as the terrain, from wild rhododendrons and magnificent stands of red cedar to bears foraging along the highway, deer, beaver, chipmunks, and hoary marmots, the park symbol carved into a gigantic sign at the western entrance.

Hwy 3 bisects the park, with the primary facilities, the **Manning Park Resort⁺⁺⁺** and the **Visitor Centre⁺⁺⁺**, midway between Hope and Princeton, 68km in either direction. Resort facilities include the only indoor accommodation (chalets, cabins and hotel rooms), restaurants and supply/gift shop in the park. The Visitor Centre has a small natural history museum with free trail guides and other park information.

Manning Park Resort $$
Manning Provincial Park; tel: (250) 840-8822 or (800) 330-3321; www. manningparkresort.com

Beaver Pond *South side of the highway, 500m east of the Visitor Centre. Open all year.*

Cascade Lookout *Paved road from Manning Park Resort area. Open in summer only.*

Heather Trail *Trail head at Blackwall Peak Meadows. Open in summer only.*

Rein Orchid Trail *Trail head 100m west of Amphitheatre car park off Gibson Pass Rd.*

Rhododendron Flats $ *South side of the highway, just beyond the Summallo Grove.*

Summallo Grove *South side of the highway, 9km from the west park entrance.*

Manning is a year-round outdoor recreation centre, with alpine and Nordic skiing in winter and extensive trails for hiking, mountain biking and horse riding in summer. There are also several short, self-guiding nature trails, many accessible only in summer, as well as multi-day backpacking routes and several campgrounds accessible by car.

Two major rivers rise from the Cascades within Manning. The Skagit River curls westward through the park and the adjoining **Skagit Valley Provincial Recreation Area**❖❖❖, then disappears into a series of hydroelectric reservoirs south of the US border to drain into Puget Sound near Seattle. The Similkameen River runs east through the Cascades and eventually drains into the Okanagan River and then into the Columbia River in Washington State.

Beaver Pond❖❖, created by beavers damming a small stream, offers excellent birdwatching during May and June. The sometimes paved, sometimes gravel trail stretches 500m.

A summer-only paved road leads 9km from the highway at the Lodge to **Cascade Lookout**❖❖❖, with grand views back to the valley surrounding the Manning Park Lodge and Visitor Centre and nearby mountains. A good gravel road climbs another 6km to **Blackwall Peak Alpine Meadows**❖❖❖ and sublime vistas invisible from lower lookouts. The meadows shimmer with wild flowers from late July to mid-August.

Heather Trail❖❖❖ follows a carpet of wild flowers more than 24km long and up to 5km wide stretching from Blackwall Peak to Third Brother Mountain and beyond. Road access is from the Blackwall Peak Alpine Meadows car park.

Rein Orchid Trail❖❖❖ explores bog and riverside terrain filled with native orchids, ferns and other wetland flora. The flat, 15-minute trail is only 500m long.

Rhododendron Flats❖❖❖, a flat 2-km walking trail, goes through one of the few naturally occurring groves of rhododendrons in the Cascades. Red blossoms are at their height early–mid-June most years.

A 700m trail (wheelchair accessible in most seasons) in **Summallo Grove**❖❖❖ circles through a towering riverside grove of red cedar and Douglas fir.

PRINCETON❖❖

Princeton and District Chamber of Commerce *57 Hwy 3 (east end of town); tel: (250) 295-3103; http://town. princeton.bc.ca. Open daily Jun–Sept; Oct–Apr Mon–Fri.*

The town was originally called Vermillion Forks for the red pigment mined by First Nations bands. The name 'Princeton' dates from an 1860 visit to Eastern Canada by the Prince of Wales. Once a mining and cattle town, Princeton has become the commercial centre of the south Cascades region. Most of the major mines have closed in recent years, prompting residents to turn their colourful history into profitable tourism. Several downtown buildings sport new western-themed murals, while the Chamber of Commerce promotes walking tours and gold panning.

Princeton and District Pioneer Museum and Archives
$ 167 Vermillion Ave; tel: (250) 295-7588; http://town.princeton.bc.ca/museum/museum.htm. Open daily, Apr–Oct.

Gold panning $ Check with the Chamber of Commerce for location and pan hire.

Vermillion Bluffs $ Behind Home Hardware, Bridge St and Fenchurch Ave.

Princeton and District Pioneer Museum and Archives*** has an outstanding collection of fossils, including some of the earliest known examples of fossilised citrus trees, apple trees and salmon. There are also exhibitions of local mining equipment, fluorescent minerals and pioneer artefacts.

Gold prospectors followed the Similkameen River northward in the 1850s, panning and dredging as they went, but small flakes of gold continue to wash out of the Cascades with every spring melt. The Chamber of Commerce can recommend where to pan on the river.

The Okanagan First Nations bands who lived at **Vermillion Bluffs*****, when Hudson's Bay Company explorers first appeared in the early 1800s, called the place *Yak Tulameen*, 'place where red earth is sold'. The band mined red ochre, vermilion sulphate, from cliffs along the Tulameen River, just west, and sold it at a well-established marketplace where Princeton now stands.

Accommodation and food in Princeton

Princeton Hotel Pub $$ *258 Bridge St; tel: (250) 295-7773*, is the oldest restaurant in Princeton, *open 1200–1500*.

Villager Motel $$ *Hwy 3; tel: (250) 295-6996*, is the largest and newest motel in town.

The Dewdney Trail

In the 1860s, it was easier to travel east–west through the United States than through BC, and easier still to travel north–south along the many river valleys that connected the two countries. When gold was discovered at Wild Horse Creek, near **Cranbrook** (see page 250), American miners and merchants flooded north, threatening to undermine already tenuous British authority. The solution: Surveyor Edgar Dewdney blasted a mule trail 1.2m wide through 400km of mountains, desert and forests from Hope to the East Kootenays in just seven months.

The Dewdney Trail opened the southern reaches of BC to the coast for the first time. As mining grew, so did the trail, expanding from mule trail to wagon road and automobile road, Hwy 3. With a boost from the Kettle Valley Railway, road access slowly focused the province's southern communities on Vancouver and Victoria and away from closer, more accessible commercial centres in the United States.

Opposite
Coquihalla Highway

Above
Keremeos Mill

Suggested tour

Total distance: 240km.

Time: Allow half a day to drive from Hope through the Cascades to the Okanagan Valley and 2–4 days to explore Manning Provincial Park.

Links: Go west to the **Lower Fraser River Valley** (*see page 122*) and Vancouver (*see page 42*), north to **Kamloops** (*see page 138*), the **Gold Rush Trail** (*see page 186*) or the **Okanagan Valley** (*see page 148*).

Route: From **HOPE** ❶ (*see page 127*), go east on Hwy 3, the Crowsnest Highway, named for the Crowsnest Pass near the BC–Alberta border. The freeway turns north toward **Kamloops** at Hwy 5, the **Coquihalla Highway** (*see page 144*), while Hwy 3 reverts to two lanes. Hwy 3 largely follows the **Dewdney Trail**, the first rough mule track cut through the wilderness to supply Kootenay gold fields in the 1860s.

Look for the raw scar of the **Hope Slide** looming above the north side of the highway 10km beyond the junction. One side of the mountain, 1983m high by 1km wide, slid into the valley in 1965. The slide raised the valley floor by 70m and blocked the highway for weeks.

Continue east past the wooden carving of a hoary marmot into **MANNING PROVINCIAL PARK** ❷, the most scenic (and the slowest) section of the Crowsnest. The road is winding and occasionally steep, the scenery distracting and the wildlife sometimes close enough to cause traffic jams.

The road turns north after leaving the park, heading for the former mining town of **PRINCETON** ❸. The highway follows the Similkameen River as it cuts through increasingly dry terrain eastward toward **HEDLEY** ❹. By **KEREMEOS** ❺, the mountains have taken on the look of desert, although streambeds and river courses are still lined with green – as are growing tracts of fruit orchards and vineyards. The highway takes a final plunge over **Richter Pass** (682m) before dropping into the true desert of the **Okanagan Valley** (*see page 148*) at **Osoyoos** ❻ (*see page 152*).

Detour: From Keremeos, take Hwy 3A north and east to **Skaha Lake** (*see page 153*) in the central **Okanagan Valley** (*see page 148*).

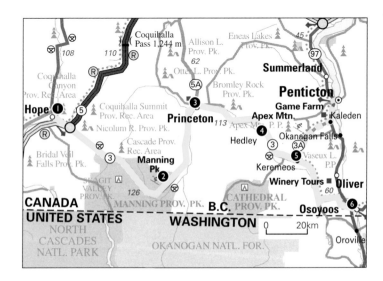

Kamloops

Ratings

Cowboys	●●●●●
First Nations	●●●●●
History	●●●●○
Outdoor activities	●●●●○
Scenery	●●●●○
Beaches	●●●○○
Parks	●●●○○
Sport	●●●○○

B C's largest city, at least in terms of area, takes its name from a Secwepemc First Nations word, *Kamloopa*, the 'meeting of the rivers'. Straddling the junction of the North Thompson and South Thompson rivers, Kamloops spreads across 31sq km of river valley and hillside that have become the centre of BC's ranching industry.

In prior decades, scarlet-clad huntsmen rode to hounds across the rolling hills in noisy pursuit of wild foxes (or coyotes, depending on the luck of the hunt). Those same hills today are sprouting housing estates or provincial parks, depending on the luck of conservationists.

In the old city centre, on the low south bank of the Thompson River, dozens of stately brick buildings rise along shady streets that lead to sandy riverfront beaches. Outlying districts have more ice-rinks, playing fields, gymnasiums and tennis courts than many countries can claim.

Kamloops, proud of being the Tournament Capital of Canada, holds at least one major sport competition every weekend of the year.

Sights

ⓘ **Kamloops Visitor Info Centre** *1290 W. Trans Canada Hwy (exit 368); tel: (250) 374-3377 or (800) 662-1994; www. adventurekamloops.com. Open daily.*

🏛 **City of Kamloops Fire Hall Museum $** *1205 Summit Dr; tel: (250) 372-5131. Open Mon–Fri; tours Tue, Thur.*

Farmers Market $ *Tel: (250) 573-3981; late May–Oct: Victoria St between 4th–5th Ave, 0800–1400; St. Paul St between 2nd–3rd Ave, 0800–1200.*

City of Kamloops Fire Hall Museum*
The museum is part of the city's main fire hall, with tours occasionally interrupted by genuine emergency calls. Fires excepted, there's almost always a fire-fighter on hand to explain the intricacies of fire suppression equipment and technologies dating back to 1884.

Farmers Market*
The weekly farmers market started as a place for local farmers to sell their products, but has become a popular cultural and educational venue. Look for anything from a 4-H Club parade with chickens and rabbits to live music, square dancing and suggestions on how to control garden bugs without pesticides – plus a better selection of fresh fruits, vegetables, breads, cheese and picnic supplies than any store in town.

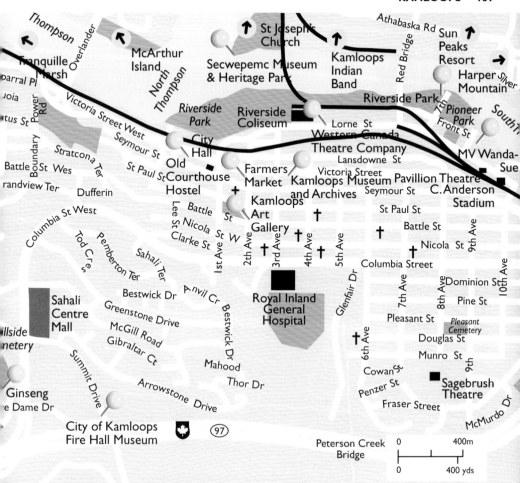

Canadian Imperial Ginseng
1274 McGill Rd; tel: (250) 851-2880. Open daily.

Sunmore Ginseng Factory
925 McGill Pl; tel: (888) 289-8222 or (250) 374-3017; www.sunmore.com. Open daily.

Harper Mountain $$
2042 Valleyview Dr; tel: (250) 979-3939 or (888) 676-9977; www.skibc.com/skiresorts_harper.html. Open approx. early Dec–late Mar.

Ginseng◆◆◆

Kamloops has become a major ginseng-growing region – the areas of black sunscreens protecting the shade-loving plants from the fierce summer sun are the world's largest single source of ginseng. Few ginseng growers welcome visitors, but the processors do. The two biggest, **Canadian Imperial Ginseng◆◆◆** and **Sunmore Ginseng Factory◆◆◆**, offer daily tours and product samples as well as display gardens.

Harper Mountain◆

Kamloops' traditional family ski hill is a short drive from town with alpine and Nordic skiing in winter. There are day-use only facilities, and lifts are less developed than newer competitor Sun Peaks, but prices are also considerably lower.

Kamloops Art Gallery $ 465 Victoria St; tel: (250) 828-3543; www.kag.bc.ca. Call for hours.

Kamloops Heritage Railway $$ 510 Lorne St; tel: (250) 374-2141; www. kamloopsheritagerailway.com. Operates weekends mid-Jun–mid-Sept, mid Dec.

Kamloops Indian Band 200-355 Yellowhead Hwy; tel: (250) 828-9700; www.kib.ca

Kamloops Museum and Archives $ 207 Seymour St; tel: (250) 828-3576; www. city.kamloops.bc.ca/parks/ museum. Open Tue–Sat 0930–1630.

Kamloops Symphony Orchestra $$ 335 Victoria St; tel: (250) 372-5000; www.kamloopssymphony.com. Concerts Nov–Apr.

Kamloops Water Slide $$ Hwy 1, 19km east; tel: (250) 573-2213. Open late May–Labour Day.

Kenna Cartwright Park Trans Canada Hwy to Exit 366 north on Copperhead Dr, west on Hillside Dr.; tel: (250) 828-3580; www.city. kamloops.bc.ca/parks/kenna

McArthur Island North Kamloops via McKenzie Ave or 12th St; tel: (250) 828-3580; www.city.kamloops. bc.ca/parks/parks/ macislandpark.html. Open daily.

Kamloops Art Gallery*

The gallery, which claims to be the largest public art exhibit in interior BC, concentrates on local artists and publishes a free walking tour to private downtown galleries.

Kamloops Heritage Railway*

Summer weekends are the time to board for the 70-minute carriage or open-air car trips pulled by the restored steam engine No 2141, *The Spirit of Kamloops*. A restoration shop is located one block away in Pioneer Park.

Kamloops Indian Band***

The Kamloops Band is one of 17 modern Secwepemc (Shuswap) bands and the most economically successful. Much of the Band's land along the North Thompson and South Thompson rivers has been leased out to thriving industrial parks, farming and grazing operations. Profits support a successful Band community as well as the **Kamloopa Powwow Days***, held each August, one of the largest First Nations gatherings in North America.

Kamloops Museum and Archives**

Three floors of displays explore local Secwepemc First Nations history, Hudson's Bay Company activities, gold rushes, ranching and cowboy history, local Chinese culture, Victoriana and natural history. The museum's collection of Secwepemc baskets is one of the best in the province. Exhibits include an 1842 log building from the HBC fort on what is now the Kamloops Indian Reserve on the north bank of the South Thompson River, two Victorian-era house interiors, a Victorian medical office and a late 19th-century general store.

Kamloops Symphony Orchestra*

The 50-member orchestra presents a full concert schedule from autumn to spring, plus outdoor summer concerts at Sun Peaks and other area venues.

Kamloops Water Slide*

Kamloops' only water park has slides, hot tubs, wading pools and miniature golf next to the area's largest RV park.

Kenna Cartwright Park

BC's largest municipal park (800 hectares) is in the southwestern section of Kamloops, spread around Mount Dufferin. A number of nature trails offer hikers year-round views of the convergence of the North and South Thompson Rivers, Kamloops Lake and the Thompson Valley. It's mixed grassland–forest wilderness within the city, home to bears, coyotes, deer, and several provincially identified vulnerable species, including the Great Basin Spadefoot Toad.

McArthur Island**

Recreation is big business in Kamloops, with 84 baseball diamonds, 73 soccer fields, 53 tennis courts, 5 ice arenas, 40 gymnasia, 18 golf

Old Courthouse Hostel $ 7 W Seymour St; tel: (250) 828-7991 or (866) 782-9526; www.hihostels.ca. Open daily.

Riverside Park South bank, Thompson River, east and west from the foot of 3rd Ave; tel: (250) 828-3580; www.city.kamloops.bc.ca/parks/parks/body.shtml. Music concerts nightly Jul–Aug.

Secwepemc Museum & Heritage Park $ 355 Yellowhead Hwy; tel: (250) 828-9801; www.secwepemc.org/museum.html. Open Open Labour Day–May Mon–Fri 0830–1630, Jun–Labour Day Mon–Fri 0830–2000, Sat–Sun 1000–2000.

St Joseph's Church Off Chilcotin Avenue, Kamloops Indian Band Reserve; tel: (250) 374-7323. Open daily Jul–Sept; year-round for services.

Sun Peaks Resort $$$ 50km and 45 minutes north of Kamloops off Hwy 5; tel: (250) 578-7222 or (800) 807-3257; www.sunpeaksresort.com. Open all year.

courses in the region ... and McArthur Island. The North Shore island is all recreation, with golf course, cycling trails, swimming, tennis, football, soccer, rugby, baseball and more. McArthur is also a wildlife mecca, with a butterfly garden, viewing platform to spot beavers, muskrats, yellow-bellied marmots, squirrels, red foxes and river otters, hides for birdwatching and an extensive native-plant walk.

Old Courthouse Hostel◆◆◆

Kamloops' 1904 courthouse has been restored as a youth hostel, retaining the original Gothic-style arched windows and stained glass. The main courtroom, with the judge's bench, jury seats, witness box and prisoner's box intact, has become the dining area and lounge.

Riverside Park◆◆◆

The city's first riverfront park features a rose garden, tennis, swimming, walking trails, water park and a 5000-seat coliseum.

Secwepemc Museum & Heritage Park◆◆◆

The Secwepemc (pronounced she-whep-m,) or Shuswap First Nations controlled a vast territory from Kamloops west to the Fraser River, north to Soda Springs and east to the Rockies for millennia before the Hudson's Bay Company built its first fur-trading fort at Kamloops in 1812.

The Secwepemc traditionally lived a semi-nomadic life, following fish, game and food plants from spring to autumn and returning to permanent villages with the first winter snows. One of the largest and oldest of the villages occupied the northeastern shore of the confluence of the two Thompson Rivers, land that eventually became the Kamloops Indian Reserve.

A 4-hectare Heritage Park covers the ancient village site, which includes remains of dwellings at least 2400 years old. Reconstructed houses and archaeological excavations show changes in house styles and sizes from 5000 years ago to first contact with the HBC in the early 19th century. The Park also has exhibits of heritage and native food plants and a traditional salmon fishery. In summer, band performers offer traditional song, dancing, theatre and story-telling as well as salmon barbecues in a traditional summer lodge.

The museum building was once part of the Kamloops Indian Residential School. Exhibits include most of the artefacts found in the Heritage Park outside, as well as artefacts from digs throughout traditional Secwepemc lands and a fine collection of archival photographs. Museum displays put a distinctly Secwepemc spin on local history, detailing the legal and moral transgressions committed by White settlers that are largely ignored by the Kamloops Museum.

St Joseph's Church◆◆◆

The white steeple of St Joseph's was first raised in 1846, but the current building has been restored to its early 1900s look, complete with stained-glass windows and bright interior paintings. Don't miss

Tranquille Marsh
10km west of North Kamloops on Tranquille Rd; tel: (250) 371-6200. Open daily.

Western Canada Theatre Company $$
1025 Lorne St; tel: (250) 372-3216 or (866) 374-5483; www. westerncanadatheatre.bc.ca. Regular productions Oct–Mar.

the cemetery, directly across the car park, with grave markers ranging from simple wooden crosses to ornate totemic carvings.

Sun Peaks Resort◆
Sun Peaks has skiing in winter (882m vertical drop, groomed runs, open glades and snowboarding) and fishing, golf, hiking, horse riding, mountain biking, music festival, swimming and tennis in summer. Base facilities include hotels, condominiums, lodges, restaurants and shopping.

Tranquille Marsh◆◆
This BC Wildlife Watch viewing site overlooks an extremely active waterfowl habitat. Look for trumpeter swans, Canada and snow geese, herons, ducks and dozens of other species, especially during the spring and autumn migrations. Follow Red Lake Road a few kilometres to spot bighorn sheep.

Western Canada Theatre Company◆◆
Kamloops has one of the few professional theatre companies in the province outside Vancouver and Victoria. The programme emphasises well-known productions that have already garnered a following in London or New York.

Accommodation and food

Accommodation is usually easy to find, although advance booking is wise during the summer holiday period. Motels are concentrated along Hwy 5 and off Hwy 1 at exits 366–369. For more expensive digs, try along Columbia St (exit 369), which curves from the highway down to the old town centre near the river.

South Thompson Inn Guest Ranch $$$ *3438 Shuswap Rd, North of the South Thompson River, 15 minutes east off Hwy 1; tel: (250) 573-3777 or (800) 797-7713; www.stigr.com,* is an expansive horse-farm-cum-resort next to the **Rivershore Estates & Golf Links** – guests get preferred tee times.

A growing population has brought new life to Kamloops' restaurants. Don't expect the cutting edge Northwestern fare found in Vancouver and Victoria, but there's more than steaks, burgers and meatballs.

Apollon $$ *369 Victoria St; tel: (250) 372-5852,* in the old town centre, is a good choice for Greek dishes.

Bagel Street Café $ *428 Victoria St; tel: (250) 372-9322; www. bagelstreetcafe.com,* in the old town centre, is popular for breakfast and light lunches.

Taka $$ *270-1210 Summit Dr (Columbia Place Mall); tel: (250) 828-0806,* has Kamloops' best Japanese cuisine.

Warunee's Thai Restaurant $$ *413 Tranquille Rd; tel: (250) 554-7080; www.ocis.net/~dturner/thai,* is the city's first Thai restaurant, with a cheerful website filled with descriptions of Thai culture, recipes, and the menu.

Right
Kamloops countryside

Weather The BC interior is given to extremes: +40°C (104°F) and blazing sun in summer; –40°C (–40°F) and drifting snow in winter. Both extremes are arid.

Suggested tours

Total distance: 3km.

Time: 2 hours' walking, 4 hours' cycling. The Kamloops Museum has self-guiding maps and brochures for both tours.

Route: The North Kamloops cycle tour has seven stops between Riverside Park and the **Tranquille Sanitarium** by way of McARTHUR ISLAND ❶.

The museum's recommended walking tour includes 30 stops in the old city centre, Nicola Street–Riverside Park and Fourth Street–Lee Road. Start at the old **Calvary Temple** (185 Seymour Street, across 2nd Avenue from the **KAMLOOPS MUSEUM AND ARCHIVES ❷**), the oldest public building in town. It opened in 1887 as St Andrew's Presbyterian Church. Just uphill was Kamloops' posh residential district between the 1880s and 1914, with imposing residences along St Paul, Battle and Nicola streets between 1st Avenue and Lee Road.

Walk west along Seymour Street to the English-Gothic-style **OLD COURTHOUSE HOSTEL ❸** (7 W Seymour Street), now a youth hostel. Diagonally across 1st Avenue is the **Cigar Factory** (297 1st Avenue), built in 1895 and converted to a bakery in 1913. Continue down 1st Avenue to the **Bank of Commerce** (118 Victoria

Coquihalla Highway

Created for Expo '88, the World's Fair that put Vancouver on the international map, the Coquihalla shaves 90 minutes and uncounted grey hairs off the drive between Hope and Kamloops. Cruise smoothly from four-lane Hwy 1 on to four-lane Hwy 5 at Hope and you can make the run from Vancouver to BC's inland capital in a comfortable 5 hours – without bending a single speed limit!

BC's only toll road is actually a second attempt to conquer the Cascade Range between Hope and Kamloops. The first try, the Kettle Valley Railway (see page 151), was plagued by runaway trains, washouts, rockslides, avalanches and massive snowfalls until Canadian Pacific Railways finally gave up and closed the line in 1959. The Coquihalla follows much of the old KVR route through the Cascades, but a panoply of modern engineering marvels keeps the highway open through the same choke-points where the railway failed year after year: massive snow sheds, avalanche diversion channels, snow dams, arcing bridges and howitzer emplacements to blast hanging snowpacks are well worth the $10 toll.

The highway is a microcosm of BC scenery. From the lush forests and rough coastal mountains around Hope, the roadway climbs sharply into the older, more rounded peaks of the Cascades. As the climate becomes drier toward the interior, trees become smaller and moss is displaced by the sparse, semi-arid grasses of the Fraser Plateau.

Street), which looks almost as it did when built in 1904. Straight ahead is **RIVERSIDE PARK ❹**, originally the site of a sawmill, gristmill and brickyard.

Victoria Street is one of the most scenic sections of Kamloops, lined with well-preserved buildings. One of the most imposing is the **Fuoco Block** (No 219), erected during the boom years between 1910 and 1914. The 1905 **Kamloops Inn** (No 345) was the site of the city's first fire hall. The **Ellis Goodman Block** (No 371) was home to a successful drugstore partnership, with an apothecary shop at street level and professional offices on the floors above. The **Plaza Hotel** (No 405), opened in 1927 in pseudo-Spanish style, was the first hotel in Kamloops built specifically for automobile traffic. Turn uphill along 4th Avenue to Seymour Street. The **Elks Lodge** (409 Seymour Street), also built in 1927, shows similar Spanish design details. Continue west along Seymour Street back to the Calvary Temple.

Also worth visiting

Lac de Bois Grasslands Provincial Park *North of Kamloops; tel: (250) 851-3000; http://wlapwww.gov.bc.ca/bcparks/explore/parkpgs/lacduboi.htm.* Open daily, no developed facilities or water.

Above
Lac du Bois

Eastern unit Take exit 374 from Hwy 1 at Kamloops. Follow Hwy 5 north over the South Thompson River to Halston Avenue (second set of traffic lights). Take Halston west (left) over the North Thompson River. At the first traffic signal beyond the river, turn right (uphill) to Westsyde Road. Move to the left-hand lane and drive straight up the hill through the housing estates on Lac du Bois Road. Enter the park when the road turns to gravel at the cattle guard.

Western Unit Take Hwy 1 exit 369 or 374 toward the Kamloops Airport via Tranquille Road. From the airport, continue west toward Tranquille. At the Tranquille Sanatorium, turn right, over the railway tracks, and up a long hill.

Dewdrop Lake is straight ahead, along the flats; **Tranquille River Canyon** is uphill.

To explore the grasslands, head for the eastern unit, accessible from Hwy 5. For lakes and canyons, drive the western unit, off Tranquille Road beyond the Kamloops Airport. Either way, Lac du Bois is what Kamloops looked like before it was Kamloops, complete with sweeping vistas, red lava cliffs, canyons ringing with waterfalls, arid grasslands, dry forests, hidden lakes and rolling fields of wild flowers stretching to the horizon.

Lac du Bois is also BC's largest publicly owned grassland. Established in 1996, it accommodates multiple and not always compatible uses, from walking and mountain biking to grazing, logging, all-terrain vehicle driving, fishing, hunting and no-entry ecological preserves in three separate grassland communities.

Ecologists go dewy-eyed over the only-in-Kamloops opportunity to see all three types of bunchgrass native to North America west of the Rocky Mountains. Flower lovers rave about the variety: buttercups, biscuit root, mariposa daisies and yellow sagebrush are only the beginning, with flowering seasons that can range from May into July, depending on rainfall, exposure and elevation.

Birdwatchers think they're in heaven: sharp-tailed grouse, sapsuckers, hairy woodpeckers, flammulated owls and dozens of other species use the grasslands in every season. It's nearly impossible not to see cows, or at least evidence of their recent presence; visitors who know where to look can expect to spot California bighorn sheep, coyotes, foxes, moose, mule deer, rattlesnakes and waterfowl.

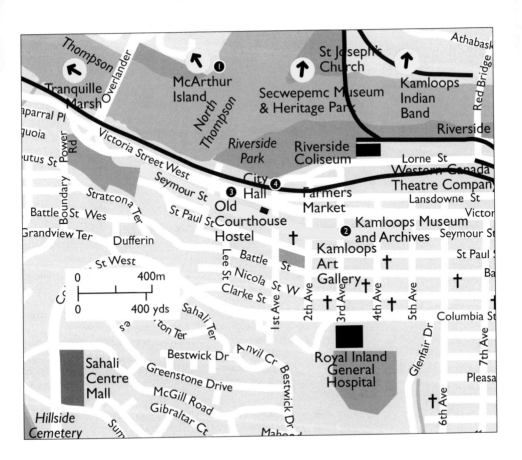

Okanagan Valley

Ratings

Food and drink	●●●●●
Wineries	●●●●●
History	●●●●○
Scenery	●●●●○
Beaches	●●●○○
Children	●●●○○
Outdoor activities	●●●○○
Wildlife	●●●○○

The Okanagan Valley is touted as one of Canada's two true deserts (the other is in the Yukon Territory), but leave the sand shoes at home – true desert is all but impossible to find anywhere in the valley. Decades of irrigation have pushed cacti and other desert creatures into a few isolated ecological reserves, as lush fruit orchards, vegetable fields and vineyards spread from the Okanagan River up every arable hillside, bench and plateau.

The valley itself follows a string of lakes linked together by the Okanagan River, the remnants of an immense glacial river that carved a broad north–south rift through the mountains. The Cascade Range blocks most rain-bearing clouds from the Pacific Ocean; the even higher Monashee Mountains to the east capture what moisture remains. The Okanagan sits in the rain shadow of both ranges, a desert that has blossomed into BC's fruit basket, wine cellar and most popular interior holiday destination.

BRITISH COLUMBIA WINE INFORMATION CENTRE✦✦✦

ⓘ Thompson Okanagan Tourism
1332 Water St, Kelowna;
tel: (250) 860-5999;
www.totabc.com

This is the single most complete source of information about wine in BC, with experimental plantings, a tasting room and the best commercial selection of BC wine in the province. (**British Columbia Wine Information Centre** $ *888 Westminster Ave W, Penticton; tel: (250) 490-2006; www.bcwineinfo.ca. VQA Wine Shop open Mon–Fri 1000–1800, Sat–Sun 1000–1600.*

DOMINION RADIO ASTROPHYSICAL OBSERVATORY✦✦✦

Sitting at the bottom of a shallow valley, DRAO's towering white radio dish, surrounded by an array of smaller antennae, looks more like *Star Wars* than the Okanagan. (**Dominion Radio Astrophysical Observatory** $ *White Lake Rd, 9km from Kaleden Jct; tel: (250) 493-2277; www.drao.nrc.ca. Open Mon–Fri 0830–1630.*)

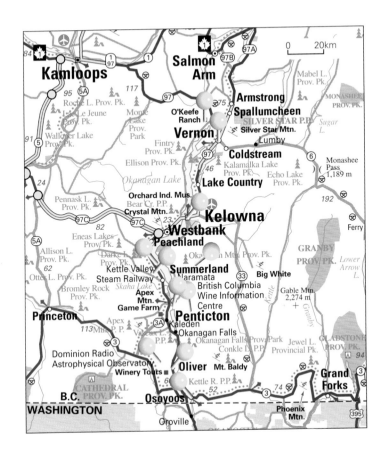

KELOWNA❖❖

ⓘ Tourism Kelowna Visitor Info Centre
544 Harvey Ave (Hwy 97), Kelowna, BC V1Y 6C9; tel: (250) 861-1515 or (800) 663-4345; www.tourismkelowna.org. Open Mon–Fri 1000–1700, Sat–Sun 1000–1500.

Kelowna's Cultural District A self-guided 6-block walking tour brochure is available at the Visitor Info Centre and galleries, museums and restaurants, or by request: tel: 866-903-3384; www.artsinkelowna.com

Kelowna began as an 1850s Roman Catholic mission, but soon expanded into lumber and fruit. The 128-km² expanse of Okanagan Lake moderates winter weather while the dry, sunny climate produces dependable crops of apples, peaches and grapes.

Lake and sun have also made Kelowna a popular holiday destination. Vast areas of beaches, parks and mountain forests offer sailing, fishing, hiking, house-boating and skiing.

The 1917 Laurel Packing House, now the **BC Orchard Industry and Wine Museum**❖❖❖, displays the history of Okanagan fruit growing and packing with period photographs and hands-on equipment displays. The Wine Museum has a few wine-related displays in a retail shop.

Pleasant **City Park**❖❖❖ stretches 1km from the foot of the floating bridge across Lake Okanagan to the white sculpture, *The Sail*, merging into the waterfront and marina.

Father Pandosy Mission❖❖❖, a rough-hewn Oblate Mission, founded in 1859 by Fr Charles Pandosy, was the first non-Native settlement in

BC Orchard Industry and Wine Museum $ *1304 Ellis St; tel: (250) 763-0433; www. kelownamuseum.ca/om/index. htm. Open Tue–Sat 1000–1700.*

City Park $ *Lakeshore, from the floating bridge to the white sculpture 'The Sail'.*

Father Pandosy Mission *3685 Benvoulin Dr., southeast from the city centre; tel: (250) 860-8369. Open daily Apr–Oct.*

Geert Maas Sculpture Gardens and Gallery $ *250 Reynolds Rd; tel: (250) 860-7012; www.geertmaas.org. Open May–Oct Mon–Sat, or by appointment.*

Kelowna Art Gallery *1315 Water St; tel: (250) 762-2226; www.kelownaartgallery.com. Open Tue–Sat 1000–1700, Thur to 2100, Sun 1300–1600.*

Kelowna Museum $ *470 Queensway; tel: (250) 763-2417; www.kelownamuseum. ca/km/index.htm. Open Tue–Sat 1000–1700.*

Kelowna Land & Orchard $ *2930 Dunster Rd; tel: (250) 763-1091; www.k–l–o.com. Tours daily May–Oct.*

KVR Bike Trails *Myra Canyon, June Springs and Chute Lake are undergoing reconstruction. Check with the CVB for current conditions. When restored, access roads may or may not be passable by passenger cars.*

the Okanagan. The original log buildings have been heavily but accurately restored.

The **Geert Maas Sculpture Gardens and Gallery✧** complements the sculptor's more traditional indoor gallery, while the **Kelowna Art Gallery✧** has a growing collection of BC art and artists. Exhibits at **Kelowna Museum✧✧** include an 1861 trading post, a traditional First Nations pit house and Kelowna's first radio station.

One of the Okanagan's orchard giants, **Kelowna Land & Orchard✧✧**, offers regular tours, fruit and juice samples, Raven Ridge Cidery, a petting zoo, and a small museum.

KVR Bike Trails✧✧✧, railbeds from the abandoned **Kettle Valley Railway**, now under reconstruction to restore the trestles and path destroyed by fire in 2003, shall, when restored, offer spectacular canyon and mountain views for walkers and mountain bikers with a maximum 2 per cent grade. **Myra Canyon✧✧✧** offers the best views; the first trestle is an easy 15-minute walk from the car park. The next 12km to **June Springs✧✧✧** crosses 17 trestles and two tunnels.

Elysium Garden–Nursery✧✧ transformed an apple orchard with mountain views into display gardens, and a Japanese garden, with a water-efficient xeriscape garden using plants from this desert region.

Right
Kettle Valley Railway bike trail

Elysium Garden–Nursery $$ 2834 Belgo Rd; tel: (250) 491-1368; www.elysiumgardennursery.com. Open May–mid-Oct 0900–1700.

Gray Monk 1055 Camp Rd; tel: (250) 766-3168 or (800) 663-4205; www.graymonk.com. Open daily.

Mission Hill Winery 1730 Mission Hill Rd; tel: (250) 768-7611; www.missionhillwinery.com. Open daily.

Quail's Gate Estate Winery 3303 Boucheire Rd; tel: (250) 769-4451; www.quailsgate.com. Open daily.

Summerhill Pyramid Winery 4870 Chute Lake Rd; tel: (250) 764-8000 or (800) 667-3538; www.summerhill.bc.ca. Open daily.

Wineries*** Most of the dozen or so in the area offer free tours and tastings. **Gray Monk***** is one of the oldest wineries in the Okanagan and still among the best. **Mission Hill Winery***** has spectacular views across Okanagan Lake from the winery tasting room. **Quail's Gate Vineyard Estate Winery***** doesn't have a grand building, but some of the Okanagan's grandest ice wines. Its wine shop is in a refurbished log cabin. **Summerhill Pyramid Winery*****, BC's largest producer of sparkling wines also, has stunning views across the valley from a deck just outside, and a four-storey pyramid-shaped aging cellar.

Accommodation and food in Kelowna

Wicklow by the Lake Bed & Breakfast $$ 1454 Green Bay Rd, Westbank; tel: (250) 768-1330, overlooks Okanagan Lake.

Bohemian Café & Catering Co. $ 363 Bernard Ave; tel: (250) 862-3517, is family-owned and known for speciality coffees.

Ric's Grill $$ 210 Lawrence Ave; tel: (250) 869-1586, is a great place to have steak.

Woodfire Bakery $ 2041 Harvey Ave; tel: (250) 762-2626, is a local favourite for breakfast and lunch.

KETTLE VALLEY STEAM RAILWAY***

Kettle Valley Steam Railway $$ 18404 Bathville Rd, Summerland; tel: (250) 494-8422 or (877) 494-8424; www.kettlevalleyrail.org. Operates weekends May–Oct; check schedule.

This 10-km section of track is all that remains of the Kettle Valley Railway that once linked Nelson with Hope. The train, pulled by a 1924 Shay steam locomotive engine, offers stupendous views across the Okanagan Valley, on two-hour tours.

O'KEEFE RANCH***

O'Keefe Ranch $ 12km North of Vernon; tel: (250) 542-7868; www.okeeferanch.bc.ca. Open May–Sept, daily 0900–2000.

Started in 1867, the O'Keefe became one of the largest cattle ranches in the region. The ranch headquarters (Hwy 97, 12km north of Vernon) grew into a small town with church, general store and post office. Living history interpreters sound as if they just stepped off the range.

OLIVER**

This orchard and vineyard town lived by ranching until a Provincial irrigation project turned jobless World War I veterans into farmers.

Oliver & District Chamber of Commerce and Visitor Info Centre *End of 36205 93rd St near Okanagan River; tel: (250) 498-6321; www.oliverchamber.bc.ca*

Oliver and District Museum *$ 9728 356 Ave; tel: (250) 498-4027. Open Mon–Sat 0900–1600 in summer.*

Wineries: Gehringer Bros *Road 8; tel: (250) 498-3537 or (800) 784-6304.*

Hester Creek *13163 326th Ave; tel: (250) 498-4435; www.hestercreek.com*

Inniskillin Okanagan Vineyards *$ Road 11; tel: (250) 498-6663 or (800) 498-6211; www.inniskillin. com/en/vineyard/vineyards Okanagan.asp?location= vineyard&secondLocation= vineyardsOkanagan*

Tinhorn Creek *Road 7; tel: (250) 498-3743 or (888) 484-6467; www.tinhorn.com*

The Ditch, the original irrigation canal, is still used. Most of the Okanagan River was canalised in the 1950s for more irrigation and flood control. Exhibits in **Oliver and District Museum**◆, the former Provincial Police building, cover natural history, early mining activities and irrigation.

Wineries◆◆◆ Oliver created the **Golden Mile** as a marketing ploy to lure visitors to a string of award-winning wineries located on the west side of Hwy 97 just south of town. **Gehringer Bros**◆◆◆ leans toward traditional German-type wines. **Hester Creek**◆◆◆ expanding in 2004–2005, produces more modern styles, influenced by California rather than Europe. **Inniskillin Okanagan Vineyards**◆◆◆, co-owned by the Inkameep Indian Band (Okanaqueen Tribe), produces intense, flavourful wines. **Tinhorn Creek**◆◆◆ shines with reds and has Valley views from the winery deck.

Okanagan wine

Wine has been a familiar Okanagan product for decades, but high-quality wine is a new arrival. The change started in 1988, when Provincial authorities encouraged grape growers to pull out old vineyards that were filled with table grapes and high-yield, low-quality wine grapes. The replacements were Cabernet Sauvignon, Chardonnay, Riesling, Merlot, Sauvignon Blanc, Pinot Noir and similar varieties. The province also revised antiquated licensing laws that favoured high production over high quality and introduced the **VQA**, the Vintners Quality Alliance, BC's answer to appellation and quality control schemes in France, Germany, Italy and California.

OSOYOOS◆

Osoyoos Chamber of Commerce *Jct of Hwys 3 and 97; tel: (250) 495-7142; www.osoyooschamber.bc.ca. Open daily.*

Beaches *$ Downtown and lakeside parks.*

Desert Centre *$ West on 146 Ave; tel: (250) 495-2470 or (877) 899-0897; www.desert.org. Open daily.*

Just north of the US border, Osoyoos sits in the same Sonoran desert made famous by Sonora, Mexico. Osoyoos Lake draws visitors eager to bake on sandy beaches and water-ski in almost-warm water, but irrigation has turned the desert into a literal fruit basket: apples, peaches, pears, grapes, plums and cherries from surrounding hillsides appear in roadside fruit stands in summer.

Sandy strands are a way of life. **Gyro Beach**◆ and **Community Beach**◆ are in the centre of town. **Desert Centre**◆◆◆, one of the Okanagan's few surviving pockets of desert, has 3km of boardwalks and interpretative kiosks. Look for greasewood, rabbit brush, sage, burrowing owls, spadefoot toads, yellow badgers and rattlesnakes. **The Nk'Mip Desert & Heritage Centre**◆◆ is the Okanagan First Nation's own desert interpretation, with self-guided trail walks, reptile encounters, a rattlesnake research centre, traditional village, and craft demonstrations.

Osoyoos Museum◆, an 1891 log schoolhouse, has exhibits on Inkaneep settlement and local irrigation projects.

Nk'Mip Desert & Heritage Centre $
1000 Rancher Creek Rd, Hwy 3 east of downtown; tel: (250) 495-7901; www.nkmipdesert.com. Open mid-Apr–Oct.

Osoyoos Museum $
Community Park; tel: (250) 495-2582; www4.vip.net/ osoyoosmuseum. Open daily May–Sept.

Osoyoos Oxbows Fish and Wildlife Management Reserve
Road 22 E, 7.5km north from Osoyoos; tel: (250) 490-8200. Open daily.

Osoyoos Oxbows Fish and Wildlife Management Reserve✲✲✲ is all that remains of the natural Okanagan River, with marshes, ponds and open channels providing vital wildlife habitat.

Accommodation and food in Osoyoos

Motels are concentrated along Hwy 3 E (Main St), the spit crossing Osoyoos Lake at the south end of town.

Best Western Sunrise Inn $$ *5506 Main St; tel: (250) 495-4000 or (877) 878-2200; www.bestwesternosoyoos.com*, is close to Osoyoos Lake. Continental breakfast is included.

Campo Marina $$ *Richter Pass Motor Inn, Hwy 3 E; tel: (250) 495-7650; open Tue–Sun 1700–2100*, has the best Italian food in the South Okanagan.

Newton Observatory B&B $$ *# 3 Observatory Rd on Anarchist Mountain; tel: (250) 495-6745; www.jacknewton.com/canada.htm.* From late April to mid-October, Jack & Alice Newton operate a 3-suite bed and breakfast 500m above the valley, with Jack's expertise in viewing the sky through telescopes a bonus.

PENTICTON✲✲✲

Penticton Visitor Information Centre *888 Westminster Ave W; tel: (250) 493-4055 or (800) 663-5052; www.penticton.org. Open Mon–Fri 0900–1700, Sat–Sun 1000–1700.* **South VIC** *on Hwy 97 south of Penticton. Open summer 0900–1700.*

Penticton Museum and Archives $ *785 Main St; tel: (250) 490-2451. Open Tue–Sat 1000–1700, Jul–Aug Mon–Sat.*

Rafting $ *Okanagan Lake–Skaha Lake. Summer only.*

Skaha Lake $ *South of Penticton.*

Skaha Climbing Bluffs $ *South of town, off S Main St.*

Sitting between Okanagan Lake and Skaha Lake, Penticton has beaches on two sides and mountains behind. The traditional lure – peaches and beaches – is being pre-empted by vineyards, wineries and outdoor recreation.

Look for First Nations artefacts and pioneer memorabilia in the **Penticton Museum and Archives**✲.

The screams of summer delight are coming from tyre tubes and rafts floating 7km down the canalised Okanagan River from Okanagan Lake to Skaha Lake. Operators set up temporary shop on the south shore of Okanagan Lake; prices include transport back to the starting point.

Skaha Lake✲✲✲ remains popular for sailing, boating, fishing, sightseeing and swimming off beaches at the north end, near Penticton. **Skaha Climbing Bluffs**✲✲✲, overlooking Skaha Lake, have pleasant hiking trails through the sage and Ponderosa pine as well as granite slabs, chimneys, faces and overhangs for rock monkeys.

The 72-m restored sternwheeler **SS *Sicamous*✲✲✲** sailed Okanagan Lake between 1914 and 1935.

Accommodation and food in Penticton

God's Mountain Crest Chalet $$ *South of town above Skaha Lake; tel: (250) 490-4800; www.godsmountain.com*, is a whimsical, whitewashed villa perched between vineyards and a sheer drop into Skaha Lake.

SS Sicamous $ *On the beach off Lakeshore Dr; tel: (250) 492-0403; www.sssicamous.com. Open daily Apr–Oct, Nov–Mar Mon–Fri.*

Granny Bogners' $$ *302 W Eckhardt Ave; tel: (250) 493-2711*, has an excellent local wine list to match its Northwest cuisine.

Naramata Heritage Inn & Spa $$$ *3625 1st St, 19km north of Penticton, east side of Okanagan Lake; tel: (250) 496-6808 or (866) 617-1188; www.naramatainn.com*, is ultimate luxury in a restored heritage hotel.

Penticton Lakeside Convention Centre & Casino $$ *21 Lakeshore Dr. W; tel: (250) 493-8221 or (800) 663-9400; www.rpbhotels.com*, spreads along Okanagan Lake.

Villa Rosa $$ *795 Westminster Ave W; tel: (250) 490-9595; www. thevillarosa.com*, concentrates on northern Italian dishes.

SUMMERLAND⁂

Chamber of Economic Development and Tourism *15600 Hwy 97; tel: (250) 494-2686; www. welcometosummerland.com. Call for hours.*

Pacific Agri-food Research Centre $ *4200 Hwy 97 S (across from Sunoka Beach); tel: (250) 492-5466; http://res2.agr. ca/parc-crapac/summerland /index_e.htm. Gardens open daily 0800–dusk.*

Summerland Museum $ *9521 Wharton St; tel: (250) 494-9395; http://www2.vip. net/~smhschin. Open Jun–Aug Mon–Sat 1000–1600; Sept–May Tue–Sat 1300–1600.*

Cellar Door Bistro *$$ Sumac Ridge Estate Winery; tel: (250) 494-0451*, offers Northwest dishes and picnic items. Open daily.

The small town is a major fruit-growing centre, sitting at the junction of three fertile valleys. The name was coined by an early developer who made a fortune subdividing the lakeside, adding irrigation and luring winter-weary farmers from Manitoba and Alberta. The Kettle Valley Steam Railway (*see page 151*) still steams over 10km of track.

The **Pacific Agri-food Research Centre**⁂ opened as Dominion experimental farm in 1914 to develop fruit varieties better suited to the semi-arid Okanagan climate. English-style Ornamental Gardens soon followed, all open to the public.

The hilltop **Sumac Ridge Estate**⁂ winery (*17403 Hwy 97 (north of town); tel: (250) 494-0451; www.sumacridge.com. Open daily*) is worth a visit just for the valley view – the outstanding wines are a bonus.

If it's sweet and based on fruit, you'll find it at **Summerland Sweets**⁺ (*Canyon View Rd; tel: (250) 494-0377 or (800) 577-1277; www. summerlandsweets.com*): candies, syrups, jams, wines and more, all from local orchards. *They are open most of the year for sampling, and there are tours May–Aug Mon–Fri 1000–1600.*

The artefacts at the **Summerland Museum**⁑ are local, but the KVR, irrigation and fruit-growing history are valley-wide.

VERNON❖❖

Vernon Tourism
701 Hwy 95; tel: (250) 542-1415 or (800) 665-0795; www.vernontourism.com. Open daily.

Greater Vernon Museum Archives $
3009 32nd Ave; tel: (250) 542-3142; www.vernonmuseum.ca. Open Tue–Sat 1000–1700.

Sen'klip Native Theatre Company $
www.geocities.com/Broadway/Stage/6598

Outdoor recreation and original red brick buildings at affordable rents have turned Vernon into a thriving and surprisingly trendy town at the north end of the Okanagan Valley. The city sits between three lakes, **Kalamalka**❖❖❖, **Okanagan**❖❖❖ and **Swan**❖❖❖, all lined with sandy beaches. The acclaimed O'Keefe Ranch (*see page 151*) is northwest.

Greater Vernon Museum and Archives❖❖ is the best place for agricultural history, including the region's first commercial orchards, planted in 1891 by Lord Aberdeen, later Governor-General of Canada.

Sen'klip Theatre Company❖❖❖, one of Canada's few First Nations theatre groups, is gaining a reputation worldwide for blending traditional themes and modern arts.

Accommodation and food in Vernon

The Best Western Vernon Lodge $$ *3914 32nd St; tel: (250) 545-3385 or (800) 663-9400; www.bestwesternvernonlodge.com*, has a real stream, BX Creek, running through the lobby.

Café Asiago $$ *3202 31st Ave; tel: (250) 542-3970*, is Northwestern with Italian touches.

Italian Kitchen Company $$ *2916 30th Ave; tel: (250) 558-7899*, offers unalloyed Italian.

Left
Summerland peaches

Above
O'Keefe Ranch, near Vernon

Above
Kalamalka Lake looking to
Vernon

Suggested tour

Total distance: 160km.

Time: 4 hours to drive; 2–5 days for winery touring.

Links: The Okanagan Valley connects west through the **Cascade Mountains** (*see page 130*) to **Vancouver** (*see page 42*), via Hwy 97C to **Kamloops** (*see page 138*) or via Hwy 97/97A to the **Shuswap Lakes** (*see page 158*).

Route: From **OSOYOOS** ❶ , take Hwy 97 north through a mixture of fruit orchards, vegetable fields and vineyards coaxed from the desert by intensive irrigation. Irrigation projects have been so successful that Canada's 'arid' desert has been reduced to a few endangered pockets of cacti and burrowing owls. Continue north to Oliver.

Detour: From the Osoyoos Oxbows Fish and Wildlife Management Reserve, continue east a few hundred metres to the main road and turn left. Follow the eastern shore of the river past some of the newest vineyards and wineries in the Okanagan to **OLIVER** ❷ .

From Oliver, the Okanagan Valley narrows toward **Vaseux Lake**, a bird, mountain goat and California bighorn sheep sanctuary. Beyond the lake lies **Okanagan Falls**, now a minor rapid at the south end of Skaha Lake. The road climbs the hillside above the lake before dropping back down to water level at **PENTICTON** ❸ , perched between **Skaha Lake** and **Okanagan Lake**.

Detour: From Penticton, follow secondary roads to the east of Okanagan Lake to **Naramata** for additional winery visits.

Continue north on Hwy 97 past **SUMMERLAND** ❹ and **Peachland** to **KELOWNA** ❺ and **VERNON** ❻ .

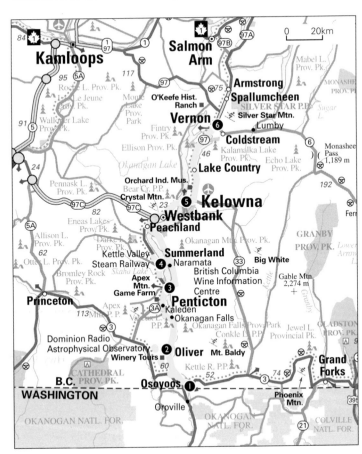

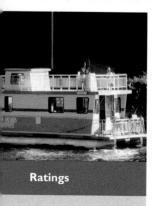

Shuswap Lakes

Ratings

Lakes	●●●●●
Mountain scenery	●●●●●
Children	●●●●○
Outdoor activities	●●●●○
Parks	●●●●○
History	●●●○○
Nature	●●●○○
Towns	●●●○○

There's more than meets the eye – or the main highway – in the Shuswap Lakes region: lakes, long and narrow, more like flat, calm rivers than broad lakes, but also soaring mountains, breathtaking runs of salmon, sandy beaches and eye-popping scenery that is easy to reach and forever beyond the touch of even rough logging roads.

The Shuswap is arguably the most scenic section of the entire 8047-km stretch of Highway 1 between St Johns, Newfoundland and Victoria, BC. Wild, historic, filled with tiny towns, the Shuswap welcomes bald eagles and grizzly bears with the same equanimity it shows to fleets of luxury houseboats and some of the best ice cream on either side of the Rocky Mountains. Highways follow rail lines, which traced lakeshores and river canyons past rugged peaks and foaming waterfalls. If you can't find it in the Shuswap, it may not exist.

CHASE✦✦✦

ℹ **Chase and District Chamber of Commerce Visitor Information Centre** *400 Shuswap Ave; tel: (250) 679-8432; www.chasechamber. com. Open daily late May–Aug; Sept–Jun Mon–Fri.*

🏕 **Niskonlith Lake Provincial Park** $
8km northwest from Chase on Niskonlith Lake; tel: (250) 955-0861; http://wlapwww. gov.bc.ca/bcparks/explore/ parkpgs/niskonli.htm. Open Apr–15 Sept.

A carpenter from New York who was lucky enough *not* to strike gold in the Cariboo instead found fortune building a timber and cattle town. Chase is better known today for its outdoor recreation opportunities – canoeing down 58km of calm water to Kamloops, fishing, houseboating, hiking, swimming, golf and winter skiing. The town is surrounded by calm pine forests at the head of Little Shuswap Lake. The municipal beach is particularly scenic and popular.

The **Chase Museum & Archives**✦✦, the former Blessed Sacrament church, is filled to the rafters with the town's first physician's office, the gleaming mahogany bar from an early hotel, an antique barber's chair and everything in between. (**Chase Museum & Archives** $ *1042 Shuswap Ave; tel: (250) 679-8432. Open Jun–Aug, daily.*)

Niskonlith Lake Provincial Park✦✦✦ has camping, magnificent wildflower displays from May to June and good rainbow-trout fishing year-round.

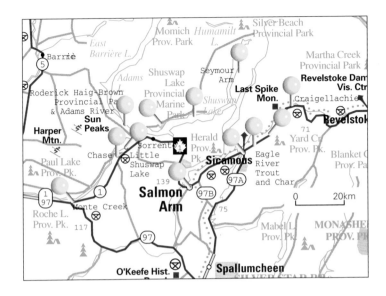

CRAIGELLACHIE*

A stone cairn and railway-station-type souvenir shop commemorates the driving of the last spike to complete the Canadian Pacific Railway in 1885 (**$** *Hwy 1, east from Sicamous at a place named for a Morayshire, Scotland Peak.*

EAGLE RIVER TROUT AND CHAR***

This small fish farm sells fresh trout and char, as well as smoked fillets or whole fish, a fine addition to any picnic (**$** *Hwy 1, 1km east from Yard Creek Provincial Park; tel: (250) 836-4245; open daily in summer*).

LITTLE SHUSWAP LAKE***

Little Shuswap is the smallest of the Shuswap Lakes, but has the most accessible beaches from Hwy 1 (**$** *North and east from Chase to the Adams River and Little River*).

MONTE CREEK*

The small town and railway station are best known as the site of an abortive railway robbery by 'Gentleman Bandit' Bill Miner in 1906 that netted around $15. Miner was captured, sentenced to life in

Monte Creek $ *Hwy 1, 31km east from Kamloops.*

prison, escaped, and eventually landed in a US prison for later robberies. A romantic version of his story surfaced in a 1980s Hollywood film, *The Grey Fox*, filmed in the area.

RODERICK HAIG-BROWN PROVINCIAL PARK & ADAMS RIVER✦✦✦

Roderick Haig-Brown Provincial Park & Adams River *North from Hwy 1 at Squilax; tel: (250) 955-0861; http:// wlapwww.gov.bc.ca/bcparks/ explore/parkpgs/roderick.htm*

The park surrounds and protects 11km of the Adams River between Adams Lake and Little Shuswap Lake. The river has one of the heaviest runs of sockeye salmon in the world, well over a million of the bright-red fish fighting their way up the Fraser and North Thompson rivers to spawn every fourth year. (The next major, or dominant, run occurs in 2006.) Off-years merely feature a few hundred thousand salmon, plus attendant bears, eagles, ravens, mink, gulls and other wildlife. Observation decks provide a clear view of spawning with naturalists on hand during the height of the late summer–autumn salmon runs. Hikers have 26km of trails used for wintertime cross-country skiing.

SALMON ARM✦

Salmon Arm & District Chamber of Commerce *200 Trans Canada Hwy SW; tel: (250) 832-6247, (250) 832-2230 or (877) 725-6667; www.visitsalmonarm.com*

RJ Haney Heritage Park & Museum $ *751 Hwy 97B, 4km east from Salmon Arm; tel: (250) 832-5243; www.sjs.sd83.bc. ca/rjhaney/index.htm. Open daily Jul–Aug (with dinner theatre Wed, Fri, Sun), mid-May–Jun Wed–Sun, Sept Mon–Fri.*

Rotary Peace Park and Public Wharf *Marine Park Dr. at the lake.*

MV *Wanda-Sue* $$ *departs from Twin Anchors Marina; tel: (888) 374-7447 or (250) 374-7447; www.wandasue.com. Cruises daily May–Oct.*

The commercial centre of the Shuswap Lakes region, Salmon Arm was born as a fruit and dairy town on the rich flood plain of the Salmon River, which enters Shuswap Lake here. The town and the south arm of Shuswap Lake were named 'salmon' for the massive runs of salmon that made their way from the Pacific Ocean each year. The salmon disappeared when faulty railway construction blocked the Fraser River at Hells Gate (*see page 190*) in 1912, destroying the fish run. Even without the salmon, Salmon Arm is a popular port to hire house-boats, floating RVs, to explore the far reaches of Shuswap Lake.

The **RJ Haney Heritage Park & Museum**✦✦✦ includes a historic church farm buildings, schoolhouse and a rebuilt forest lookout tower with fine views of farmland to Bastion Mountain.

Rotary Peace Park and Public Wharf✦✦✦, a 250-m pier and walkway, curves out from the park with excellent views of shorebirds and waterfowl. At least 150 different species of birds nest around the mouth of the Salmon River each spring. Best breeding displays are April to June.

Long-time area resident George Slack dreamed of seeing a paddle wheel boat on the Thompson River. Now cruising on Shuswap Lake, the **MV *Wanda-Sue***✦✦, his 100 passenger 26-m sternwheeler makes summer festive on this holidaymaker lake.

Accommodation and food in Salmon Arm

Motels line Hwy 1 through town, there is some lakeside lodging, or, to explore Shuswap Lake by water, hire a houseboat.

Salmon Arm & District Chamber of Commerce lists houseboat operators at *www.sachamber.bc.ca*, in members' directory, under 'houseboats'.

Twin Anchors Houseboats $$ *tel: (250) 836-2450 or (800) 663-4026; www.twinanchors.com*, is the largest of several local operators.

SEYMOUR ARM❖❖❖

A few old buildings still line the streets, but the restaurant, pub, general store and a small hotel are all at the wharf on Bughouse Bay. The town is accessible by road in summer and by ferry from Sicamous all year. (**Seymour Arm** *North end of Seymour Arm, the northernmost arm of Shuswap Lake, 47km north from Anglemont by logging road.*)

SHUSWAP LAKE❖❖❖

Shuswap Lake $
The lake stretches from Sorento, south to Salmon Arm, east to Sicamous and north to Seymour Arm.

The narrow, H-shaped lake is the most popular houseboating destination in BC, perhaps in Canada. The 1000km of shoreline tends to be steep, with no shoals or reefs, or soft and sandy. Warm summer weather means few storms and no heavy waves. Nineteen species of fish keep anglers busy all year.

SHUSWAP LAKE PROVINCIAL MARINE PARK❖❖❖

Shuswap Lake Provincial Marine Park *26 sites around Shuswap Lake; tel: (250) 955-0861; http://wlapwww.gov.bc.ca/bcparks/explore/parkpgs/shus–mar.htm*

The park has less than 1000 hectares, but is scattered around 26 sites on the shores of Shuswap Lake. Most of the units are accessible only by water and are extremely popular with summer houseboaters.

Right
Shuswap Lake

David Thompson

The Thompson River is named for David Thompson, Canada's most important and least acknowledged White explorer. In two decades of travel, this North West Company trader logged 90,000km by canoe, foot and horse, mapping four million square kilometres of Western Canada plus major sections of Washington, Idaho, Oregon and Montana in the US.

Along the way, Thompson found the source of the Columbia River at Columbia Lake (1807), pioneered Athabasca Pass through the Rockies (1811) and mapped the entire length of the Columbia River.

Thompson's greatest achievement, travelling the Columbia River to the Pacific Ocean, was also his greatest disappointment. He arrived just in time to find American fur traders, who had sailed from Boston, feverishly building Fort Astoria. Their 1811 post eclipsed British claims to what would become Oregon and Washington and led to the division of Western America along the 49th parallel. Thompson's precise maps were used well into the 20th century, but the explorer, having retired to Montreal, died in poverty.

SICAMOUS❖❖

ℹ Sicamous and District Chamber of Commerce
110 Finlayson St (near Government Dock); tel: (250) 836-3313; www. sicamouschamber.bc.ca. Open daily in summer, Mon–Fri in winter.

🍴 D Dutchman Dairy
$ Hwy 1, 1km east from Sicamous; tel: (250) 836-4304. Open daily.

🚢 Shuswap Lake Ferry Service $$
tel: (250) 836-2200. Service to Seymour Arm all year.

The name comes from a Secwepemc word that means 'narrow' or 'squeezed in the middle', a good name for the tiny narrows between Mara and Shuswap lakes. The one-time railway camp has become a resort town that is especially popular with houseboaters – local operators have more than 300 vessels for rent, no experience required. **D Dutchman Dairy❖❖❖**, a local dairy, has 50 flavours of what aficionados call BC's best commercial ice cream. Even coach tours stop for a cone – highly recommended is the banana and black walnut.

Right
The SS *Sicamous*

For those who don't want to drive their own boats, **Shuswap Lake Ferry Service**✧✧✧ offers regular vehicle and passenger ferry (all year) services on the tug, *Stephanie*, between Sicamous and Seymour Arm.

Accommodation and food in Sicamous

Motels and restaurants line Hwy 1 and Hwy 97A from Vernon.

Sicamous Inn $$ *tel: (250) 836-4117 or (800) 485-7698; www. sicamousinn.ca*, is the largest in town, with the best facilities.

YARD CREEK PROVINCIAL PARK✧✧✧

Yard Creek Provincial Park $
*Hwy 1, 15km east from Sicamous; tel: (250) 851-3000; http://wlapwww.gov. bc.ca/bcparks/explore/ parkpgs/yard.htm. Park operated by **Columbia Shuswap Regional District** 781 Marine Dr. NE, Salmon Arm; tel: (250) 832-8194 or (888) 248-2773; www.csrd.bc.ca. Open May–Sept.*

This wet, upland forest has excellent birdwatching and pleasant hiking trails beneath hemlock and cedars along a sparkling creek, and is a popular camping and picnic spot.

Suggested tour

Total distance: 160km.

Time: 3 hours to drive; 2–5 days to explore.

Links: Kamloops (*see page 138*) is just west on Hwy 1; **Revelstoke** (*see page 236*) and the **Columbia River** (*see page 230*) just west.

Route: Hwy 1 follows the **South Thompson River** west past **MONTE CREEK ❶**. The high cliffs on the north side of the river have been eroded into an irregular series of columns and buttresses that can take on fantastic shapes in the late afternoon light. The earliest known human remains in BC, a man trapped in a mudflow about 8000 years ago, were found along **Gore Creek**, near the north end of the bridge at **Pritchard**.

Road and river climb slowly to **CHASE ❷**, a ranching and lumber town on the south shore of Little Shuswap Lake, the west end of a vast lake system that extends north (Adams Lake) and west (Shuswap Lake).

Just east of Chase is a lay-by for **Chase Falls**, an easy and popular short hike. Just beyond is **Squilax Mountain**, home to a herd of Rocky Mountain bighorn sheep which often descend the bluffs on the south side of Hwy 1. The **Jade Mountain Lookout**, 2km east, offers broad views of Little Shuswap Lake. Just beyond is the **North Shuswap (Squilax) Bridge** over the **Little River**. The 4-km river between the two Shuswap lakes was once a thriving trade centre for Secwepemc (Shuswap) First Nations. The river is better known today for trout fishing in February, March and October.

Above
Black bear

🅟 **Quaaout Lodge
Resort $$** *PO Box
1215 Chase, BC; tel: (800)
663-4303 or (250) 679-
3090; http://quaaout.com*

Detour: Little Shuswap Lake Road runs west around the north side of Little Shuswap Lake to **Quaaout Lodge**, a resort and outdoor recreation centre owned by the Squilax/Little Shuswap First Nation. The popular resort is jammed mid-July when the Nation hosts the annual **Squilax Powwow**, drawing attendees from across North America.

Squilax-Anglemont Road runs northeast from the bridge to a turn for the **RODERICK HAIG-BROWN PROVINCIAL PARK** ❸ and the Adams River, or continue along the north shore of **SHUSWAP LAKE** ❹.

A 40-km paved road links the hamlets of **Lee Creek**, **Scotch Creek**, **Magna Bay** and **Anglemont**, all with campgrounds, bed and breakfasts and cabins for rent. **SEYMOUR ARM** ❺ is another 45km north on a good gravel road. Return to Hwy 1 at the Squilax Bridge or take the Shuswap Lake Ferry to Hwy 1 at Sicamous.

Hwy 1 continues east from the bridge to **Squilax**, little more than a general store and hostel, and on to **Sorrento**. The tiny community swells to more than 4000 in summer when motels, resorts, RV parks and campgrounds fill up. Hwy 1 climbs south from Sorrento.

Also worth visiting

Turn downhill at **Canoe Point Road** to Shuswap Lake at **Sunnybrae Provincial Park, Herald Provincial Park** and **Paradise Point**, one of the few sites in **SHUSWAP LAKE PROVINCIAL MARINE PARK** ❻ that can be reached by land. Return to Hwy 1.

The main highway emerges on a hillside high above Shuswap Lake and sweeps down into the rich agricultural valley leading to **SALMON ARM** ❼. Continue along the lakeshore past the junction with Hwy 97B, which leads south to **Vernon** and the **Okanagan Valley** (*see page 148*). If the valley seems hazy, blame the lumber mill at Canoe, which still burns sawdust and other waste. The best place to admire Shuswap Lake is the **Shuswap Rest Area**, a picnic area 15km east from Canoe on the north side of Hwy 1.

SICAMOUS ❽ is just beyond, straddling the narrow junction of Shuswap Lake and **Mara Lake**, stretching southward. Hwy 97A leads south into the Okanagan Valley. Hwy 9 continues eastward past the Dutchman Dairy, a must-taste ice-cream stop, following the **Eagle River** past **YARD CREEK PROVINCIAL PARK** ❾. **EAGLE RIVER TROUT AND CHAR** ❿ is a good stop for smoked trout and char just 11km before **CRAIGELLACHIE** ⓫, where the transcontinental Canadian Pacific Railway was completed in 1885.

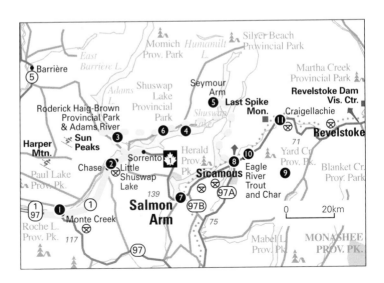

Railway journeys

Ratings

Children	●●●●●
Heritage	●●●●●
Railways	●●●●●
Scenery	●●●●●
Mountains	●●●●○
Desert	●●●○○
Food and drink	●●●○○
Forests	●●●○○

No industry was more influential in the development of South-western Canada, especially British Columbia, than the railways. Settlers, miners, gold rush prospectors and immigrants raced west to claim land or resources; many took the trains. Returning to developed Eastern Canada were the raw materials from the land, forests, ocean and rivers, along with cultivated crops and cattle. The *quid pro quo* for BC's entry into the Canadian Confederation as a province in 1871 was the assurance from the Canadian Pacific Railway and the Federal government in Ottawa that a transcontinental railway would be built. Fifteen years later, Vancouver was quickly transformed from a backwater to a full-fledged city when the promise was fulfilled and it became the terminus railway hub controlling the overland flow of passengers and freight.

Present-day routes, demarcated by Mile Markers, wind through craggy mountain massifs, crawl through river canyons, traverse deserts and ranchlands, and skirt shimmering lakes.

THE CANADIAN✦✦

The Canadian $$
VIA Rail Canada, 1150 Station St, Vancouver; tel: (604) 640-3741 or (888) 842-7245; www.viarail.ca/Canadian. Runs three times weekly.

Route: Jasper–Kamloops–Vancouver

The Canadian is Canada's original transcontinental rail line stretching from Toronto to Vancouver that convinced British Columbia to join the nascent Canadian Confederation in the first place. The complete journey takes three days in each direction, but the scenic section between Jasper and Vancouver is less than one day, non-stop.

The VIA Rail train rides the same rails as the Rocky Mountaineer, but without the frills of steady narration, a printed guide to the route and travel timed to provide the best views of the stunning mountain scenery both westbound and eastbound. But for travellers on a budget, VIA Rail is less expensive.

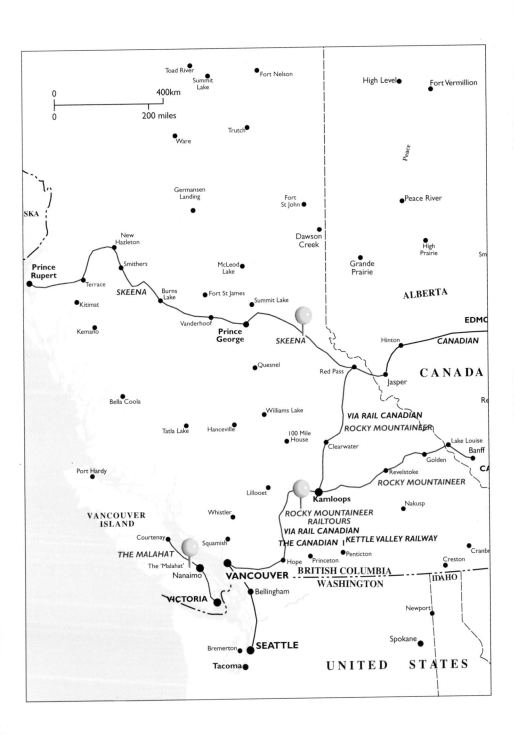

THE MALAHAT❖❖

The Malahat $$ *VIA Rail Canada, 450 Pandora Ave, Victoria; tel: (888) 842-7245; www.viarail.ca/malahat. Runs daily. There is no baggage check.*

Route: Victoria–Duncan–Nanaimo–Parksville–Courtenay

The *Malahat* has been running up and down Vancouver Island since the E & N, Esquimalt and Nanaimo Railway, began operations in 1886. It provided the first predictable land link between Victoria and Nanaimo. Service was later extended north to Courtenay. The train is named for the Malahat Ridge, a steep mountain range west of Saanich Inlet that frustrated road builders and limited travel north from Victoria for decades.

Just what the Saanich Indian word malahat means is open to debate. One camp says, 'infested with caterpillars', referring to a year when an infestation of tent caterpillars stripped trees of their leaves. Another camp prefers 'place where one gets bait'.

Either way, the *Malahat* makes scheduled stops on its 4½-hour point-to-point journey, but will also stop on request, a fine way to venture beyond Duncan's totem poles, Nanaimo's Bastion near the marina and Parksville's swimming beach. The Chemainus murals are worth a stop, a wall side composite history of First Nations, first settlers, Chinese merchants, lumberjacks, fishers, and the rails.

It's a train remarkable for its engineering and its scenic route. Instead of a locomotive engine, the *Malahat* uses lightweight, self-propelled passenger cars called Budd Cars. Unlimited stopovers are permitted with standard ticketing, but there is no provision to check baggage, so travel light. Bring your own provisions and non-alcoholic beverages, or get them at the Nanaimo stop.

ROCKY MOUNTAINEER RAILTOURS✦✦✦

ⓘ Rocky Mountaineer Vacations *1755 Cottrell St at Terminal Ave, Vancouver; tel: (604) 606-7245 or (800) 665-7245; www.rockymountaineer.com. Runs mid-Apr–early Oct, and winter trips in Dec; www.WinterRailtours.com*

Below
The Rocky Mountaineer train passes through Banff National Park

Route: Vancouver–Kamloops–Jasper/Banff

The *Rocky Mountaineer* trains, always photographed against stunning Banff National Park scenery in brochures, live up to their billing as the 'Most Spectacular Train Trip in the World'. Self-adulation aside, the *RM* took a route abandoned by VIA Rail in 1989 and in a decade built a heavily booked tourist train which offers good steward service, food, and above all, stunning scenery. Stewards called Onboard Attendants also provide a narrated history of points of interest en route, interpret natural history, provide books and talk about their personal research of the region.

Expect occasional stops or slow-downs for wildlife spotting. The *RM* waits for commercial traffic, so schedules are not precise, enhancing

the feeling of travelling back in time when nature (rockslide, avalanche or flood) or business (a railway with more priority) could affect railway operations.

GoldLeaf Service, with roomy seats, has much-coveted dome car views, kept clean despite often misty or rainy weather. White linen and flower-vase dining is below the dome car level. RedLeaf Service passengers see the view from closer to ground level and can access landings between cars, a spot favoured by photographers. Meals served at the seat are box lunches of excellent quality. Snacks are non-stop.

The *Rocky Mountaineer* provides a tabloid newspaper upon boarding, a Mile Marker by Mile Marker key to the routes, scenery, historic men, engineering feats, commercial development and ethnology the train passes through. With the tabloid guide, it's impossible to be lost even though the *RM* traverses about 1000km over track controlled by two railway companies, the Canadian National and Canadian Pacific.

The *RM* trains to Jasper or to Banff follow the same route from Vancouver as far as Kamloops. Leaving Vancouver, the train also leaves urban density behind for the green grass suburbs and lakes east. At Hope, the *RM* travels up the Fraser River Canyon, gathering a collective gasp at gondolas moving across the river almost into the train at Hell's Gate. As the train criss-crosses the Fraser and Thompson River Canyons, who can resist the sight of an occasional raft upriver near Suicide Rapids or the evocatively named Jaws of Death Gorge?

The route turns east to Kamloops where passengers disembark, have

Below

VIA train crossing the North Thompson River at Kamloops

dinner, take in the local Two River Junction musical review, and spend the night.

Kamloops–Jasper Along the Jasper Route on the second day, the *RM* follows the North Thompson River past Blue River and halts briefly at the lovely Pyramid Falls for photographers. Mountains begin to fill the view, with the Premier and Cariboo Ranges to the west and the Monashees to the east. Eastward, the *RM* approaches the Rockies and enters Mount Robson Provincial Park, with 3954m Mount Robson ahead. Yellowhead Pass, used by the Grand Trunk Pacific and Canadian Northern Pacific Railways in prior days, is the crossing rejected by the CPR as not southerly enough to protect Canadian interests against American railways. Mount Edith Cavell is on the right as the train approaches Jasper.

Kamloops–Banff The route to Banff from Kamloops skirts the edge of the Shuswap Lakes and Sicamous' house-boat population. Eighteen km east at Craigellachie, a cairn commemorates the driving of the final spike to inaugurate the transcontinental railway by the CPR in 1885. A graceful bridge crosses the Columbia River to Revelstoke, gateway to Mount Revelstoke and Glacier National Parks. Lights dimmed, the *RM* heads through the arrow-straight 8-km-long Connaught Tunnel through Mount MacDonald, built in 1913 to avoid the avalanche disasters constantly plaguing Rogers Pass. There is

another pause to admire the 149m-long Stoney Creek Bridge arching 100m over the creek. Having crossed the Columbia Mountains, the route briefly follows the Columbia River south to Golden.

The *RM* moves east up into Yoho National Park to Field along the Kicking Horse River. There is a short train stop at Field, which is surrounded by dramatic golden mountains with hanging glaciers where fossils are rife (*see sidebar on page 266*). The CPR used the town as a stopping point for transcontinental trains and passengers. *RM* passengers stay aboard the train, this being merely a short wait for clearance on the track for the final haul over the Rockies.

Just east of Field are the Lower and Upper Spiral Tunnels, the double figure-8 solution to a too-steep grade up a mountain called the Big Hill. The Lower Spiral through Mount Ogden turns 230 degrees over its 900m, and the 1001-m long Upper Spiral Tunnel through Cathedral Mountain swivels 250 degrees – before both emerge 15m higher than when the train entered either tunnel. The RM crosses into Alberta and Banff National Park at the Continental Divide, passing close to but not within viewing distance of Lake Louise before heading down the Bow River Valley to the town of Banff.

Passengers not returning by train to Vancouver can continue to Calgary on the *Rocky Mountaineer*.

Below
Royal Hudson steam train

An exhausting but rewarding all-day Brewster coach tour (*www. brewster.ca*) taking in the Icefields Parkway and the TransCanada Hwy to between Banff and Jasper can be booked in either direction, with stops at Athabasca Falls, Sunwapta Falls, Peyto Lake and Lake Louise.

THE SKEENA❖❖❖

The Skeena $$$
tel: (888) 842-7245
or (604) 640-3741;
www.viarail.ca/skeena.
Runs three times weekly,
year-round.

Route: Jasper–Prince Rupert

A stop in Prince George is a welcome pause along the 1160km route that follows the track of the early 20th century Grand Trunk Pacific Railway. *The Skeena* leaves Jasper National Park heading west over the Yellowhead Pass, passing by the landmark, Mount Robson, generally following the Fraser River to Prince George. West is the land of First Nations and the Gitxsan, preserving the world's largest collection of standing totem poles in the Hazeltons. For the last 225km to Prince Rupert, *The Skeena* threads through its namesake river canyon, often giving credence to the Skeena's meaning as 'a river of mists'.

Other Railway Rides in BC

American Orient Express $$$ tel:
(800) 320-4206 or (630)
663-4550; www.
americanorientexpress.com

Royal Canadian Pacific
$$$ tel: (877) 665-3044 or
(403) 508-1400;
www.cprtours.com

VIA Rail offers the only railway passenger service, but there are other privately-operated ultra-luxury summer options: **American Orient Express'** Canadian Rockies Route and **Royal Canadian Pacific's Royal Canadian Rockies Experience** that follows the Columbia River Valley south to Crowsnest Pass, the boundary between BC and Alberta, and into southern Alberta's prairielands. British Columbia has a number of lovingly preserved or restored trains still in operation.

One of the most beloved is the **Royal Hudson**, now at the West Coast Railway Heritage Park (*see page 180*) in Squamish. The CPR steam locomotive engine No. 2860, built in 1940, carries the royal British coat of arms in tribute to its engine class (H14-6-4). King George VI and Queen Elizabeth had this class of engine to pull their train on a 1939 Canadian visit, and the king designated its type 'Royal Hudson'. Only five Royal Hudsons survive.

The **Alberni Pacific Railway** restored 1929 2-8-2 Baldwin Locomotive No 7 pulls a steam train to the MacLean Mill National Historic Site on central Vancouver Island in summer (*see page 91*).

A 1924 Shay steam locomotive engine plies the last 16km of track remaining on the **Kettle Valley Steam Railway** (*see page 151*) route through the Okanagan Valley. Even older is the **Fort George Railway** (*see page 224*) 1912 six-tonne Davenport 0-4-0 locomotive engine operating on a narrow gauge railway on summer weekends in Prince George. A **Fort Steele steam train** ride (*see page 253*) is one of the highlights at Fort Steele Heritage Town in eastern British Columbia. Not far away, alpine Kimberley uses the **Bavarian City Mining Railway** (*see page 254*) cars for a scenic 9km train ride to the Sullivan Mine.

BC Railway Museums:
Canadian Museum of Rail Travel⁺ Cranbrook (see **The Crowsnest** page 250); **Kwinitsa Railway Station Museum**⁺⁺ Prince Rupert (see **Prince Rupert** page 209); **Prince George Railway and Forestry Museum**⁺⁺⁺ Prince George (see **Prince George** page 225); **Revelstoke Railway Museum**⁺ Revelstoke (see **Columbia River** page 236); **West Coast Railway Heritage Park**⁺⁺⁺ Squamish (see **Howe Sound & Whistler** page 180).

BC Ferries tel: (888) 223-3779 or (250) 386-3431; www.bcferries.ca. Provides connections with The Skeena at Prince Rupert, and Vancouver Island's The Malahat to Vancouver.

Suggested tours

Time: 4–7 days depending on connections and season.

Links: For major stations, see **Vancouver** (*see page 42*), **Victoria** (*see page 62*), **Kamloops** (*see page 138*), **Jasper** and **Banff** (*see* **Alberta Rockies** *page 270*), **Prince George** (*see page 222*) and **Prince Rupert** (*see page 206*). **Central Vancouver Island** (*see page 86*) covers stops on *The Malahat*. At Prince Rupert, disembarking *Skeena* passengers can take an Inside Passage **Ferry Voyage** (*see page 113*) to Port Hardy, then a coach to Courtenay to board *The Malahat*.

Route: The railway companies offer combination packages with each other, as well as motorcoach and ferry connections where appropriate. Most tourist rail excursions run from approximately May to September. Regular routes such as VIA Rail's transcontinental 'Canadian' train from Vancouver to Toronto with stops en route in Kamloops, Jasper, Edmonton, Saskatoon, Winnepeg, Sioux Lookout and Sudbury Junction run all year.

A cross-province railway excursion provides an excellent introduction to geography before hiring a car and taking to the road. Rail buffs will want to take the train to see the two western provinces with varied scenery and rolling stock.

Coast to Rockies Triangle: Eastern Loop

Fly or drive from **Vancouver** to **Prince George**. The next morning, board **THE SKEENA** , continuing its run to **Jasper**. The following day, board the **ROCKY MOUNTAINEER** ❷ on its northern route from **Jasper** to **Kamloops**. Overnight and re-board the Rocky Mountaineer to **Vancouver**.

Interior to Coast: Western Loop

Fly or drive from **Vancouver** to **Prince George**. Board **THE SKEENA** ❸ going west. At **New Hazelton**, the route begins to follow the curls and curves of the broad, high-walled super-scenic **Skeena River Valley** to **Prince Rupert**. Catch a **BC Ferry** to **Port Hardy** at the north end of **Vancouver Island**. Take a motor coach to **Courtenay** and board the **THE MALAHAT** ❹ to **Victoria**. BC Ferries connect **Victoria** and **Vancouver**.

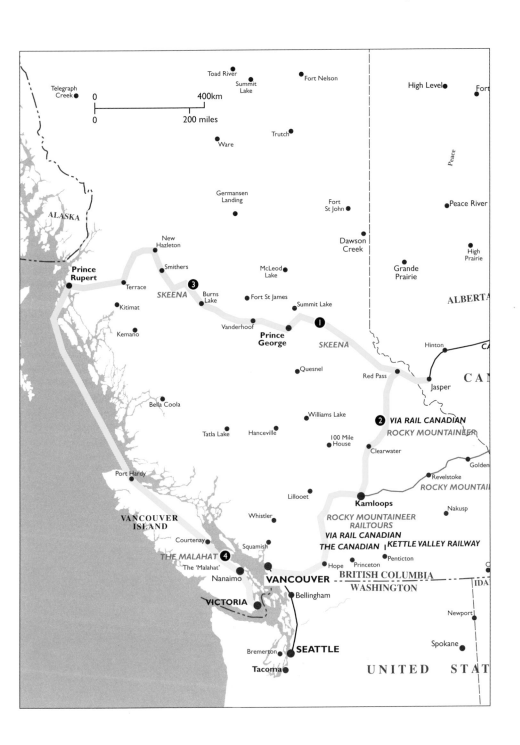

Ratings

Coastal scenery	●●●●●
Outdoor activities	●●●●●
Skiing	●●●●●
Children	●●●●○
Nature	●●●●○
Entertainment	●●●○○
Food and drink	●●●○○
Villages	●●●○○

Howe Sound and Whistler

They call it the Sea to Sky Highway, Hwy 99 on most maps. By either name, it curls and twists along the glacier-carved shores of Howe Sound, north of Vancouver, to the base of Whistler Mountain, one of North America's most acclaimed, most visited and most challenging mountain resorts. It is also one of the most scenic drives in southern BC, if not the easiest.

Much of the roadway is carved into the sheer cliffs hugging Howe Sound. The frequent 'No Stopping' signs warn of rockfalls and avalanche hazard, not lack of lay-bys. The few legal stopping spots provide picture-postcard views of BC Ferries plying the protected waters of the sound with trackless mountains rising barely beyond reach. More mountains rise just behind the highway, some pocked with the remains of enormous mining operations, some never touched and all cut by streams rushing from the sky back to the sea.

The Sea to Sky Highway is currently undergoing reconstruction (*tel: (877) 472-3399 or (604) 660-1088; www.th.gov.bc.ca/seatosky/index.htm*) to widen it two to four lanes and straighten the route, all in anticipation of traffic for the 2010 Olympic and Paralympic Winter Games. Traffic congestion is expected until late 2009. Allow extra time to reach your destination.

BRACKENDALE EAGLE RESERVE✦✦✦

Brackendale Eagle Reserve *Brackendale, Government Rd. Best eagle viewing Dec–Feb.*

Brackendale Art Gallery *41950 Government Rd; tel: (604) 898-3333; www.brackendaleartgallery. com, spearheaded the eagle reserve creation, hosts annual January eagle counts, and is the information centre.*

The 550ha Eagle Reserve lies along both banks of the Squamish River north of Squamish, providing winter habitat and food for between 2000 and 3000 bald eagles in mid-winter. Eagles flock to the river to feed on spawning Salmon, a feeding frenzy that usually peaks around Christmas and tapers into mid-February, when the eagles disperse. Eagles can be observed from a riverside walk and observation point on the east bank or from the water with rafting and kayaking operators out of Squamish.

BRANDYWINE FALLS PROVINCIAL PARK❖❖❖

Centrepiece of the park is Brandywine Falls, a 66-m cataract erupting from atop an ancient lava bed. The falls viewpoint is an easy 10-minute walk through the forest. The name dates from an early brandy versus wine bet over the height of the falls by two early railway surveyors – neither had cash, so one bet brandy and the other wine. (**Brandywine Falls Provincial Park** *Hwy 99, 37km north of Squamish; tel: (604) 986-9371; http://wlapwww.gov.bc.ca/bcparks/explore/parkpgs/ brandywi.htm. Open daily.*)

BRITANNIA BEACH❖

This wide spot in the beach along Howe Sound was once a busy support and supply town for the Britannia Mine, the largest producer of copper in the British Empire between 1930 and 1935. Today, it's a centre for arts and crafts shops, small galleries, a general store and an

Britannia Beach *Hwy 99, 33km north of Horseshoe Bay.*

BC Museum of Mining National Historic Site *$$ tel: (604) 896-2233 or (800) 896-4044; www. bcmuseumofmining.org. Open May–mid-Oct daily 0900–1630, mid-Oct–Apr Mon–Fri 0900–1630.*

ever-changing list of restaurants and bistros. The car park just east of Hwy 99 is also a popular spot for RCMP radar speed traps.

During some 70 years of operation, the massive Britannia Beach Mine produced more than 600 million kg of copper. The facility closed in 1974 but has re-emerged as the **BC Museum of Mining National Historic Site✧✧✧**, with nearly the entire plant battered but intact. Facilities include mining museum displays in the heritage support buildings just off the highway to the east. Outdoor displays include a 235-tonne 'Super Haul' truck and other massive equipment. Guided tours take visitors inside the 1910 mine and tunnels to see slushers, muckers, drills and one of the last surviving gravity-fed ore concentrators in the world. If the site looks familiar, it probably is. The spooky, rust-stained shop that seems to spill down the mountainside has starred in nearly 100 cinema and TV productions in recent years.

BROHM LAKE INTERPRETATIVE FOREST✧

Brohm Lake Interpretative Forest *Hwy 99, 13km north of Squamish; tel: (604) 898-2100; www.for.gov.bc.ca/ dsq/interpForests/BrohmLk/ Brohm.htm*

There's fishing in the shallow lake and swimming in clear water that seldom warms to more than frigid. Eleven kilometres of trails lead through 400 hectares of forest with spreading views of the **Tantalus Mountain Range✧✧✧** and one of the largest ice fields in North America.

GARIBALDI PROVINCIAL PARK✧✧✧

Garibaldi Provincial Park *East of Hwy 99, Squamish–Whistler; tel: (604) 898-3678; http://wlapwww. gov.bc.ca/bcparks/explore/ parkpgs/garibald.htm. Highway signs indicate trail access. Open daily but weather may make access difficult.*

There is no road access into the wilderness park, but well-developed trail systems lead to five of the most popular camping and hiking areas – **Black Tusk/Garibaldi Lake, Cheakamus Lake, Diamond Head, Singing Pass** and **Wedgemount Lake** (all✧✧✧). In summer, look for azure-blue lakes, vast meadows of wild flowers, untouched stands of

Right
Timber bridge

Douglas fir, yellow and red cedar, mountain hemlock and lodgepole pine, depending on altitude. The park gets heavy snow in winter, but Diamond Head is particularly popular with experienced Nordic skiers and snow campers. The park is also accessible via trails from Whistler and Blackcomb.

HORSESHOE BAY❖❖

ⓘ North Vancouver InfoCentre *131 East 2nd Street, Horseshoe Bay, North Vancouver; tel: (604) 987-4488; www.nvchamber. bc.ca/nvtourism*

Named for its shape, this protected bay opens on to the head of Howe Sound, a convenient terminal for service to **Nanaimo** (*see page 90*) on Vancouver Island, as well as more local services from **BC Ferries**. The small town just above the ferry docks offers restaurants, pubs, shopping and a pleasant park with views across the harbour from beneath spreading shade trees. (**BC Ferries** *End of Hwy 1; tel: (250) 386-3431 or (888) 223-3779; www.bcferries.bc.ca*)

MURRIN PROVINCIAL PARK❖

ⓘ Murrin Provincial Park *Hwy 99, 3km north of Britannia Beach; tel: (604) 986-9371; http:// wlapwww.gov.bc.ca/bcparks/ explore/parkpgs/murrin.htm. Open daily.*

The park was named for a former general superintendent of the Britannia Beach Mine, who shared his summer cottage, tiny Brown Lake and surrounding trails with mine employees. It is popular for walking, picnicking, swimming, fishing, sunbathing and novice to intermediate rock climbing. More experienced climbers head for **Stawmus Chief**, just up the road.

PORTEAU COVE PROVINCIAL PARK❖❖❖

ⓘ Porteau Cove Provincial Park *Hwy 99, 25km north of Horseshoe Bay; tel: (604) 986-9371; http://wlapwww. gov.bc. ca/bcparks/explore/ parkpgs/porteau.htm. Open daily.*

The cove was once an important ferry landing on Howe Sound, but is better known today for beachcombing, fishing and scuba diving. Several ships have been scuttled just off the beach to the north of the pier for divers to explore. Look for the bouys floating off the right-hand side of the pier. The actual cove is at the more protected south end of the park, beyond the camping area.

SHANNON FALLS PROVINCIAL PARK❖❖❖

ⓘ Shannon Falls Provincial Park *Hwy 99, 7km north of Britannia Beach; tel: (604) 986-9371; http://wlapwww.gov.bc.ca/ bcparks/explore/parkpgs/ shannon.htm. Open daily.*

You can hear Shannon Falls, the third highest in BC, from the car park. The 335-m cataract is a five-minute walk along a pleasant but well-worn forest trail. Best time to visit is shortly after noon, when the sun highlights the falls dropping from the cliff high above. Expect crowds in summer, including motor coach tours en route to Whistler.

SQUAMISH❖❖

Squamish Chamber of Commerce *37950 Cleveland Ave (the main street); tel: (604) 892-9244 or (866) 333-2010; www.squamishchamber.bc.ca. Open daily.*

Soo Coalition for Sustainable Forests *1498 Pemberton Ave; tel: (604) 892-9001.*

West Coast Railway Heritage Park $$ *3km north on Hwy 99 to Centennial Way, then 1km west; tel: (604) 898-9336; www.wcra.org/heritage. Open daily 1000–1700.*

Squamish Estuary *West from Third Ave beyond Vancouver St, just southwest of town.*

The word *squamish* means 'Mother of the Winds' in the language of the Coast Salish, the local First Nations group – it's an accurate description of local weather. Daytime sun heats the sheer rock faces surrounding Squamish, creating afternoon updrafts that build into world championship windsurfing gusts.

Squamish is also a timber town of two minds. Forestry jobs and incomes are slowly declining while hiking, kayaking, cycling, fishing, rock climbing and other outdoor activities are growing in economic importance – and luring a growing number of outsiders who hate nothing so much as the sight of logging trucks, pulp mills and clear-cuts. Outdoor recreation is winning, but timber interests are stringing out their measured withdrawal as long and as gracefully as possible.

Soo Coalition for Sustainable Forests❖❖❖, the timber industry advocacy group, arranges mill and forest tours.

The **West Coast Railway Heritage Park**❖❖❖ is a must-see for rail buffs, with more than four dozen vintage railway carriages and locomotive engines. Highlights include a gleaming 1890 Executive Business Carriage panelled in hand-rubbed teak, a restored Colonist Car that once carried migrants across the prairies on hard benches, the only surviving steam locomotive engine from the Pacific Great Eastern Railway that once served Howe Sound and a gargantuan orange snowplough.

ⓘ Squamish Estuary Conservation Society, *www.squamishestuary.org, provides trail maps on its website.*

Squamish Estuary✦✦✦ has excellent birdwatching, especially during the spring and autumn migrations.

Accommodation and food in Squamish

Howe Sound Inn & Brewing Company $$ *37801 Cleveland Ave; tel: (604) 892-2603 or (800) 919-2537; www.howesound.com*, the only brewpub on the Sound. Local fish, seasonal vegetables, rooms upstairs.

Sunflower Bakery $ *38086 Cleveland Ave; tel: (604) 892-2231*, is a good source for light lunches or picnic supplies.

STAWAMUS CHIEF PROVINCIAL PARK✧

ⓝ Stawamus Chief Provincial Park *Just north of Shannon Falls; tel: (604) 898-3678; http:// wlapwww. gov.bc.ca/ bcparks/ explore/parkpgs/stawamus.htm*

Below Howe Sound

The 652-m Chief lures thousands of climbers and hikers every year. There are at least 180 different ascent routes, including a rugged walking trail that gains 550m in just 2.5km. The rocky plug is the second largest granite monolith in the world after Gibraltar. Best spot to watch rock climbers is from a lay-by on the eastern side of the highway, about 1km north of the park entrance. Some climbing routes are closed Mar–July for Peregrine Falcon nesting.

WHISTLER✧✧✧

ℹ️ **Tourism Whistler**
*4010 Whistler Way,
Whistler, BC V0N 1B4; tel:
(604) 938-2769, (877) 991-
9988 or (800) 944-7853;
www.mywhistler.com. Open
daily.*

**Whistler 2010 Info
Centre** *Whistler Village on
walkway between Brewhouse
and Esquire's Coffee; tel:
(604) 932-2010; open
Thur–Mon 1100–1700.*

Created in the hope of luring the Olympic Winter Games to Canada in the 1960s, Whistler developers scored as the alpine and Nordic events venue for the 2010 Olympiad. North America's most successful mountain development may have started as a ski resort, but it has become just as successful – and just as busy – in summer.

Two mountains, Whistler and Blackcomb, have been trimmed and groomed for just about every mountain activity known to man or estate developer: skiing, golf, hiking, mountain biking, fishing, kayaking, rafting, canoeing, shopping, eating, drinking, climbing and snowboarding are only the beginning. The ski season extends well into summer, thanks to lifts that access high-altitude glaciers. A few hundred metres below, families with hiking boots and backpacks can watch for deer, marmots, bears and other wildlife amid alpine meadows and open forest.

At the base is Whistler Village, an entirely artificial and hugely successful European-style pedestrian village packed with hotels, restaurants, shops, cafés, clubs, plazas, bridges, creeks, gazebos, musicians and magicians, none of them more than a 10-minute stroll away. Relaxing? No, but Whistler was designed for excitement, glamour and glitz and has very largely succeeded.

Right
Whistler Mountain

Whistler Museum and Archives $
4329 Main St; tel: (604) 932-2019;
www.whistlermuseum.org.
Open Sept–Jun Fri–Sat 1000–1600, Thur 0900–2000; Jul–Aug Fri–Wed 1000–1600, Thur 0900–2000.

Golf Whistler $$$ boast four highly-rated designer championship courses; tel: (866) 860-4653; www.golfwhistler.com

Whistler Mountain Bike Park $$ has 1200m of vertical run, with more than 200km of lift-served track, two jump parks and three levels of skill centres; tel: (866) 218-9690, (604) 932-3434 or (604) 938-7275; www.whistler/blackcomb.com/bike. Open daily in summer 1000–1500, Wed, Fri–Sat to 2000.

The original activity centre was Whistler Village, at the foot of Whistler Mountain. The Village still has more restaurants, more shops and more variety than the rest of the resort. A short walk across the valley is Upper Village, a more expensive, more exclusive and less frenetic enclave surrounding Fairmont Chateau Whistler. Smaller valleys to the south are filled with condominium developments that rely largely on the Village for services and entertainment.

For activity information in any season, contact the **Tourism Whistler** and the **Whistler Activity and Information Centre** in the **Whistler Village Conference Center**. Shops near the gondola base in Whistler Village hire out bikes, skates and other equipment in summer and skis or snowboards in winter.

Summer is Whistler's value season, as well as its most active. At the base, five lakes are strung like turquoise and green beads on a necklace, woven together with 20km of mostly paved trails for easy walking, cycling and rollerblading. Six lakeside parks offer broad lawns, sandy beaches and full picnicking facilities with sailing, windsurfing, boating and fishing.

Both Whistler and Blackcomb lifts remain open (except for short maintenance periods in autumn), with summer skiing on Blackcomb and hiking or mountain biking on both mountains. Other possibilities include golf, climbing, backpacking, hang-gliding, heli(copter)-hiking, jet boating, flightseeing and hayrides.

Winter is Whistler's *raison d'être*, with 200-plus named runs and 33 lifts. Blackcomb has the longest lift-serviced vertical in North America, 1609m, as well as the longest uninterrupted fall-line skiing on the continent. Whistler comes a close second, with 1530m of vertical served by lifts. Then there's Nordic skiing on valley golf courses and trails, ice-skating, snow shoeing and sleigh rides.

Even if you're only spending the day at Whistler, check out **Fairmont Chateau Whistler***◆◆ in the mountains. Canadian Pacific didn't break the bank building Canada's grandest 20th-century resort hotel, but it looks like they did. It's an enormous castle-like building beneath a copper-green roof that still manages to feel comfortable, thanks to touches such as Mennonite hooked rugs and quilts and First-Nations-inspired twig furniture. The Great Hall and the Mallard Bar are best for gawking.

Whistler is short on history, but the **Whistler Museum and Archives**◆ makes the best of skiing gear from the 1960s, fishing souvenirs from the 1920s and local logging paraphernalia.

Accommodation and food in Whistler

Most Whistler hotels, inns and other accommodation have their own booking number, but it's easier to book through **Tourism Whistler** *tel: (604) 664-5625 or (800) 944-7853; www.mywhistler.com*. Expect two- to three-night minimum stays in high season (Dec–Mar), the lowest rates Sept–Nov and Apr–Jun, and mid-range rates the rest of the year.

Araxi Ristorante $$ *Whistler Village; tel: (604) 932-4540; www.araxi.com*, gets justified raves for its menu, service and wine list.

Caramba $$ *Town Plaza; tel: (604) 938-1879*, is the liveliest Italian restaurant at Whistler.

Crepe Montagne $ *Market Pavillion; tel: (604) 905-4444; www.bc-biz. com/crepemontagne*, is a crepe restaurant that overflows with bonhomie.

Fairmont Chateau Whistler $$$ *4599 Chateau Blvd, Upper Village; tel: (604) 938-8000 or (800) 257-7544; www.fairmont.com/whistler*, is undisputed Queen of the Mountain.

Pan Pacific Whistler $$$ *4320 Sundial Cres, Whistler Village; tel: (604) 905-2999 or (888) 905-9995; http://whistler.panpacific.com*, has full-kitchen suites a few steps from both Whistler and Blackcomb gondolas.

Residence Inn Whistler $$$ *4899 Painted Cliff Rd, Upper Village; tel: (604) 905-3400 or (800) 331-3131; http:marriott.com*, has a prime ski-in, ski-out location midway up the base of Blackcomb Mountain.

Thai One On $$ *Upper Village; tel: (604) 932-4822*, is a calm refuge with Thai dishes as good as any in Vancouver.

Westin Resort & Spa Whistler $$$ *4090 Whistler Way, Whistler Village; tel: (604) 905-5000 or (800) 228-3000; www.westin.com*, reigns supreme over Whistler Village.

Zeuski's Taverna $ *Town Plaza; tel: (604) 932-6009*, is cheerful, cheap and always busy.

WHISTLER INTERPRETATIVE FOREST❖❖

Whistler Interpretative Forest *Hwy 99, 9km north of Brandywine Falls Provincial Park; tel: (604) 898-2100 or (604) 932-5535; www.for. gov.bc.ca/dsq/interpForests/ whistlerinformation.htm*

There's an extensive and well-marked network of hiking and mountain biking trails throughout a working forest between Hwy 99 and Garibaldi Provincial Park. Watch for logging trucks and be sure to park entirely off the roadway. Almost directly across Hwy 99 is **Function Junction**, a catchy name for a perfectly ordinary service area for Whistler Resort. There are bakeries, hardware stores, a brewery, plumbers, electrical supplies and all the other mechanical and service functions that resorts like to keep out of sight and out of mind.

Suggested tour

Total distance: 120km.

Time: 2–4 hours, depending on traffic.

Links: The Sea to Sky Highway connects to **Vancouver** (*see page 42*) to the south, or continue north on Hwy 99 to the **Gold Rush Trail** (*see page 186*) near **Hat Creek Ranch** (*see page 190*).

Route: From Vancouver, take the **Lion's Gate Bridge** north over the

First Narrows to **West Vancouver**. Take Hwy 1, the TransCanada Highway, westbound, following signs for the BC Ferries terminal at **HORSESHOE BAY** ❶ , Squamish and **WHISTLER**.

Hwy 1 runs to the ferry line-up at Horseshoe Bay. Hwy 99, the **Sea to Sky Highway**, continues north, hugging the cliffs above **Howe Sound**. The twisting highway is narrow and verges are almost non-existent, especially in winter when snowbanks crowd the road. There are a number of scenic lay-bys, none of them accessible from the northbound lanes. If time permits and the weather is clear, continue to **PORTEAU COVE**, north of Horseshoe Bay, and turn back for the views.

The roadway opens up just south of Porteau Cove, a one-time ferry landing for Howe Sound ferry service that has become a popular park for beachcombing, fishing, boating and scuba diving. Eight kilometres north is **BRITANNIA BEACH** and the Britannia Mine, a museum that was once the largest copper producer in the British Empire. Just north is **SHANNON FALLS PROVINCIAL PARK**, with one of the highest waterfalls in BC, a five-minute walk from the car park, and **STAWMAUS CHIEF**, a massive peak that is a favourite with rock climbers.

Continue north to **SQUAMISH** ❷ , a timber town that is turning towards outdoor recreation. The highway turns inland past **BROHM LAKE** and **BRANDYWINE FALLS PROVINCIAL PARK** before passing Function Junction, a small service community for **WHISTLER** ❸ .

The Gold Rush Trail

Ratings

Historical sights	●●●●●
History	●●●●●
Outdoor activities	●●●●●
Scenery	●●●●●
Children	●●●●○
Museums	●●●●○
Parks	●●●●○
Nature	●●●○○

The Fraser River and Cariboo Gold Rush transformed BC from a distant source of furs into a major presence on the world stage. Nearly every product, every place, every attitude that is a part of BC today has its roots in Gold Rush. Most of the province's major highways began as Gold Rush trails, many interior towns exist because they once filled Gold Rush needs. Even timber, largest of BC's traditional industries, owes much to the insatiable Gold Rush demand for wooden buildings, railway sleepers and fuel.

Who made the first gold discovery and where may never be known. First Nations traders brought small amounts of gold to the Hudson's Bay Company for years, but the fur-trading giant hid its shining secret, rightly fearing that an influx of gold miners would disrupt its profitable monopoly. The Gold Rush that created the province broke the company.

ALEXANDRA BRIDGE PROVINCIAL PARK❖❖❖

🏛 Alexandra Bridge Provincial Park $
Hwy 1, 22km north from Yale; tel: (604) 795-6169; http://wlapwww.gov.bc.ca/ bcparks/explore/parkpgs/ alexandra.htm. Access on the park's west side only.

The small park surrounds the 1926 **Alexandra Suspension Bridge❖❖❖** that still spans the Fraser Canyon. An easy walking path follows the original roadbed down to the old bridge and across the foaming river visible through an open grating. The suspension bridge replaces an 1863 bridge at the same spot, which itself replaced a ferry downstream at Spuzzum. The new Alexandra Bridge is 2km north of Spuzzum.

ASHCROFT MANOR❖❖

🏛 Ashcroft Manor $
10km south of Cache Creek; tel: (250) 453-9983. Open daily.

Built in 1862 as a roadhouse for the Cariboo Wagon Road, Ashcroft grew into a prosperous farm, ranch, mill and social centre in the sagebrush and cactus desert south of Kamloops. The manor also served as one of BC's earliest courthouses. Most of the complex burned down in 1943, but a church and the roadhouse, now a tearoom and museum, survived.

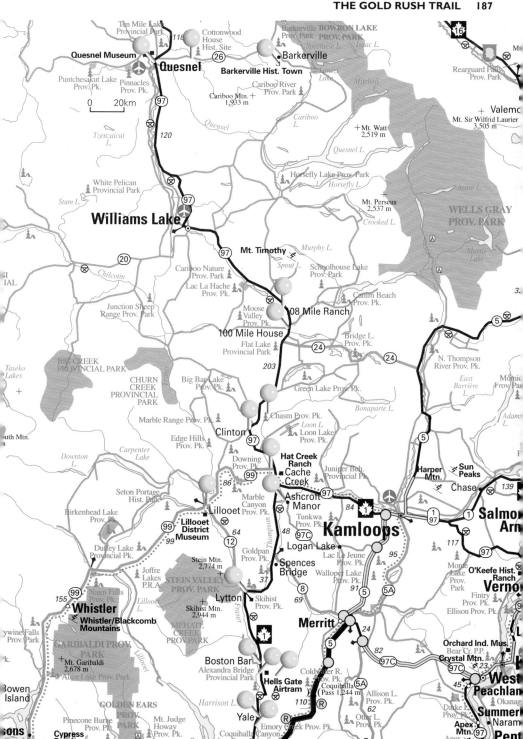

BARKERVILLE HISTORIC TOWN***

Barkerville Historic Town $$ *Hwy 26, 8km east from Wells; tel: (250) 994-3302; www.heritage.gov. bc.ca/bark/bark.htm. Open daily 0800–2000; costumed interpreters and full services mid-Jun–Sept.*

For most of the 1860s, Barkerville was the biggest town north of San Francisco and west of Chicago. More than 100,000 hopeful miners and hangers-on travelled the Cariboo Wagon Road to Barkerville between 1862 and 1870. They turned what had been a shanty town into a city so rich and so confident that it very nearly outdid Victoria in a bid to become the capital of BC.

The gold along Williams Creek ran out in little more than a decade, but the town survived to become a thriving heritage site. More than 125 buildings remain, most of them original, if heavily restored. The bordellos and dance halls never reopened, but restaurants, theatres, churches, stores, bakeries, photographers and a Chinese grocery are back in business during the summer months. In winter, the only residents are park wardens and ground squirrels.

For a better sense of just how far Barkerville lies from the rest of BC, walk (or ski in winter) the last 1.6km of the old wagon road west to Richfield with *A Walk to Richfield*, a self-guiding map keyed to 18 historic sites. The map is available at the Barkerville Visitor Centre. Most visitor facilities are in Wells.

Below
Barkerville's main street

BOSTON BAR✤

Boston Bar *Hwy 1,*
11km north from Hells
Gate.

Local First Nation residents named the settlement for the 'Boston men', or Americans, who swarmed over the gravel bar in search of gold. The town survived as a supply centre for later traffic and is now a lumber town.

CHASM PROVINCIAL PARK✤✤✤

Chasm Provincial
Park *Hwy 97, 20km*
northeast from Clinton; tel:
(250) 397-2523; http://
wlapwww.gov.bc.ca/bcparks/
explore/parkpgs/chasm.htm

The Painted Chasm (*open Jun–Sept*) is an enormous orange-pink river-carved gash through 120m and 15 million years of lava atop the Fraser Plateau. The 1.5km gorge shows multiple layers of reds and yellows that are especially brilliant in late afternoon sun.

CLINTON✤

Village of Clinton
1423 Cariboo Hwy;
tel: (250) 459-2261;
www.village.clinton.bc.cam

South Cariboo
Historical Museum
(Clinton Museum) $
1419 Cariboo Hwy;
tel: (250) 459-2442.
Open daily 0800–2000.

Straddling the junction of two wagon roads, Clinton was originally called Junction, a name discarded when Queen Victoria decided her Colonial Secretary needed a town named in his honour. Little has changed in the years since.

Clinton remains a quintessential cowboy town where everyone knows everyone else and if you have to ask directions, you most definitely don't belong. Most of the horseback trail riding, hiking, rafting and other outdoor activities take place at guest ranches scattered in the hills and valleys to the west.

South Cariboo Historical Museum (Clinton Museum)✤✤✤, set in an 1890s schoolhouse, chronicles the transition from Gold Rush to cowboy country. Most of the people featured in displays can be found at the **Pioneer Cemetery**, just north from town.

Accommodation and food in Clinton

Many area ranches have discovered that guests are more profitable (and less laborious) than huge cattle herds. The self-proclaimed Guest Ranch Capital of BC has facilities ranging from rustic to ritzy.

Big Bar Guest Ranch $$ *tel: (250) 459-2333; www.bigbarranch.com*, was one of the first and is still among the best for families – horse-riding, hiking, river rafting, backcountry camping trips, Nordic skiing and similar activities are geared for beginners.

Moondance Guest Ranch $$$ *tel: (250) 459-7775 or (888) 459-7775; www.moondanceguestranch.com*, is a luxury ranch with private cabins, gourmet meals and wood-fired saunas.

COTTONWOOD HOUSE HISTORIC SITE✧✧

Another of the roadhouses en route to Barkerville, Cottonwood was a family residence from 1874 to 1951. Period buildings include the main house, root cellar and a double barn, all explained by costumed interpreters (**$** *Hwy 26, 28km east from Hwy 97; tel: (250) 992-2071 or (250) 983-6911; www.cottonwoodhouse.ca; open daily late May–early Sept*).

EMORY CREEK PROVINCIAL PARK✧

Once the site of Emory City, the park commemorates the thousands of Chinese workers who built the Canadian Pacific Railway. When White miners abandoned the town, Chinese workers moved in and reportedly recovered twice as much gold from tailings, the refuse left from mining operations, as the Whites had found in the first pass (**$** *Hwy 1, 18km north from Hope; tel: Yale First Nation, (604) 863-2443; http://wlapwww. gov.bc.ca/bcparks/explore/parkpgs/emory.htm; open Apr–Oct*).

HAT CREEK RANCH✧✧✧

Hat Creek Ranch $
Hwys 99 & 97; tel: (250) 457-9722 or (800) 782-0922; www. hatcreekranch.com and www.heritage.gov.bc.ca/hat/ hat.htm. Open mid-May– mid-Oct 0900–1700.

Still a working ranch, Hat Creek is the last intact roadhouse on the Cariboo Wagon Road. The 20 heritage buildings include one of the largest barns in BC. Stagecoaches and wagon trains used ranch facilities until automobiles began using the road in 1916. Facilities include trail rides, ranching demonstrations, museum displays and a summer Shuswap First Nation village.

HELL'S GATE✧✧✧

Hell's Gate *Hwy 1, 10.5km north from Alexandra Bridge Provincial Park; tel: (604) 867-9277; www.hellsgateairtram.com. Open early Apr–mid-Oct.*

An average of 850,000 cubic metres of water blasts through a space about the width of a city street every second. River rafters run the rapids daily in summer, but only one steamboat, the *Skuzzy*, ever made it upstream, winching through the raging narrows with bolts driven into the rock.

The rapids are more fearsome now. In 1913, a careless Canadian National Railway construction crew touched off a landslide that choked the river and blocked the salmon run for years. Fish ladders built between 1945 and 1946 helped, but modern salmon runs are less than one-third the pre-1913 volume, even in the best of years.

For the best view of the rapids, ride the **Airtram**✧✧✧ 152m down and across the canyon to a museum, restaurant, gift shop and viewing platform. A suspension bridge crosses the river just downstream and railway trains pass every half-hour.

100 MILE HOUSE❖

ℹ South Cariboo Visitor Info Centre
422 Cariboo Hwy 97 S; tel: (250) 395-5353 or (877) 511-5353; www. southcaribootourism.com. Look for the 12-m Karhu racing skis that make the VIC.

This small town is the service centre for the Central Cariboo and a major Nordic skiing area in winter. It began as a Cariboo Road stage stop in the 1860s. Seventy years later, Lord Martin Cecil, Marquis of Exeter, began and headquartered his Emissaries of Divine Light here. The Marsh Wildlife Sanctuary, adjacent to the Visitor Info Centre has bird identification signage, helpful when spotting bald eagles and sandhill cranes.

108 MILE RANCH❖❖❖

ℹ South Cariboo Visitor Info Centre
(see 100 Mile House) has information for 108 Mile Ranch and nearby resorts. Find more information online: www.108ranch.com

The one-time roadhouse has become a museum with a collection of heritage buildings moved to the site, including one of the largest log barns in Canada (*$ Hwy 97, 13km north from 100 Mile House; tel: (250) 971-5288; www.historical.bc.ca/main.html; open late May–mid-Sept 0900–1700*). The **Hills Health Ranch** (*tel: (250) 791-5225 or (800) 668-2233; www.spabc.com*) has lodging, a spa using rose hips grown on the ranch, and other activities.

LILLOOET❖❖

ℹ Lillooet and District Chamber of Commerce
790 Main St; tel: (250) 256-4289 or (800) 217-3487; www. lillooetchamberofcommerce. com. Open daily May–Oct.

🏛 Lillooet Museum $
790 Main St; tel: (250) 256-4308; www. lillooetbc.com/page11.html. Open May–Oct.

☾ Mile-0-Motel $$
616 Main St; tel: (250) 256-7511 or (888) 766-4530; www.mileomotel.com, is central and comfortable.

The main streets of Lillooet are extraordinarily wide to allow the 20-team ox wagons that worked the Cariboo Wagon Road to turn around. The **Mile Zero Cairn**❖❖❖ opposite the Visitor InfoCentre is Mile 0 for the roadhouses and supply points north.

Lillooet Museum❖❖❖ shares a former Anglican church with the Visitor InfoCentre and a trove of mining and pioneer artefacts. A self-guiding museum map lists 15 historical sites on Main Street alone.

Right
Hell's Gate mural

LYTTON✣

ℹ **Lytton Tourism Info Centre** *400 Fraser St; tel: (250) 455-2523; www.lytton.ca*

Lytton lives by logging and **river rafting✣✣✣**. Companies based here put in up and down the Fraser and North Thompson rivers for trips that last a few hours to a few days. Five kilometres of riverfront have also been set aside as a **Gold Panning Recreational Reserve✣✣✣** with hand-panning only. Ask for information and pans at the **Lytton Museum✣✣✣**, which is devoted to the Cariboo Wagon Road and mining history (*$ Fraser St, next to the InfoCentre; open daily in summer*).

QUESNEL✣✣✣

ℹ **Quesnel & District Chamber of Commerce and Visitor Info Centre** *679-B Hwy 97 south; tel: (250) 747-0125; www. quesnelchamber.com or www.northcariboo.com*

📍 **Heritage Corner** *Carson and Front Sts.*

Quesnel & District Museum & Archives $ *705 Carson Ave; tel: (250) 992-9580; www.city.quesnel. bc.ca/museum2004. Open daily May–Aug, Sept–Apr Tue–Sat.*

Sitting at the confluence of the Quesnel and Fraser rivers, Quesnel was the last river town before the final overland trek to the gold fields at Barkerville. There's still enough gold in the rivers to keep prospectors busy. Much of the river has been staked, or claimed, but there's public panning at the river junction.

Heritage Corner✣✣✣ is the centre of town, marked by massive steamboat and mining machinery in the riverfront park and a scenic 1929 bridge across the Fraser River.

Highlight of the **Quesnel & District Museum & Archives✣✣✣** is an extraordinary collection of area photographs from 1865 onwards.

Accommodation and food in Quesnel

Cariboo Hotel $$ *254 Front St; tel: (250) 992-2333*, is central.

Heritage House $$ *102 Carson Ave; tel: (250) 992-2700*, serves meals in the original Hudson's Bay Company trading post.

Ramada Limited Quesnel $$ *383 St Laurent Ave; tel: (250) 992-5575; www.ramada.com*, is near the river.

Below
Hell's Gate

YALE❖❖❖

🅱 Historic Yale Museum $ *31179 Douglas St; tel: (604) 863-2324; www.heritage. gov.bc.ca/yale/yale.htm. Open daily May–mid-Sept 1000–1700.*

St John the Divine Church *Next to the museum.*

A handful of people still live in this Gold Rush boom town, though most of the town centre is a pleasant historic district. The interior of the 1863 Anglican **St John the Divine Church**❖❖❖ remains almost unchanged since its consecration. It's the oldest church in BC still on its original foundations. **Yale Museum**❖❖❖, in an 1868 house, is filled with period photographs and exhibits concentrating on the two Sto:lo villages that were once here and Gold Rush memorabilia. Ask about gold panning at **Foreshore Park**❖❖❖, on the riverfront. Costumed interpreters give guided tours in summer, including lantern tours of the pioneer cemetery.

Suggested tour

Total distance: 600km.

Time: Allow 2 days to drive from Hope to Barkerville and a week to explore along the way.

Links: From Hope, Hwy 3 runs east through the **Lower Fraser River Valley** (*see page 122*) to **Vancouver** (*see page 42*) and west to the **Cascades** (*see page 130*) and the **Okanagan Valley** (*see page 148*). From Cache Creek, Hwy 1 leads east to **Kamloops** (*see page 138*) and the **Shuswap Lakes** (*see page 158*). At Quesnel, Hwy 97 continues north to **Prince George** (*see page 222*).

Route: From Hope ❶ (*see page 127*), Hwy 1 follows the **Fraser River** north into the **Fraser River Canyon** past EMORY CREEK PROVINCIAL PARK to YALE ❷, as far upriver as First Nations canoes and later steamboats ever travelled. Simon Fraser walked down the Fraser Canyon in 1806, complaining that 'We had to pass where no human being should venture. Yet in those places there is a regular footpath impressed, or rather indented, by frequent travelling upon the very rocks.' Gold discoveries along the Fraser River and further north brought calls for a road through the canyon.

By 1864, Royal Engineers had blasted the **Cariboo Wagon Road** through to Lytton, opening the interior to miners, loggers and settlers. Hwy 1 follows the same route, and usually the same roadbed.

Hwy 1 continues north past **ALEXANDRA BRIDGE PROVINCIAL PARK** ❸ to HELL'S GATE ❹, the narrowest spot along an already narrow canyon. The Sto:lo First Nation pegged logs to the canyon wall to create a trail along the sheer rock face. Today, a tram crosses the narrow rapids, a popular summer destination for kayakers and river rafters.

BOSTON BAR ❺ is one of the few Gold Rush towns along the Fraser River to survive into the modern era. Hwy 1 snakes high above the

Skihist Provincial Park *tel: (250) 315-2771; http://wlapwww. gov.bc.ca/bcparks/explore/ parkpgs/skihist.htm. Open Apr–Oct.*

river toward **Siska**, one of 11 Nlaka'pamux Nation communities along the Fraser Canyon. Several tribal artists are building worldwide reputations carving soapstone from traditional quarries near by. **Siska Art Gallery and Band Museum** (*tel: (250) 455-0072*) displays and sells local art as well as CDs by the Siska Halaw Singers and Drummers.

The highway continues along the canyon to **LYTTON** ❻, at the confluence of the coffee-coloured Fraser and the icy-blue Thompson rivers. The Gold Rush wagon road crosses the river to Hwy 12, climbing through increasingly arid country along the Fraser to **LILLOOET** ❼ and HAT CREEK.

Alternative route to Hat Creek: Continue north on Hwy 1 along the canyon of the **North Thompson River. Skihist Provincial Park**, 8km north, has fine views of the semi-desert canyon, rafters floating downstream and trains passing on the opposite bank. Lay-bys 5km north

BC gold rushes

Hollywood epics have cast trappers, farmers and Mounties as the romantic heroes of Western Canada, but gold miners deserve the credit for transforming a frontier into a Province.

The story begins with the Hudson's Bay Company, which occasionally accepted bits of gold from its First Nations trading partners but decided not to publicise its steady trickle of mineral wealth. HBC governors feared the kind of rush that had spelt disaster for established businesses in California, which had been wrecked by the tens of thousands of Argonauts who flooded west in 1849.

In early 1858, the HBC relented and shipped about 20kg of raw gold to the nearest mint, San Francisco. The shipment ignited a frenzy. Every craft that could float sailed north, jammed with miners headed for the Fraser River to Hope and beyond.

More than 30,000 miners flooded through Victoria between May and July 1858, nearly all of them Americans. Business prospered, but Government trembled. British authority was little more than a thin line of HBC trading posts. There was nothing to prevent the unruly American mobs from seizing BC as easily as they had taken California from Mexico a decade before.

Britain replaced HBC commercial control with direct rule in November 1858, throwing the company into a decline from which it never recovered. James Douglas, former chief agent for HBC, then governor of Vancouver Island, became governor of the newly created Crown Colony of British Columbia. He promptly requested British road builders, British troops and British magistrates to enforce British law.

The gambit succeeded. Bewigged justices backed by a handful of soldiers, and eventually the Royal Canadian Mounted Police, kept BC British through waves of miners rushing north to mineral strikes on the Boundary, Similkameen and Thompson rivers, the Okanagan Valley, Cariboo Mountains, the Yukon and the Kootenay Mountains. By the time the dust had settled around the turn of the 20th century, Gold Rush trails had grown into a network of roads, railways and ferry routes that is still recognisable today.

Above
Fraser Canyon

**Goldpan Provincial Park** tel: (250) 315-2771; http://wlapwww.gov.bc.ca/bcparks/explore/parkpgs/goldpan.htm. Open year-round.

overlook **Little Hells Gate**, a popular spot to watch salmon leaping upstream in autumn and rafters shooting the same rapids in summer. Most rafts launch just upstream from **Goldpan Provincial Park**.

Eleven kilometres north are **Spences Bridge** and **Murray Falls**, tumbling over red cliffs directly into the river. Watch for ospreys nesting in tall trees along the river (the nests look like untidy piles of sticks) and California bighorn sheep on nearby cliffs. In winter, sheep often descend to lick salt from the highway. There are several seasonal ice-cream and fruit stands north of town.

ASHCROFT MANOR ❽, 13km north, is a welcome splash of shady green against the desert hills on the way to Cache Creek and the junction with Hwy 97. Hwy 1 turns east toward **Kamloops** (*see page 138*). Continue north on Hwy 97 to Hat Creek Ranch.

At Lillooet, turn on to Hwy 99, which corkscrews up rolling benchlands along the original wagon road track. Some of the natural terraces are irrigated, others are covered by low black sheets of plastic that shade crops of ginseng. Near the top of the grade is the hamlet of **Pavilion** and the **Pavilion General Store**, one of the oldest buildings in BC still on its original site. The mountain vistas are stunning and the store is the only ice-cream and cold-drink stop in the dusty summer heat.

The Cariboo Wagon Road continues north to **Kelly Lake** and Clinton as Pavilion Mountain Road, a steep gravel road that is passable in good weather. The highway loops east and south into **Marble Canyon**, named for 1000m cliffs of red and yellow marble, before emerging at **HAT CREEK RANCH ❾** and Hwy 97.

The hills turn green as the road climbs and conifers replace sagebrush on the way to **CLINTON ⑩**, a centre for cattle and guest ranches. Just north is **CHASM PROVINCIAL PARK ⑪**, a vast gorge cut through 15 million years of lava eruptions. Increasing rainfall brings denser forests on the way north to **100 MILE HOUSE ⑫** and **108 MILE RANCH ⑬**, one-time roadhouses named for the distance from Lillooet on the Cariboo Wagon Road.

Further north through the forests is **150 Mile House**, the last stop before **Williams Lake** (*see page 202*) and Hwy 20 west across the Chilcotin to **Bella Coola** (*see page 200*).

Hwy 97 continues north to **Soda Creek**, the terminus of the Cariboo Wagon Road and the head of navigation along 650km of the Upper Fraser River to Quesnel and **Prince George** (*see page 222*). Rails replaced steamboats in the 1920s, but carbon dioxide still bubbles into the creek from calcium carbonate in the streambed.

There are few signs of settlement to the north until **Marguerite Ferry**, an unpowered ferry across the Fraser and the **Fort Alexandria Monument**. The monument marks the end of Alexander Mackenzie's 1793 journey down the Fraser and the site of an 1821 North West Company trading post. Mackenzie turned back on the advice of Dalkeh traders, and returned upstream to **QUESNEL ⑭** and struck out overland to reach the Pacific Ocean at Bella Coola.

From Quesnel, turn east on Hwy 26 through the mountains to **COTTONWOOD HOUSE HISTORIC PARK ⑮**, another Gold Rush roadhouse. Eleven kilometres east is **Blessing's Grave Historic Park**, surrounding the isolated grave of one of the handful of miners murdered during the hectic years of the Cariboo Gold Rush. Just east is **Wells**, born in a second Cariboo Gold Rush during the 1930s, and **BARKERVILLE ⑯**, the gold mining centre so many thousands of miners laboured so long to reach.

Publican creates backwater

Williams Lake (*see page 202*) missed the Cariboo Gold Rush when a pub owner declined a short-term loan to Cariboo Wagon Road builders. Instead, the contractors built through 150 Mile House, where a more obliging publican made the loan and a quick fortune on the new road traffic. Williams Lake languished until the 1920s when the railway, now known as BC Rail, arrived from Lillooet, on the way north to Prince George.

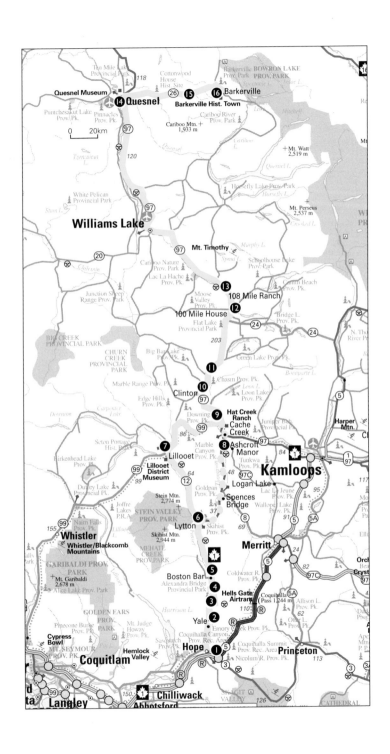

Cariboo–Chilcotin

Ratings

Mountains	●●●●●
Nature	●●●●●
Outdoor activities	●●●●●
Parks	●●●●●
Scenery	●●●●●
Children	●●●●○
History	●●●●○
Wildlife	●●●●○

This is Canada's answer to the Wild West, a semi-wilderness of forests, mountains, lakes and prairies, a land where towns are small, few and *very* far between. It's a land where ghosts of gold seekers haunt decaying ghost towns that once eclipsed Vancouver, a land where cattle outnumber people and dreams grow as big as the sky is wide.

The Cariboo lies east, dense forests that stretch from the Cariboo Mountains, in eastern BC, to the Fraser River. The Chilcotin is west, a great grassy plain rising from the Fraser and running to the feet of the Coast Range, home to some of the largest cattle ranches on earth and vast tracts that have yet to be properly mapped.

West again is the glacial crest of the Coast Range, dropping precipitously into the Pacific Ocean. It's hard to get here, and once arrived, even harder to forget.

ALEXIS CREEK❖

ⓘ **Cariboo Chilcotin Coast Tourism Association** *118A N First Ave, Williams Lake; tel: (800) 663-5885 or (250) 392-2226; www.landwithoutlimits.com*

🅱 **Alexis Creek** *112km west of Williams Lake.*

With nearly 250 people, this Chilcotin metropolis has petrol, an RCMP station, post office, grocery store and a BC Forest Service office.

Accommodation in Alexis Creek

Chilcotin Hotel $$ *tel: (250) 394-4214,* is the only hotel and restaurant in town.

ANAHIM LAKE❖❖❖

This largely First Nations village is the largest in the West Chilcotin and a centre for fishing the Dean and other

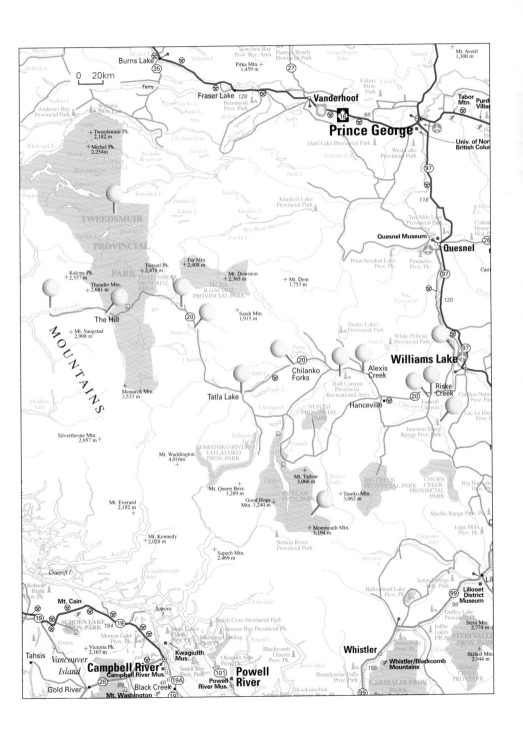

AC Christensen General Store tel: (250) 742-3266, is the best source of area information and supplies.

nearby rivers. **Anahim Lake Resort** (*$$ Hwy 20; tel: (800) 667-7212 or (250) 742-3242; www.anahimlakeresort.com*) offers fishing, air taxi service, hiking, riding and general relaxation. The renowned July Stampede is authentic, less commercial than July's Calgary Stampede.

BELLA COOLA✦✦

Bella Coola Valley Tourism tel: (250) 982-2212; www.bellacoola.ca. **Cariboo Chilcotin Coast Tourism Association** tel: (800) 663-5885 or (250) 392-2226; www. landwithoutlimits.com

Acwsalcta Nuxalk Nation School 4km east off Hwy 20.

The Art House $ Sir Alexander Mackenzie Secondary School, S. side of Hwy 20, Hagensborg; tel: (250) 799-5752. Open daily 1100–1630.

Hagensborg Hwy 20, 18km east of Bella Coola.

Sir Alexander Mackenzie Provincial Park and Mackenzie Rock 65km north west on Dean Channel; tel: (250) 398-4414; http://wlapwww. bc.ca/bcparks/explore/ parkpgs/alex_mack.htm. No land access. Ask about transport at the museum.

Thorsen Creek Petroglyphs Off Hwy 20, east of Bella Coola. Ask for directions at the museum.

Captain George Vancouver sailed up fjord-like North Bentinck Arm to Bella Coola in 1793, just weeks before Alexander Mackenzie walked down the narrow valley to the sea. Norwegian farmers arrived in 1894 to share the valley with Nuxalk (Bella Coola) First Nations. Town and fjord are ringed by sheer mountains, providing endless opportunities for fishing, hiking and outdoor adventure.

The **Acwsalcta Nuxalk Nation School**✦✦✦ has some of the finest First Nations artwork on public display along the coast. **The Art House**✦✦ combines gallery and teahouse in the former Principal's Residence. Works by local artists are for sale and the views are hard to beat.

Bella Coola Valley Museum✦ (*open mid-June–mid-Sept Sun–Fri 1000–1700*), in a 19th-century schoolhouse and surveyor's cabin, has Hudson's Bay Company relics and Norwegian goods. Norwegian farmers at **Hagensborg**✦ were Bella Coola's first non-Native residents in modern times. Many of the century-old homes and barns show adze marks produced by the original builders.

Mackenzie Rock in **Sir Alexander Mackenzie Provincial Park**✦✦✦ was the final stop of Mackenzie's 1793 trek across Canada. He painted a message in vermilion and bear grease, *Alexander Mackenzie, from Canada, by land, the twenty-second of July, one thousand, seven hundred and ninety-three*, later chiselled into the rock. The **Thorsen Creek Petroglyphs**✦✦✦ are dozens of carvings lining rocks along the creek. Engage a Nuxalk First Nation guide for safety.

Accommodation and food in Bella Coola

Bella Coola Valley Inn $$ *Mackenzie St; tel: (250) 799-5316 or (888) 799-5316; www.bellacoolavalleyinn.com*, is the best motel in town and the closest to the BC Ferries dock.

Tallheo Cannery Inn $$ *Across the harbour from Bella Coola; tel: (250) 982-2344; http://centralcoastbc.com/tallheocannery*

BULL CANYON PROVINCIAL RECREATIONAL AREA✦✦✦

This pleasant picnic and camping stop (*$ Hwy 20, 6km west of Alexis Creek; tel: (250) 397-2523; http://wlapwww.gov.bc.ca/bcparks/explore/ parkpgs/bullcan.htm; open mid-May–Sept*) was a cattle round-up point and the site of a decisive battle between Tsilhqot'in and Secwepemc bands.

CHILANKO FORKS✦✦✦

Chilanko Forks
62km west of Alexis Creek.

Chilanko Forks is a traditional Chilcotin town with a general store and petrol station. A marsh by the airport access road is good for beaver and muskrat-spotting.

FARWELL CANYON✦✦✦

Farwell Canyon
19km south of Hwy 20 from Riske Creek.

Right
Farwell Canyon

The Chilcotin River has cut a deep canyon through soft golden cliffs, creating flat-topped hoodoos (columns of rock formed by erosion) capped by sand dunes that shift with the wind.

THE HILL✦✦✦

The Hill *Hwy 20, east of Bella Coola.*

The final barrier to land travel between Bella Coola and the rest of BC was finally breached in 1953 – by local bulldozer operators who were tired of government highway engineers saying a road down the sheer western face of the Coast Range was impossible. Views from the single-track gravel road are stupendous, but there are no verges or lay-bys.

JUNCTION SHEEP RANGE PROVINCIAL PARK✦✦✦

This isolated park at the junction of the Fraser and Chilcotin Rivers protects the world's largest herd of California bighorn sheep, as well as some 40 or so butterfly species and countless birds (**$** *15km south of Hwy 20; tel: (250) 398-4414; http://wlapwww.gov.bc.ca/bcparks/explore/parkpgs/junction.htm; open Apr–Nov, requires high-clearance vehicle*).

NIMPO LAKE✦✦✦

The Dean on Nimpo $$ *1145 Hwy 20 West; tel: (888) 646-7655 or (250) 742-3332; www.thedeanonnimpo.com*

This 12-km lake claims to be BC's floatplane capital for the many daily charter flights to remote rivers and lakes. **The Dean on Nimpo** is the most comfortable of several lake-front fishing resorts.

RISKE CREEK✦

Riske Creek *46km west of Williams Lake.*

The tiny farming town of Riske Creek is named after a 19th-century Polish farmer, an early settler in the area.

Accommodation and food in Riske Creek

Chilcotin Lodge $$ *Riske Creek; tel: (250) 659-5646 or (888) 659-5688; www.chilcotinlodge.com,* is a former hunting lodge turned B&B, restaurant and campground, *open May–Dec.*

TATLA LAKE***

 **Tatla Lake** *109km from Alexis Creek.*

Lake and the 400-resident town provide the half-way point between Williams Lake and Bella Coola. Nordic skiing is a popular winter activity, rivalling lake diving in the summer for appeal.

TS'YL-OS PROVINCIAL PARK***

Lakes and streams in this undeveloped wilderness (pronounced 'sigh-loss') produce a quarter of the entire Fraser River salmon run. Apart from two gravel roads off Hwy 20, the only access is by air, boat, horse or foot (*100km south of Hwy 20 from Lees Corner; http://wlapwww.gov.bc.ca/ bcparks/explore/parkpgs/ts.htm*).

TWEEDSMUIR PROVINCIAL PARK***

Tweedsmuir is 981,000 hectares of wilderness outside a narrow corridor along Hwy 20. The best easy walks are on the Bella Coola side along the **Atnarko River Spawning Channels***, where grizzly and black bears *always* have the right of way (*$ Headquarters on Hwy 20 east of Bella Coola; tel: (250) 398-4414; http://wlapwww.gov.bc.ca/bcparks/ explore/parkpgs/tweed.htm*) [North Tweedsmuir Provincial Park and Protected Area] *and http://wlapwww.gov.bc.ca/bcparks/explore/parkpgs/ tweedsmu.htm* [South Tweedsmuir Provincial Park].

WILLIAMS LAKE*

ⓘ Williams Lake District Chamber of Commerce *1148 S Broadway (Hwy 97, south end of town); tel: (250) 392-5025; www. williamslakechamber.com*

This is the only real town between Hope and Quesnel, a cowboy city that has expanded into forestry, mining, agriculture and tourism.

Williams Lake's public gallery, the **Stationhouse Gallery***, concentrates on BC artists, while **Museum of the Cariboo–Chilcotin***, focuses on the ranching, rodeo and cowboy history of the Cariboo–Chilcotin region.

Scout Island Nature Centre*, a small marsh, has lakeside walking paths, wildlife watching and a summer nature centre. **Xats'ull Heritage Village**** a short drive from town, has daily cultural tours and programmes and extended educational stays in a pit house or tepee.

Fraser Inn Hotel
$$ 285 Donald Rd;
tel: (250) 398-7055
or (800) 452-6789;
www.fraserinn.com, is the
largest hotel in town.

**Rowat's Waterside
B&B** $$ 1397 Borland Rd;
tel: (250) 392-7395 or
(866) 392-7395;
www.wlakebb.com, is a bed
and breakfast a short walk
from Scout Island.

**Great Cariboo
Steak Company** $$
Fraser Inn, 285 Donald
Road; tel: (250) 398-7055,
is known for oversized
steaks.

Hearth Restaurant $$
99 5th Ave; tel: (250) 398-
6831, in the Cariboo
Friendship Society, has
open-beam First Nations
décor.

**Stationhouse
Gallery** $ | N
Mackenzie Ave (old BC Rail
Station); tel: (250) 392-6113.
Open daily.

**Museum of the
Cariboo–Chilcotin** $
113 N 4th Ave; tel:
(250) 392-7404;
www.cowboy-museum.com

**Scout Island Nature
Centre** West end of town,
off Hwy 97 east of city
centre; tel: (250) 398-8532.
Open daily.

**Xats'ull Heritage
Village** $$ 3405 Mountain
House Rd (Hwy 97 37km
north of Williams Lake); tel:
(250) 989-2323;
www.xatsull.com/Heritage%
20Village/tour_and_program_
rates.htm

Suggested tour

Total distance: 465km.

Time: Allow 10–12 hours to drive; 2–5 days to explore.

Links: From Bella Coola, BC Ferries **Discovery Coast** route (*see page 106*) leads south to **Port Hardy** and **North Vancouver Island** (*see page 96*). From Williams Lake, the **Gold Rush Trail** (*see page 186*) leads north toward **Prince George** (*see page 222*) or south toward **Hope** (*see page 127*).

Route: From **WILLIAMS LAKE** ❶, take Hwy 20 west to the **Fraser River**. The river marks the edge of the **Chilcotin Plateau**, which stretches west toward the **Coast Range**. **Becher's Prairie** forms the eastern section of the plateau, rolling grasslands dotted with boulders deposited by retreating glaciers. Nest boxes on fence posts help attract birds which feast on the clouds of mosquitoes hovering above the thousands of tiny lakes and ponds scattered across the Chilcotin.

The enormous antennae rising from the prairie form part of the Loran-C navigation system. A good gravel road 9.5km west leads 16km east to the fairy-tale hoodoos of Farwell Canyon and **JUNCTION SHEEP RANGE PROVINCIAL PARK** ❷.

Detour: Follow the gravel road along the rolling curves of the almost treeless plain to **FARWELL CANYON** ❸ and a wooden bridge over the **Chilcotin River**. There are early First Nations rock paintings on the overhang at the south end of the bridge. Local Tsilhqot'in fishers net salmon from the river in summer and autumn, drying their catch on racks near by. The road loops 50km loop back to Hwy 20 at **Lees Corner**.

The bright yellow log buildings 1.5km west of the turn-off are the town of **Riske Creek** ❹. Continue west, following traditional wooden fences snaking along the road. One of the best views across the Chilcotin is from a hilltop rest area 35km west of Chilcotin Lodge and Riske Creek. Another gravel road leads south to **Hanceville**, named for Tom Hance, the first rancher in the area, and **TS'YL-OS PROVINCIAL PARK** ❺.

Hwy 20 continues westwards to **ALEXIS CREEK** ❻, the largest town in eastern Chilcotin, 10km west. **BULL CANYON PROVINCIAL RECREATION AREA** ❼ is another 9km west. Views westward are stunning as the road gradually rises toward **CHILANKO FORKS** ❽ and a section of gravel highway.

Continue west toward Tatla Lake. There's a wonderful view across the lake and valley from a hilltop viewpoint 15km west of Chilanko Forks. **Pollywog Marsh**, 12km west of the lay-by, is a pleasant lakeside rest stop. **TATLA LAKE** ❾, another 10km west, is the edge of the Chilcotin Plateau and halfway to Bella Coola. It's a pleasant drive in summer, but don't be taken in by the weather. Winter temperatures regularly hit -50ºC with 50kph winds driving blinding blizzards.

Kleena Kleene is well into the slowly rising foothills of the Coast Range. The road continues up toward **NIMPO LAKE** ⑩ , where pavement begins again for the benefit of several lakeside fishing lodges.

Just west is the **Dean River**, famed for fine steelhead and trout fishing. A highway marker commemorates the 1864 **Chilcotin War**, when Tsilhqo'tin warriors killed 18 roadbuilders, packers and settlers who were attempting to cut a route from Bute Inlet (opposite Campbell River on Vancouver Island) across the Chilcotin to the Cariboo gold fields. Five of the warriors, including the war chief, were executed by Colonial troops, but the road was abandoned, sparing the Chilcotin from smallpox and land-hungry settlers for a few more years. A provincial enquiry in 1993 granted five posthumous pardons and a memorial was erected.

The pavement disappears again at **ANAHIM LAKE** ⑪ , the closest the Chilcotin has to a modern town. Gravel roads lead north along the Dean River, but check locally for conditions before setting out. Beyond the last tyre tracks lies the Nuxalk-Carrier Grease Trail east to the Fraser and west to Bella Coola.

From Anahim Lake, the gravel road climbs into the Coast Range and **TWEEDSMUIR PROVINCIAL PARK** ⑫ , which begins at 1524-m **Heckman Pass**. There are good views of the multicoloured **Rainbow Mountains** from the **Tsulko River**, east of the pass. Local First Nations bands mined obsidian from the Rainbows, a string of ancient volcanoes stained red, yellow and purple by mineral deposits.

Just west of Heckman Pass is a brake check stop at the top of **THE HILL** ⑬ . There are no verges, no guard-rails and no lay-bys in a 19-km

Alexander Mackenzie and the Grease Trail

North West Company explorer Alexander Mackenzie has gone down in Canadian history as 'The First Man West' for his 1793 overland crossing to the Pacific Ocean at Bella Coola. Mackenzie was the first non-Native to cross North America beyond Mexico and return to tell the tale, but it was hardly a trail-breaking wilderness expedition. Mackenzie and company were shepherded every step of the way along an ancient network of trails and trade routes that spanned the continent. In the Chilcotin, he followed the Great Road, the Nuxalk-Carrier Grease Trail linking coastal Heiltsuk, Kwakwaka'wakw and Nuxalk First Nations with the interior. The trail was named for the Dakelh (or Carrier) peoples who traded oolichan oil for furs, obsidian and other goods from the Coast Range to the Rockies. Part of the rugged route has been reborn as the **Alexander Mackenzie Heritage Trail/Nuxalk-Carrier Grease Trail**, 420km from Quesnel (see page 192), on the Fraser River, to Bella Coola. The foot and horse track parallels Hwy 20 from Tweedsmuir Provincial Park at **Burnt Bridge**, 49km east of Bella Coola, to the sea.

stack of single track, hairpin turns that drops 1300m to the head of the Bella Coola Valley. Use low gear to creep down (or up) the 18 per cent grade to prevent brakes from overheating and failing.

A hard road surface begins again at the bottom of The Hill, running through dense forest along the Atnarko and Bella Coola rivers. The valley opens and broadens toward the sea. **Hagensborg** still has many of the square-cut, hand-hewn buildings left by early Norwegian settlers a century ago. The town of **BELLA COOLA** ⑭ sits at the mouth of the Bella Coola River, at the head of **North Bentinck Arm**.

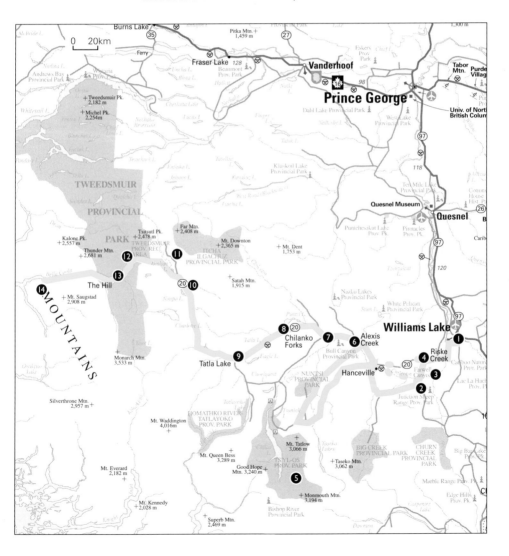

Prince Rupert

Ratings

Children	●●●●●
Nature	●●●●●
Scenery	●●●●●
Art	●●●●○
History	●●●●○
Museums	●●●●○
Outdoor activities	●●●○○
Parks	●●●○○

Prince Rupert is BC's most famous transit hub, the city that everyone goes through Convoys of RVers and independent travellers drive through the city on the way to and from Vancouver Island or the Queen Charlotte Islands via BC Ferries. Schools of sport fishers fly through on the way to isolated lodges up and down the BC coast and along interior mountain rivers. Wildlife observation has begun to rival sportsfishing, with whale watching for humpback, grey, and orca whales matching bald eagle and black bear spotting in popularity. New cruise ship facilities have increased summertime day trippers. Even the train passengers who roll through the centre of town are on the way to somewhere else, usually a circular tour that combines rail, motor coach and ferry from Vancouver to Vancouver by way of Vancouver Island and Prince Rupert.

What they're missing is a pleasant, albeit damp, city ensconced in Canada's Northern rainforest that is big enough to offer good food, good coffee and good Internet connections but small enough to be walkable and friendly. It's a hub worth exploring.

Getting there

Tourism Prince Rupert Visitor Info Centre *Atlin Terminal, 215 Cow Bay Rd, Suite 10, Prince Rupert, BC V8J 1A2;* tel: (800) 667-1994 or (250) 624-5637; www.tourismprincerupert.com

Weather Bring rain gear. Prince Rupert gets more than twice as much rain as Vancouver, an average of 2552mm annually.

Air The Prince Rupert airport is on Digby Island, west of downtown, with ferry and bus connections to the city centre locations. If leaving by air, be sure to check bus schedules as well as airline schedules – miss the bus and you miss the flight.

Floatplane flights use the **Seal Cove Seaplane Base** east from downtown.

BC Ferries *Ferry Terminal at the end of Hwy 16, 2km west of downtown;* tel: (250) 624-9627, (250) 386-3431 or (888) 223-3779; www.bcferries.bc.ca. BC Ferries connect with **Port Hardy** (see page 101) on Vancouver Island and **Skidegate** (see page 120) in the Queen Charlotte Islands.

Alaska Marine Highway Terminal *near the BC Ferries Terminal at the end of Hwy 16;* tel: (800) 642-0066; www.alaska.gov/ferry. Prince Rupert is the southern terminus of the Alaska State Ferry system, on the Inside Passage/Southeast [Alaska] Route.

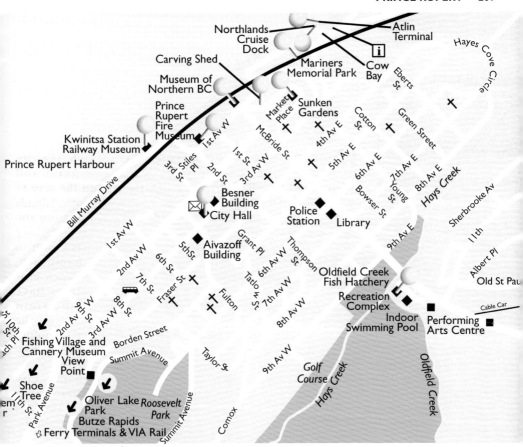

Road *Hwy 16*, the *Yellowhead Highway*, is the only road link with the rest of BC.

VIA Rail *2000 Park Ave; tel: (250) 627-7304 or (888) 842-7245; www.viarail.ca*. The *Skeena* runs between Prince Rupert and Jasper.

Cruise Ship Ocean-going cruise ships plying between southern BC and Alaska during the summer arrives at **Northlands Cruise Dock**, *Cow Bay*.

Sights

Butze Rapids❖❖
The narrow rapids reverse flow with the tide, with the boiling, foaming water at its most scenic as the tide falls. The Tsimshian called the white foam floating from the rapids *kaien*, which became the name of the island Prince Rupert occupies. The 4.8-km Butze Rapids Trail loop leads through old-growth forest to a view of the rapids.

Dreams delayed

Prince Rupert is a speculator's dream become reality, albeit several decades delayed. In the early years of the 20th century, railway baron Charles Hays envisioned a great port and gleaming city amid the rain forests of Northern BC. The commercial lure was location, days closer to Asian markets than Vancouver.

Hays sailed to England to raise capital for his grand project, then capped a successful trip by sailing home aboard the maiden voyage of the grandest ship afloat, the *Titanic*. When the *Titanic* sank, so did Hays' dreams. Planned hotels were never built. Trains rolled into Prince Rupert just in time to hit World War I. The Grand Trunk Pacific Railway came to Prince Rupert, but then disappeared in 1919, absorbed by the Canadian National Railway. Prince Rupert became a halibut fishing port and built freighters and minesweepers deployed in World War II. It took 50 years for transpacific shipping to catch up with Hays' vision. Cargo ships can dock at the railway terminal in Prince Rupert and have their cargoes halfway across the continent by the time competitors dock in Vancouver.

Butze Rapids $ *Off Hwy 16, 6km southeast of town.*

Carving Shed $ *One block east from the Museum of Northern BC; tel: (250) 624-3207. Open irregular hours Jun–Aug.*

City Hall *3rd Ave W and 3rd St.*

Cow Bay *East from downtown.*

Prince Rupert Fire Museum $ *200 1st Avenue W; tel: (250) 624-2211; www.princerupertlibrary.ca/fire. Open daily in summer; by appointment in winter.*

Laxspa'aws Pike Island Tour $$ *tour begins at the Museum of Northern BC, 100 First Ave West; tel: (800) 667-4393 or (250) 624-5645; www.pikeisland.ca. Call to verify tour dates; tickets also sold at the Museum of Northern BC.*

Carving Shed✦✦✦

Part of the Museum of Northern BC, the carving shed houses totem poles and other works in wood in the making. Carvers are usually happy to explain the significance of the traditional designs and images.

City Hall✦✦✦

Inside are ordinary municipal offices, but the outside is art deco. To the side is a small plaza with a fine totem pole and statue of city founder Charles Hays.

Cow Bay✦✦✦

Named for cattle that were made to swim ashore to a dairy in 1906, Cow Bay is a combination fishing harbour, trendy haven, and repository of historic buildings. Look for coffee shops, bistros, restaurants and boats. Mailboxes, garbage cans and other surfaces are decorated with Jersey spots and similar bovine motifs.

Kwinitsa Station Railway Museum✦✦

The 1911 building was one of 400 identical stations built on the Grand Trunk Pacific line between Prince Rupert and Winnipeg, Manitoba. Only four stations survive; this one was barged 75km down the Skeena River in 1985 and restored as a railway museum.

Laxspa'aws Pike Island Tour✦✦

In the late 1700s, ten Tsimshian First Nation bands, around 7000 people, lived in some 60 villages around present-day Prince Rupert

From mainland Alaska to Yellowstone National Park, the land of the Great Bear is sacred to native peoples and wildlife lovers. Forty-five kilometres northeast of Prince Rupert, 50 north coast grizzly bears live in an undisturbed eco-system necessary for their survival, the **Khutzeymateen Grizzly Bear Sanctuary** (tel: (250) 798-2277; http://wlapwww.gov.bc.ca/bc parks/explore/parkpgs/khutz. htm). Human visitation is severely limited for the animals' protection, with two authorized tour operators permitted several day boat access to the area from May to September. **Ocean Light II Adventures** (tel: (604) 328-5339; www.oceanlight2.bc.ca) sails a 22-m ketch; **Sun Chaser Charters** (tel: (250) 624-5472; www.citytel.net/sunchaser) has a 12.5-m sailboat.

Kwinitsa Station Railway Museum $
Pacific Place, 1st Ave and Bill Murray Way; tel: (250) 627-1915. Open Jun–Aug daily; 0900–1200, 1300–1700.

Museum of Northern BC $ 1st Ave W and McBride St; tel: (250) 624-3207; www. museumofnorthernbc.com. Open Mon–Sat 0900–2000, Sun 0900–1700 in summer; Sept–May Mon–Sat 0900–1700.

harbour, one of the largest population centres on the entire continent. The village sites are still there, complete with petroglyphs, middens and spectacular island scenery. The 3.5-hour excursion to Pike Island at Venn Passage begins with an orientation at the Museum of Northern BC, followed by a 40-minute enclosed ferry ride. After an on-island briefing, there is a 3-km guided walk on groomed cedar-chip covered forest trails. Three of five 2000 year-old archaeological village sites, middens, and beaches with canoe run marks and rock carvings are featured, though the flora of the lush rainforest alone is a great introduction to the area.

Mariners Memorial Park*
This harbour-front park commemorates a local fishing boat that disappeared in a storm with all hands. Displays include a stature depicting a fisherman at his wheel surrounded by a wall listing local sailors lost at sea and the restored Kazu Maru, a small Japanese fishing boat that drifted from Japan to BC in the 1980s.

Museum of Northern BC***
The airy, longhouse-style building is one of the finest museums in BC, The focus is 10,000 years of local Tsimshian history (the name means 'people going into the river of mists'), stretching from islands off Prince Rupert and up the Skeena River as far as Kitselas Canyon above Terrace (see page 219), and the museum covers Northwest Coast aboriginal culture in detail. Tribal Councils are heavily involved in museum research and displays, documenting village sites, artefacts and oral histories, creating databases and publishing a variety of scientific and popular books.

North Pacific Historic Fishing Village***
BC's oldest and largest surviving salmon cannery (and a National Historic Site) is the last of 19 salmon canneries that once dotted the shores of the lower Skeena River. More than 1200 canneries from Alaska south to Sacramento, California, were part of the trade at its height in the early 20th century before refrigeration and fish farms made fresh salmon fillets an everyday commodity. The cannery has been restored to show the fishing and canning process as well as daily life a century ago. The setting, a long waterfront boardwalk, docks and employee housing overlooking Inverness Pass, is one of the most scenic in the area. Don't miss the large model railroad collection in the transit shed.

Oldfield Creek Fish Hatchery*
Started as a classroom project in the late 1970s when local coho salmon runs had dwindled to just nine spawning fish, the hatchery has played a visible role in increasing the salmon population and heightening local concern over the impact that logging and other human activities can have on fish habitat and survival. Local high-

Right
Prince Rupert's shoe tree

North Pacific Historic Fishing Village $$ *1889 Skeena Dr, Port Edward (11km off Hwy 16 at south end of Kaien Island); tel: (250) 628-3538; www.district.portedward.bc. ca/northpacific. Open daily mid-May–Sept 0900–1800.*

school students convinced city authorities and local service organisations to contribute time, labour and money to build a small salmon hatchery and restore spawning beds in Oldfield Creek. Salmon spawned at Oldfield have been used to recreate runs on other local streams that had lost their entire native fish population.

Oliver Lake Dwarf Forest***

This small park protects a section of muskeg and wet forest that includes carnivorous plants and naturally stunted lodgepole pine trees

Oldfield Creek Fish Hatchery *Off Wantage Rd from Hwy 16; tel: (250) 624-6733. Open daily.*

Oliver Lake Dwarf Forest $ *Off Hwy 16, 6km south of Prince Rupert.*

Mariners Memorial Park *North and east from the Museum of Northern BC, overlooking the harbour.*

Shoe Tree *Hwy 16 south of Prince Rupert. Ask for directions at the InfoCentre.*

Sunken Gardens *East from the Carving Shed.*

Totem Tour *Self-guided walking tour.*

(visible from boardwalks) that look like carefully tended bonsai specimens.

Prince Rupert Fire Museum✦

Fire buffs make a pilgrimage just to see Prince Rupert's beautifully restored 1925 REO Speedwagon fire truck. The museum, next to the Prince Rupert Fire Hall, displays dozens of badges, patches and pins donated by visiting firemen from around the world and firefighting equipment dating back to the town's beginnings in 1906.

Shoe Tree✦✦✦

No one is quite sure how or when the *Tree of Lost Soles* got its start, but decades of mis-matched shoes have ended up nailed to the trunk, draped in the branches and piled around the base of this huge tree.

Sunken Gardens✦✦✦

The gardens were originally dug as the foundation for a 1920s provincial courthouse that was later moved a few hundred metres closer to town. The site was used for storage during World War II and later turned into a public garden.

Totem Tour✦✦✦

Tsimshian carvers have created dozens of totem poles and other wooden carvings that have been erected around Prince Rupert. The InfoCentre and Museum have self-guided tour brochures to totems throughout Kaien Island.

Accommodation and food

Hotels, motels and bed and breakfasts are scattered throughout Prince Rupert.

Breaker's Pub $$ *117 George Hills Way, Cow Bay; tel: (250) 624-5990*, is the liveliest waterfront restaurant in town.

Cow Bay Café $$ *Cow Bay; tel: (250) 627-1212*, uses local fish in Trinidadian-inspired dishes.

Cowpuccino's $ *25 Cow Bay Rd, Cow Bay; tel: (250) 627-1395*, specialises in desserts and coffees.

The Crest Hotel $$$ *222 First Ave W; tel: (250) 624-6771 or (800) 663-8150; www.cresthotel.bc.ca*, has the best water views and the most expensive hotel rooms in town.

Eagle Bluff Bed & Breakfast $$ *201 Cow Bay Rd; tel: (800) 833-1550 or (250) 627-4955; www.citytel.net/eaglebluff*, has superb harbour views.

Above
Prince Rupert harbour

Smile's Seafood Café $$ *113 Cow Bay Rd, Cow Bay; tel: (250) 624-3072*, is the oldest and best-known fish restaurant in Prince Rupert.

Crest Waterfront Restaurant $$$ *222 First Ave W (Crest Hotel); tel: (250) 624-6771*, is the most elegant eatery on the North Coast. If dinner is too dear, soak up the sunset views for the price of a drink.

Suggested tour

Total distance: 3km.

Time: 2–3 hours on foot.

Route: Prince Rupert's origins as a planned town are still obvious, at least in the downtown area, where streets are wide and boulevards grand. From the **KWINITSA STATION RAILWAY MUSEUM ❶** on the waterfront, walk up Bill Murray Drive to 1st Avenue W. Turn right, or west (1st Avenue W becomes Stiles Place) and walk one block to 3rd Street and left (south) two blocks to 3rd Avenue W. **CITY HALL ❷** is on the right with its totems and statue of Prince Rupert founder Charles Hays.

Follow 3rd Avenue W to the left (east) to McBride Street (Hwy 16). Turn left (north) to another totem. To the right are the **SUNKEN GARDENS ❸**, **CARVING SHED** and **PRINCE RUPERT ARCHIVES**. The **MUSEUM OF NORTHERN BC** is ahead, next to **MARINERS MEMORIAL PARK**, with the **FIRE MUSEUM** to the left on 1st Avenue W. The InfoCentre and Museum of Northern BC ❹ have an excellent self-guided walking tour brochure with more details and route suggestions. In summer, the museum operates guided walking tours with local tales at historic sites.

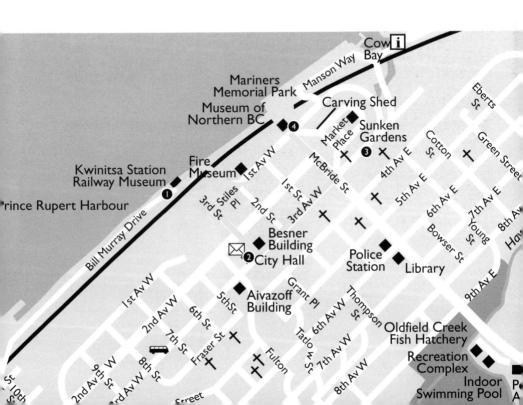

The Yellowhead Highway: Prince Rupert to Prince George

Ratings

First Nations art	●●●●●
History	●●●●●
Mountains	●●●●●
River scenery	●●●●●
Children	●●●●○
Geology	●●●●○
Outdoor activities	●●●●○
Parks	●●●●○

The northern interior is a vast plateau, in parts heavily forested, elsewhere rolling grasslands, all of it ringed by jumbled mountains that remain impassable outside the occasional river valley twisting towards the Pacific Ocean. To the west lies the Skeena, the 'River of Mists', the mystical, half-seen heartland of a vibrant First Nations enclave and a traditional route through the Coast Range. Further east lie rolling farm and forest lands dotted with lakes and marshes that eventually drain into the mighty Fraser River.

A century of logging, mining and agriculture has wrought visible changes, but the human population is as scattered today as it was when Simon Fraser paddled through on his way south in 1806. Wilderness is seldom more than a few minutes away from even the largest towns, a region where moose, deer, bears, cougars and wolves still roam a largely empty land at will.

EXCHAMSIKS RIVER PROVINCIAL PARK❖❖❖

An old-growth Sitka spruce forest dominates this small park at the confluence of the Exchamsiks and Sitka rivers. It's crowded during salmon season (thanks to excellent fishing), nearly deserted the rest of the year. (**Exchamsiks River Provincial Park** $ *Hwy 16, 56km west of Terrace; tel: (250) 638-8490; http:// wlapwww.gov.bc.ca/bcparks/ explore/parkpgs/exchamsi.htm.*)

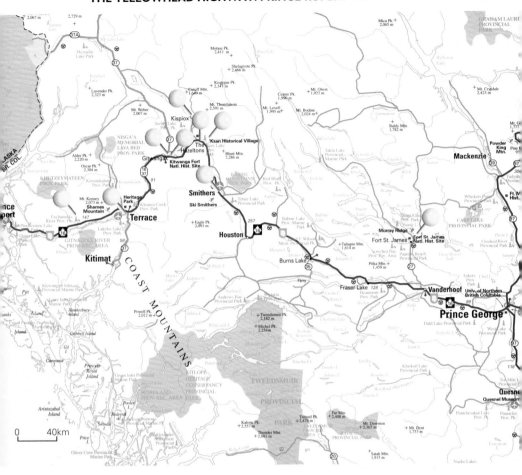

The Yellow Head

Hwy 16, the Yellowhead Highway, is named for an enigmatic French Canadian trapper, Pierre Hatsinaton. Called Tête Jaune, or Yellow Head, for his brilliant blond hair, Hatsinaton popularised a Fur Brigade route along the **Yellowhead Pass** (see page 263) through the Rocky Mountains that still serves as BC's main land link to the east. Local legend says Yellow Head hid a rich cache of furs near **Tête Jaune Cache** (see page 263), just east of today's **Mount Robson Provincial Park** (see page 262), in the early 19th century, but disappeared before he could carry them east. Both man and legend were popularised in the 1939 film classic *Tay John*, directed by Howard O'Haggan.

FORT ST JAMES✣

ⓘ Fort St James Chamber of Commerce *115 Douglas Ave; tel: (250) 996-7023; www.fsjames.com/biz/ chamber. Open daily.*

Ⓗ Fort St James National Historic Site $ *Hwy 27, 68km north from Hwy 16; tel: (250) 996-7191; www.pc.gc.ca/lhn-nhs/bc/stjames/index_e.asp. Open May–Sept 0900–1700.*

Originally called Nak'azdli, the town has been a major Dakelh (Carrier) settlement for millennia. Today, it lives on timber and tourism.

Simon Fraser paddled down Stuart Lake to Nak'azdli in 1806. He liked the 300-km string of rivers and lakes so much he dubbed it 'New Caledonia' and established the first White trading post in the territory of the Dakelh, the widest-ranging traders in interior BC. When the Hudson's Bay Company absorbed Fraser's North West Company in 1821, Fort St James became the chief post for the entire mainland area. Despite its importance, the harsh winters, gruelling isolation and monotonous diet of fresh salmon, smoked salmon and dried salmon made Fort St James the Siberia of the North American fur trade.

The HBC post, now **Fort St James National Historic Site✣✣✣**, survived until the 1930s and was later restored to its 1896 appearance. The major buildings are original, including the fur warehouse, fish cache, men's house, officers' quarters and dairy, all staffed by living-history interpreters in period costume. The Visitor Centre museum has excellent displays on the Dakelh people.

GITWANGAK✣✣

🔁 Hwys 16 and 37 junction, 50 km southwest of New Hazelton

The town and First Nation name means 'place of rabbits', but you're more likely to see **totem poles✣✣✣** dating back to the 1870s across the street from **St Paul's Anglican Church✣**, with stained-glass windows 400 years old and a Norse-style bell tower.

THE HAZELTONS✣✣✣

ⓘ Hazeltons Visitor Info Centre *Hwys 16 and 62; tel: (250) 842-6071. Open mid-May–Sept 0800–2000.*

Ⓒ Bulkley Valley Motel $$ *New Hazelton; tel: (250) 842-6817, is in the town centre.*

28 Inn $$ *New Hazelton; tel: (250) 842-6006 or (877) 842-2828; www.28inn.com, is the largest motel in the area.*

Opposite
Fort St James

There's a trio of towns: **South Hazelton✣**, a modern highway settlement; **New Hazelton✣**, an early railway town; and **Hazelton✣✣✣**, the original riverside settlement on the banks of the upper Skeena River. All three are dominated by **Mt Rocher Déboulé**, the mountain of rolling stones, named by early miners who dodged frequent rockfalls. The Gitxsan call it **Stii Kyo Kin**, 'Stands Alone', the centrepiece of an ancient city-state and still the Gitxsan cultural capital, heart and soul. There are more standing totem poles in the Hazeltons than anywhere else in BC, as well as a 'Hands of History' 113km driving loop to **Kitwanga** – follow the information signs showing a stylised hand with an all-seeing eye in the palm.

Hazelton, a busy river port from the 1860s until the Grand Trunk arrived in 1912, could be a film set today. The slow-paced town is filled with false-front wooden buildings from the more prosperous Victorian era. The Chamber of Commerce has maps of self-guiding driving and walking tours that begin at the main Tourist InfoCentre on Hwy 16.

KISPIOX✧✧✧

Kispiox *Hwy 62, 13km north of Hazelton; www.kispiox.com.* Contact **Kispiox Band Office** *tel: (250) 842-5248.*

This ancient (and now tiny) Gitxsan village, at the confluence of the Kispiox and Skeena Rivers, has a magnificent stand of 15 totem poles, including a rare carving of a crying woman, inside a grassy enclosure. Wander into galleries, both open most days in summer, feature fine local carving and other artworks. Anglers may recognise the name for the world-class salmon and steelhead fishing along the Kispiox River.

KITWANGA FORT NATIONAL HISTORIC SITE✧✧✧

This sculpted hill held one of the largest Tsimshian fortifications in the Skeena River region. The cedar plank redoubts and wood palisade protected a Grease Trail leading 100km north to the Nass River. A flaming battle in the early 1800s destroyed the complex. (**Kitwanga Fort National Historic Site $** *Hwy 37, 5km north of Hwy 16; tel: (250) 559-8818; www.pc.gc.ca/lhn-nhs/bc/kitwanga/index_e.asp*)

'KSAN HISTORICAL VILLAGE✧✧✧

'Ksan Historical Village $ *Hwy 62, 7km north of New Hazelton; tel: (250) 842-5544 or (877) 842-5518; www.ksan.org. Open daily Apr–Sept 0900–1800, shorter hours in winter.*

'Ksan is the visible heart of Gitxsan culture. The model village and museum occupy the site of Gitanmaax, a cluster of villages at the junction of the Skeena and Bulkley rivers that has been settled for at least 7000 years. A short, shady forest walk from the car park leads to seven brightly decorated cedar plank longhouses and a growing collection of totem poles. The buildings house a museum, gift and art shop, carving shed and band meeting rooms.

SMITHERS**

ℹ Tourism Smithers
*1411 Court St; tel:
(250) 847-5072 or (800)
542-6673; www.
tourismsmithers.com*

**🏛 Bulkley Valley
Museum $** *Hwy 16
and Main St; tel: (250) 847-
5322. Call for hours.*

Smithers Art Gallery
*Hwy 16 and Main St; tel:
(250) 847-3898. Open
Mon–Sat.*

**Babine Mountains
Provincial Park** *Old
Babine Lake Rd;
http://wlapwww.gov.bc.ca/
bcparks/explore/parkpgs/
babmtn.htm*

**Driftwood Canyon
Provincial Park** *Old
Babine Lake Road, 11km
northeast of Smithers; tel:
(250) 638-8490; http://
wlapwww.gov.bc.ca/bcparks/
explore/parkpgs/driftwood.
htm*

**Tyhee Lake Provincial
Park** *On Tyhee Lake, 16km
southeast of Smithers; tel:
(250) 638-8490; http://
wlapwww.gov.bc.ca/bcparks/
explore/parkpgs/tyhee.htm*

☾ Chez Josette B&B
*$$ 4259 McCabe
Road; tel: (250) 847-8743,
is a quiet bed and breakfast
that opens on to hiking
and skiing trails.*

Hudson Bay Lodge $$
*3251 Hwy 16 E; tel: (250)
847-4581 or (800) 663-
5040; www.hudsonbaylodge.
com, is the largest hotel in
the region.*

The economic centre of the Bulkley River Valley, Smithers is dominated by the classic alpine form of **Hudson Bay Mountain**, 2621m. The faux-Alpine décor along the main street, complete with red brick sidewalks and a statue of a man playing an alpenhorn, adds a kitschy touch. Like most interior towns, Smithers grew up on timber, but has diversified into agriculture, sport fishing and outdoor recreation in recent years, including winter alpine and Nordic skiing.

Bulkley Valley Museum highlights development in the Bulkley Valley. Look for local artists and local themes at the **Smithers Art Gallery**.

The 32,000-hectare **Babine Mountains Provincial Park*** offers some of central BC's finest hiking through sub-Alpine meadows, glacial-fed lakes and rugged peaks, with snowshoeing and cross-country skiing in winter.

Created to protect slate cliffs filled with plant, animal and insect fossils 50 million years old, **Driftwood Canyon Provincial Park*** also offers picnicking and pleasant forest walks. The good gravel road continues 35km west to Hwy 16 at Moricetown. Watch for moose and deer, especially early and late in the day.

Tyhee Lake Provincial Park*, a small bit of Bulkley River Valley along Tyhee Lake, provides a habitat for a variety of birds, squirrels, beaver, black bears and moose. Beach and campground are popular local getaways.

TERRACE*

ⓘ Terrace Tourism
*4511 Keith Ave;
tel: (250) 635-0832 or
(800) 499-1637;
www.terracetourism.bc.ca*

🏛 Heritage Park $
*4702 Kerby Ave;
tel: (250) 635-4546; www.
heritageparkmuseum.com.
Open May–Aug 1000–1800.*

House of Sim-Oi-Ghets
*W Kalum Rd;
tel: (250) 638-1629;
www.kitsumkalum.bc.ca/
house.html*

**Northern Lights Studio
& Gardens** *4820 Hall Ave;
tel: (250) 638-1403.*

Once a major steamboat stop, Terrace is better known now for salmon and bears. World-record salmon have been caught in the Skeena River within walking distance of the town centre. The municipal emblem, the white Kermode bear, tends to keep to the woods, but is occasionally spotted along quiet side roads.

Eight original log buildings have been collected into an excellent regional museum, **Heritage Park***, filled with period photographs and artefacts. Costumed guides lead tours in summer.

House of Sim-Oi-Ghets**, a gallery run by the Kitsumkalum Band, offers the best selection of First Nations arts and crafts in the area.

The calm Japanese-style gardens at the **Northern Lights Studio & Gardens*** attract as many visitors as the studio and gallery.

Accommodation and food in Terrace

Alpine House Motel $$ *4326 Lakelse Ave; tel: (250) 635-7216*, is a quiet motel within walking distance of downtown.

Sonbadas Steak House $$ *4402 Lakelse Ave; tel: (250) 638-1503*, provides a good selection of Greek dishes plus steaks and seafood.

Suggested tour

Total distance: 740km.

Time: One very long day driving, 3–4 days to explore.

Links: The Yellowhead Highway links with **Prince Rupert** (*see page 206*) and the **Queen Charlotte Islands** (*see page 116*) to the east and the **Gold Rush Trail** (*see page 186*) to the south via Hwy 97.

Route: From **Prince Rupert**, take Hwy 16 south. The highway passes several scenic parks with fishing, hiking and grand vistas before reaching the **Skeena River**. The name means 'river of mists' in the language of the Tsimshian and Gitxsan First Nations who have lived in the region since the end of the last Ice Age and perhaps longer. Swirling mists and low-hanging clouds often hide surrounding mountain peaks and the opposite shore.

The Skeena Canyon has been a highway for thousands of years, first for First Nations canoes, then paddlewheel steamboats, the Grand Trunk Pacific Railway and now Hwy 16. Harbour seals have been spotted 100km inland feasting on salmon and oolichan migrating upriver to spawn. Bald eagles, bears, ravens and other predators/ scavengers are common sights. The best river viewpoints (mist permitting) are **Basalt Creek**, about 20km east from the first sight of the river, and **Telegraph Point**, 33km beyond.

Above
Terrace Heritage Park

The highway passes **TERRACE ❶**, named for the natural terraces along the Skeena River, a major steamboat stop until the GTP arrived in 1912. The small timber and sport fishing town is a good place to see **Kermode** (ker-mode-ee) bears, a subspecies of black bear that is honey-blond-white in colour. The Kermode is a spirit bear in local First Nations lore, given to punishing evil-doers and rescuing the deserving in distress. These days, it's the Kermode that needs help as logging and other human activities cut into wild habitat.

From Terrace, the road swings north past **Usk**, a steamboat town that has all but disappeared, to **GITWANGAK ❷**, with a turn to **KITWANGA FORT NATIONAL HISTORIC SITE ❸**, and continues on to the three **HAZELTONS ❹**.

Detour to Kispiox: From the Visitor InfoCentre at New Hazelton, take Hwy 62 left (north) to cross over the single-track **Hagwilget Bridge**, hanging 76m above the boiling Bulkley River. The Gitxsan and Wet'suwet'en First Nations built a bridge of wooden poles lashed together with cedar bark rope over the gorge at the same site.

The highway crosses gently rolling pastures to **'KSAN HISTORICAL VILLAGE ❺** and on to Hazelton, the head of navigation on the Skeena River. The road narrows and follows the Kispiox River north to the Gitxsan village of **KISPIOX ❻**. Return to Hwy 16.

The highway leaves the Skeena just west of the Hazeltons to follow the **Bulkley River** eastward. The river is squeezed to just 15m at **Moricetown**, which has been a traditional Wet'suwe t'en fishing spot for at least the last 4000 years. The small town is named for an early missionary priest.

SMITHERS ❼ is the largest town in the Bulkley Valley, laced by several small rivers and streams. The Yellowhead climbs out of the valley to **Houston**, a sport fishing town that proudly proclaims its number-one money spinner with an 18m fly-fishing rod cocked above the **Houston and District Chamber of Commerce**; *tel: (250) 845-2238; http://district.houston.bc.ca*. The highest point on the entire Yellowhead Hwy is 40km east at **Six Mile Summit**, 1423m. Downhill lies the **Lake Country**, filled with lakes, meadows and second-growth forests.

Detour: From a turn-off just west of **Vanderhoof**, take Hwy 27 north for 68km to **Stuart Lake** and Fort St James, the former HBC post. Return to Hwy 16.

The highway rolls east through **Vanderhoof**, a logging town that has turned to ranching. The geographic centre of BC is 10km east, marked by a roadside cairn. The highway continues east through rolling forests to **Prince George** (*see page 222*).

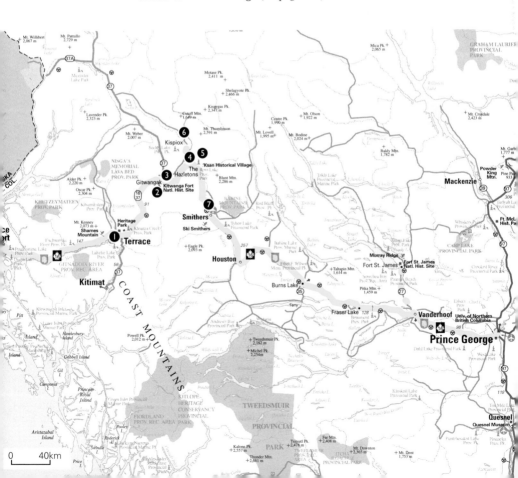

Prince George

Ratings

Children	●●●● ○
Geology	●●●● ○
History	●●●● ○
Parks	●●●● ○
Mountains	●●● ○○
Outdoor activities	●●● ○○
Scenery	●●● ○○
Wildlife	●● ○○○

Alexander Mackenzie paddled past the junction of the Fraser and Nechako rivers in 1793 without even noticing the massive confluence in a heavy morning mist. Simon Fraser had better visibility in 1807; he stopped long enough to build a small trading post on the flat bowl below looming cliffs cut by the two rivers. And that was the last most of the outside world heard of the place until the Grand Trunk Pacific Railway arrived on the way west to Prince Rupert.

Almost a century later, Prince George remains an isolated, if vital, crossroads. Roads, railways and air routes have replaced river conduits for people, goods and information, but road and rail seldom stray far from river routes in BC's rugged interior. A smoothly undulating carpet of forest cloaks a rolling plateau dotted with lakes and laced by sparkling rivers tumbling toward the Pacific.

Getting there

ⓘ **Tourism Prince George Visitor Information Centre** *1300 1st Ave; tel: (250) 562-3700 or (800) 668-7646; www.tourismpg.com, can book BC Ferries and VIA Rail. There is a second VIC at the junction of Hwys 16 and 97.*

Northern BC Tourism *303-1268 5th Ave, Prince George; tel: (250) 561-0432 or (800) 663-8843; www.northernbctravel.com*

Prince George is the primary transportation hub for northern BC. Air, rail and road routes headed north–south and east–west all cross at the junction of the Fraser and Nechako Rivers.

Air
Prince George Airport (YXS) *4141 Airport Rd, 10km south of downtown off Hwy 97 S; tel: (250) 963-2400; www.pgairport.ca.* Prince George is one of the busiest inland airports in BC, with frequent service from Vancouver and other major cities around the western side of North America. A shuttle bus and taxis serve down-town, or hire a car at the airport.

Rail
VIA Rail *1300 1st Ave; tel: (888) 842-7245; www.viarail.ca,* runs west to Prince Rupert and east to Jasper, Alberta, aboard the **Skeena**, which runs through the Skeena River Valley and through the Yellowhead Pass. The entire 1160km trip takes two days. **BC Rail** hauls freight

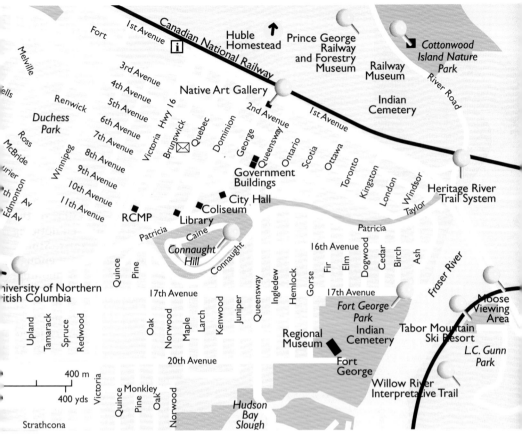

between Prince George and Vancouver, but has discontinued passenger service.

Road

Prince George sits at the junction of Hwys 97/16, two of Western Canada's most important highway corridors. Hwy 97 runs south to Hwy 1 and Vancouver and north to Dawson Creek, Fort Nelson and into Alaska. Hwy 16, the Yellowhead Highway, runs west to Prince Rupert (and, via ferry, to the Queen Charlotte Islands) and east through the Yellowhead Pass to Jasper, Alberta, and on to Eastern Canada.

Sights

Canfor Forestry Industry Tours
tel: (250) 561-5700;
www.canfor.com/1350.asp

Canfor Forestry Industry Tours*

Timber is the biggest industry in north central BC, as well as the industry with the most burdensome image problem. Many mills and forest operations offer free tours to show off their best side, and

Connaught Hill Park *Centre of town, off Queensway St, vehicles prohibited in winter.*

Cottonwood Island Nature Park *Off River Road, 2km northeast from downtown.*

Fort George Park $ *17th Ave and Taylor Dr.*

Fort George Railway $ *Fort George Park; tel: (250) 564-4764. Operates weekends and holidays May–Sept.*

Below
Fort George Railway

require advance tour bookings. This major Canadian lumber company offers year-round tours of operations around Prince George, including a tree nursery, pulp and paper mill, and sawmill.

Connaught Hill Park✦✦✦

This volcanic plug overlooking downtown has become one of the most popular parks in Prince George for its easy walking trails and 360-degree views. The park is most crowded at noontime in good weather when workers from city offices flock to the summit for an outdoor lunch and to admire floral displays.

Cottonwood Island Nature Park✦✦✦

Look for a variety of migratory birds in this 32-hectare wildlife reserve skirting the Nechako River just west of its confluence with the Fraser.

Fort George Park✦✦

Fort George was the name Simon Fraser gave to the small post he built over the winter of 1807–8, located on today's riverside park site. The park also holds the traditional burial grounds for the Lheidle T'enneh First Nations. Nearby South Fort George was the head of navigation on the upper Fraser River where paddlewheel steamboats unloaded cargo and passengers well into the 20th century.

The park has become a well-loved family playground, in large part thanks to the **Fort George Railway✦✦✦**. The narrow-gauge railway opened in 1978, but the 1912 six-tonne Davenport 0-4-0 Locomotive engine, a dinky in railway terminology, was used to build the Grand Trunk Pacific Railway Line. The station is modelled on one of GTP's standard designs that was used for more than 200 stations across BC and Alberta. Most of the original stations were built on the north side of the tracks in order to maximise sun and warmth on the south-facing platforms and block frigid winds from the north and west.

Fraser-Fort George Regional Museum $$ *Fort George Park, 333 Becott Pl; tel: (250) 562-1612 or (866) 562-1612; www. theexplorationplace.com. Open daily May–Oct 1000–1700; Nov–Apr Wed–Sun.*

Heritage River Trail System *Along the Nechako and Fraser rivers.*

Huble Homestead Historic Site – Giscome Portage Regional Park $ *Mitchell Rd off Hwy 97, 40km north of Prince George; tel: (250) 564-7033; http://parks.rdffg.bc.ca/ Giscome.html. Open daily mid-May–Labour Day.*

Moose Viewing Area *Hwy 16, 29km east from Prince George. Car park is on the north side of the highway.*

Native Art Gallery *1600 3rd Ave; tel: (250) 614-7726; www.pgnfc.com. Open daily.*

Prince George Railway and Forestry Museum $ *850 River Rd (next to Cottonwood Park); tel: (250) 563-7351; www.pgrfm.bc.ca. Open daily May–Sept.*

Sugarbowl-Grizzly Den Provincial Park & Protected Area *Hwy 16, 95km southeast of Prince George; http://wlapwww.gov.bc.ca/ bcparks/explore/parkpgs/ sugar.htm*

Also in the park, the **Fraser-Fort George Regional Museum** has a hands-on science centre for children as well as exhibits concentrating on local transportation from dugout canoes to modern railways, and a SimEx Theatre where seats move as the film action gets exciting.

Heritage River Trail System

An 11-km loop of broad gravel trails follows the Nechako River from the Cameron Street Bridge east around Cottonwood Island Park, past the confluence of the Fraser River and south to Fort George Park. The trail turns inland along Hudson Bay Slough, then cuts through town to Carrie Jane Gray Park. Follow Carney Street N back to the Cameron Street overpass.

Huble Homestead – Giscome Portage Regional Park

A vital roadhouse in the early years of the 20th century, the Homestead stood at the south end of the Giscome Portage, which connects the Arctic and Pacific watersheds over the Continental Divide. The homestead declined in importance after a 1919 road cut the portage out of commercial transportation routes. Costumed interpreters provide guided tours of the homestead and trading post.

Moose Viewing Area

A forest fire in 1961 turned Grover Forest into rolling meadows filled with the kind of tender new growth that moose love to browse. The best views are from a raised platform an easy five-minute walk from the car park.

Native Art Gallery

This is the best (but not the only) selection of both Interior and Coastal First Nations art products in the area.

Prince George Railway and Forestry Museum

Heaven for steam buffs, the museum celebrates the history of the GTP (now part of the Canadian National Railway) and the Pacific Great Eastern (now part of BC Rail). The site shows a restored section house, GTP's 1914 Penny Station, a railway worker's bunkhouse, an early BC Telephone building and a heritage fire hall. Rolling stock includes a 1903 Russell snow plough and a 1913 CPR steam crane, both in working order.

Sugarbowl-Grizzly Den Provincial Park & Protected Area

Hikers can park by trailheads along Hwy 16, to enter a wilderness area where caribou and grizzly bears are protected amid forests of old growth interior cedar-hemlock. Cross-country skiers use the same ungroomed trails in winter. In 1862, one group of Overlanders suffered hypothermia, overturned canoes, loss of provisions and death when they encountered the Grand Canyon of the Fraser here on their attempt to use the river to reach Quesnel.

 **Tabor Mountain Ski Resort $$** *Off Hwy 16, 20km east from Prince George; tel: (250) 963-7542.*

Two Rivers Gallery $ *725 Civic Plaza; tel: (250) 614-7800 or (888) 221-1155; www. tworiversartgallery.com. Open Tue–Wed Fri–Sat 1000–1700, Thur to 2100 (free 1500–2100), Sun 1200–1700.*

University of Northern British Columbia *3333 University Way; tel: (250) 960-5620; www.unbc.ca*

Willow River Interpretative Trail *Hwy 16, 34km east from Prince George.*

Tabor Mountain Ski Resort✦✦✦

Tabor Mountain is Prince George's own ski hill, a 244m vertical drop with lifts and a busy day lodge.

Two Rivers Gallery✦✦

Prince George's biggest gallery space shows touring exhibitions as well as local and regional artists. The striking civic centre building is worth a visit just for the exterior and crest (totem) pole.

University of Northern British Columbia✦✦

Canada's newest autonomous university has planted its futuristic campus atop Cranbrook Hill, overlooking Prince Rupert from the south. Choose from a self-guided indoor tour that weaves through the main buildings all year or an outdoor walk better taken in summer than in winter.

Willow River Interpretative Trail✦✦✦

The Canadian Institute of Forestry has created an excellent series of forest and streamside walking trails that explore several different hardwood, softwood and stream habitats. Allow between 45 minutes and 2 hours for the signed trails.

Accommodation and food

The University and a booming economy have given Prince George a better selection of accommodation and restaurants than might be expected in the middle of the northern forests.

Alekos Greek Taverna $$ *1232 4th Ave; tel: (250) 562-8661*, brings an authentic taste of Greece with superb service to Northern BC.

Coast Inn of the North $$$ *770 Brunswick St; tel: (250) 563-0121 or (800) 663-1144; www.coasthotel.com*, is the best hotel in town.

Credo Manor $$ *6872 O'Grady Road; tel: (250) 964-8142*, is a quiet, comfortable bed and breakfast near the University campus.

Downtown Motel $$ *650 Dominion St; tel: (250) 563-9241 or (800) 663-5729*, is just a block from the civic centre.

Pastry Chef Bakery $ *380 George St; tel: (250) 564-7034*, Prince George's oldest bakery, uses no preservatives and bakes everything from scratch.

Ramada Hotel Prince George $$ *444 George St; tel: (250) 563-0055 or (800) 830-8833; www.ramadaprincegeorge.com*, is a large city centre hotel.

Ric's Grill $$$ *547 George St; tel: (250) 614-9096; www.ricsgrill.com*, specialises in premium quality steak, but offers a wide menu selection.

Shogun Japanese Restaurant $$$ *770 Brunswick St (Coast Inn of the North); tel: (25) 563-0121*, serves sushi and teppan dishes.

Suggested tour

Total distance: 260km.

Time: Allow 1 long day or 2 days for easier sightseeing.

Links: From Prince George, the **Yellowhead Hwy** (*see page 214*) links with **Prince Rupert** (*see page 206*) to the west and the **BC Rockies** (*see page 258*) to the east. To the south, Hwy 16 links to the **Gold Rush Trail** (*see page 186*) at Quesnel.

Route: This circular tour runs north to one of the only waterfalls in north-central BC, through forest and muskeg (bog) to Fort St James and back to Prince Rupert along the Yellowhead Highway.

Take Hwy 97 north through pastoral farmlands to the **Salmon River**. About 36km north of Prince George is a marked side-road to the **HUBLE HOMESTEAD ❶** and **Giscome Portage Trail**. The homestead was established in 1904 as a waystation for travellers crossing the Arctic–Pacific Continental Divide. Waterways north of the divide, which runs between **Teapot Mountain** and **SUMMIT LAKE ❷**, 15km north, flow into the Arctic Ocean; waterways south of the divide flow into the Pacific.

At **Bear Lake**, head west on the Davie Bear Forest Service Road, an excellent gravel road that leads to the **CROOKED RIVER PROVINCIAL PARK ❸** and beyond. The meandering river was a major transport route for the Sekanni and other First Nations, as well as Alexander Mackenzie, Simon Fraser and other explorer/traders. The many lakes, rivers and streams support a wide variety of wildlife, from Canada geese, loons, blue-winged teal, ospreys, bald eagles and hawks to bears, beavers, muskrats, moose and deer. **Fisher Lake** and **Merton Lake** have particularly scenic picnic and camping sites.

Logging roads offer clear views of logging practices, including clearcuts, in which broad swaths of forest are stripped of all trees. The logged areas may be replanted or left to regenerate naturally, but either way end up looking like a disaster zone for decades. The one useful effect is to reveal the landforms hidden by dense forest. Just past the Weedon Forest Service Road (Road 300) is an area of long narrow ridges formed during the last Ice Age, around 10,000 years ago, when glaciers a kilometre thick covered this northern plateau.

The road forks just west of the **Muskeg River**. Take the south fork (1500 Road) to continue the tour. The north fork, Davie Muskeg Forest Service Road, leads 7km to **Muskeg Falls**. A short, easy trail leads from the car park to the 20-m falls, one of the few waterfalls that has developed in the area since the glaciers retreated.

The tour continues to the south end of **GREAT BEAVER LAKE ❹**, one of the most scenic lakes in the area accessible by road. Continue west, past the **MURRAY RIDGE SKI HILL ❺** to a logging truck weighing station. Take the sharp turn south to **FORT ST JAMES ❻** (*see page 216*) and Hwy 27. Follow Hwy 27 south to Hwy 16, the Yellowhead Hwy, just west of **VANDERHOOF ❼**, and turn left (east) back to Prince George.

Gravel road precautions

Some public highways are part-paved, part-gravel, while other major roads, including Forest Service roads and logging roads, are entirely gravel. Gravel roads important enough to be shown on highway and tourist maps are well maintained, but require special driving precautions, particularly in areas with active logging.

Logging trucks and other industrial vehicles *always* have the right of way. Most are equipped with radios.

In an active logging area, try to follow a log truck so the driver can notify oncoming traffic. Don't follow so close as to choke on dust, but don't fall back so far the driver loses sight of you.

Don't pass a logging truck unless the driver signals you to go around.

If a logging truck pulls over beside the road and stops, you should, too – there's almost certainly another truck headed your way along a section of road too narrow for two vehicles to pass safely.

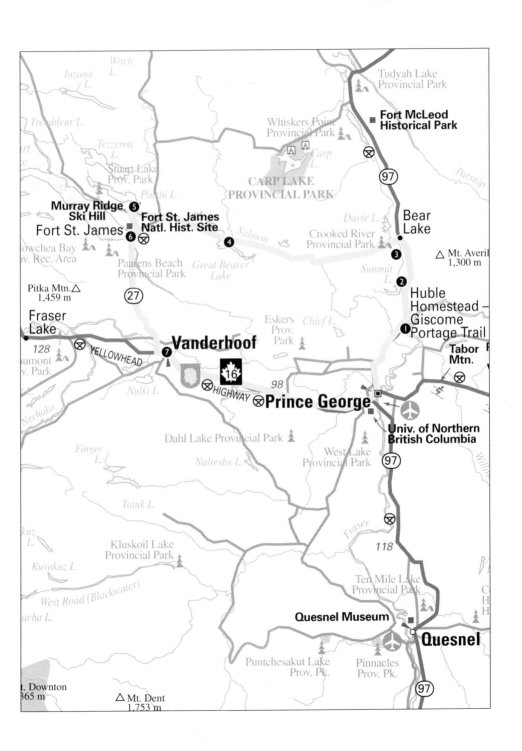

Columbia River

Ratings

Mountains	●●●●●
National parks	●●●●●
Nature	●●●●●
Scenery	●●●●●
Outdoor activities	●●●●○
Children	●●●○○
Geology	●●●○○
History	●●●○○

Subtly, the long and mighty Columbia River begins its much-dammed and thwarted route 2044km to the Pacific Ocean from Columbia Lake, a long but unprepossessing body of water visible from a lay-by along Hwy 93/95. Bird migration along the Columbia Valley is awesome in spring and autumn; migration of humans over one of the world's snowiest mountain areas at Rogers Pass is almost as awe-inspiring because of the sheer technical skill it takes to keep the pass open against avalanche.

While Parks Canada wages 'snow wars', this is railway country, from the hub at Golden at the north end of the Columbia Valley to Revelstoke west of the Selkirk Mountains along the fast-flowing Columbia River, west of Golden over Rogers Pass. Glaciers, old-growth cedars and wild-flower meadows lie in between the two towns, each claiming the distinction of Gateway to the Columbia.

CANAL FLATS❖

ⓘ **Kootenay Rockies**
*1905 Warren Ave,
Kimberley;
tel: (250) 427-4838;
www.kootenayrockies.com*

**Canal Flats Provincial
Park** *south end of Columbia
Lake; http://wlapwww.gov.bc.
ca/bcparks/explore/parkpgs/
canal.htm*

 **Doug Up Bonz**
Look for skeleton
sculptures on the east side
of Hwy 95 at Canal Flats.
Doug's a skilled bone and
fossil finder with a gift for
sculpture and humour.

There is a small lumbering community here, but the area's claim to fame is twofold: the Kootenay River and the source of the Columbia River in Columbia Lake, separated only by 2km of land (they actually join at Castlegar, *see page 241*), and an 1889 canal built to divert Kootenay River water away from valley farms. Too narrow locks were the canal's downfall. The *North Star*, only the second vessel to pass through, wrecked the locks and system in 1902. (**Canal Flats** *historic point, Hwy 93/95 at south end of Columbia Lake.*) The tiny, 6ha **Canal Flats Provincial Park** is a mecca for windsurfers.

WELCOME TO
CANAL FLATS
SOURCE OF THE MIGHTY COLUMBIA

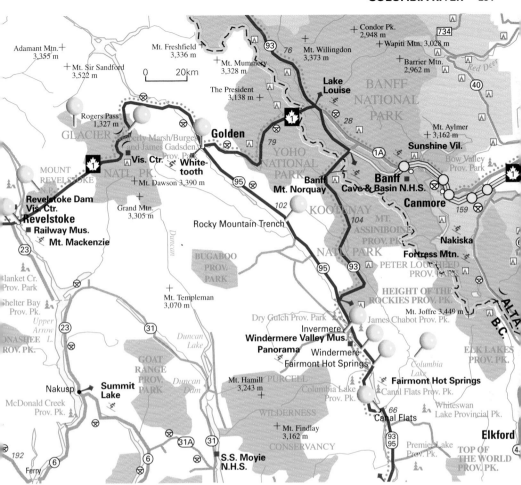

COLUMBIA LAKE❖

Columbia Lake
South of Fairmont Hot Springs on the east side of Hwy 93/95.

Look for a lay-by on the east side of Hwy 93/95 and a sign announcing 'Columbia Lake–Source of Columbia River Which Empties into Pacific Ocean at Astoria-Oregon', that is, 2044km southwest of the headwaters! Spiky golden hoodoos (eroded columns of rock) rise sheer above Dutch Creek at the lake's north end.

FAIRMONT HOT SPRINGS❖

Here you can soak in the 43°–48°C odourless hot springs, Canada's largest natural hot pools, long used by Ktunaxa (Kootenay) peoples. From several vantage points, including the Mountainside Golf Course, the forest-bound resort looks westward to the craggy line of the Purcell

Fairmont Hot Springs $$ *Fairmont Hot Springs Resort off Hwy 93/95; tel: (250) 345-6311 or (800) 663-4979; www.fairmonthotsprings.com.* Open year-round with a **Ski Hill $$**.

Hot Pools $ *Open daily 0800–1000.*

Mountainside Golf Course $$$ *Tel: (250) 345-6514 or (800) 663-4979,* one of two 18-hole courses, offering magnificent views over the Columbia River Valley. *Open mid-Mar–late Oct.*

Mountain Range. Hiking, biking, horse riding and winter downhill skiing and snowboarding supplement the pools' attraction for the RVers, lodge guests and another 750,000 visitors who make an annual pilgrimage to the resort.

Where there's a will

Ornery Major A B Rogers, described by Parks Canada as 'short, sharp and rough-tongued', was driven to find a pass over the Rockies suitable for a railway. In 1881, he tried the pass's west side, and 'Many a time I wished myself dead.' In 1882, he approached from the east and 'felt like a piece of liver'. He had found a viable pass through the mountains. The impetus? The CPR had promised to name the pass after him and paid a $5000 bonus. In ornery style he never cashed the cheque.

GOLDEN*

Golden & District Chamber of Commerce Visitor InfoCentre *500 N 10th Ave; tel: (250) 344-7125 or (800) 622-4653; www. goldenchamber.bc.ca. Open daily.*

Kicking Horse Resort $$$ *13 km west from Golden, 1500 Kicking Horse Trail; tel: (250) 439-5400 or (866) 754-5425; www. kickinghorseresort.com*

Trains, lorries, rivers, an active sawmill, tourists and outdoor enthusiasts (hang-gliders, rock climbers, whitewater kayakers and rafters, mountain bikers, hikers and anglers) all use Golden as a convenient valley-floor base. Here is the confluence of the Columbia and Kicking Horse rivers and access to Yoho National Park (*see page 264*) or Glacier National Park (*see below*). Mountains rise along both sides of the valley, causing spectacular sunsets over the Purcells, a drama much needed in this rather pedestrian service centre.

Accommodation and food in Golden

Golden Rim Motor Inn $$ *1416 Golden View Rd; tel: (250) 344-2216;* has views of the Columbia River Valley.

Kicking Horse Resort is west of Golden off Hwy 1, an all-year mountain resort with winter skiing down a 1280-m vertical, the second longest in Canada, or hiking and mountain biking the same slopes in summer. More than half of the ski runs are either expert or advanced. At any time, it's worth a ride up the mountain just for the panorama from **The Eagle's Eye**, the highest restaurant in Canada at 2335m.

Legendz $ *1405 W TransCanada Hwy; tel: (250) 344-5059,* serves delicious steak and creamy eggs, with other Marilyn Monroe and James Dean era specialities.

Sportsman Lodge $ *1200 12th St N; tel: (250) 344-2915 or (888) 989-5566; http://sportsmanlodge.ca,* is quiet and away from the highway.

GLACIER NATIONAL PARK✦✦✦

ⓘ Glacier National Park $ *Mount Revelstoke and Glacier National Parks Headquarters, 300 3rd St W (Post Office Bldg); tel: (250) 837-7500; www.pc.gc.ca/pn-np/bc/ glacier/index_e.asp. Open Mon–Fri 0830–1200 1300–1630.*

Rogers Pass Centre *Rogers Pass; tel: (250) 837-7500. Open daily Apr–mid-Jun and Sept–Oct, 0900–1700; mid-Jun–Aug 0800–1900; Nov, Thu–Mon 0900–1700; Dec–Mar 0700–1700.*

Rogers Pass National Historic Site *69km east of Revelstoke, 72km west of Golden, on Hwy 1 in Glacier National Park.*

Below Glacier National Park

The northern Selkirk Mountain Range, the birthplace of North American technical climbing – mountaineering – in 1888, is a land of snow and around 400 active glaciers, including **Illecillewaet Glacier,** visible from Hwy 1 on a clear day. Waterfalls and wild flowers are abundant in season. If travelling east, you will see 14.6-km Mount Macdonald Tunnel, North America's longest railway tunnel, built after hundreds died between 1885 and 1911 trying to keep the Rogers Pass open on the surface. A series of snowsheds protects traffic from avalanches as 'Snow Wars' keep Rogers Pass open in winter. The twin keys: constant monitoring and 105mm howitzers deployed to blast snow along avalanche paths.

Rogers Pass National Historic Site✦✦✦ Many peaks poke the sky at 3700m, catching shrouds of snow which avalanche dangerously below. Major A B Rogers, who discovered the 1382m pass, noted, 'Our eyesight caromed from one bold peak to another for miles in all directions. The wind blew fiercely across the ridge and scuddy clouds were whirled in eddies behind the great towering peaks of bare rock. Everything was covered with a shroud of white, giving the whole landscape the appearance of snow-clad desolation.' **Rogers Pass Centre** offers excellent explanations of the Snow Wars waged by the CPR and more currently by Parks Canada and the Royal Canadian Horse Artillery to keep the TransCanada Highway open. **Abandoned Rails Trail** follows Hwy 1 past side-paths and snowsheds 1.3km to the **Rogers Pass Monument**✦, which commemorates completion of the TransCanada Highway in 1962, the first alternative to rail transit over the pass.

Accommodation and food in Glacier National Park

Best Western Glacier Park Lodge $$$ *Rogers Pass; tel: (250) 837-2126; www.glacierparklodge.ca.* The only non-camping accommodation provides 50 rooms next to the Rogers Pass Centre, with a restaurant, 24-hour cafeteria and petrol station.

INVERMERE*

ⓘ Invermere Columbia Valley Chamber of Commerce Visitor InfoCentre *651 Hwy 93/95 Crossroads, Windermere; tel: (250) 342-2844; www. columbiavalleychamber.com. Open daily 0900–1700 summer, same hours Mon–Fri in winter.*

ⓘ James Chabot Provincial Park *North end of Windermere Lake; tel: (250) 422-3003; http://wlapwww.gov.bc.ca/ bcparks/explore/parkpgs/ james.htm*

At the northwest corner of Windermere Lake, the area's commercial centre south of Golden boasts September to October kokanee salmon spawning in its end of the 15km-long lake. Lakeside **James Chabot Provincial Park**** has a swimming beach, watersports and a 350-m boardwalk over the wetlands.

Opposite
Revelstoke

Right
Lake Windermere

MOBERLY MARSH/BURGES AND JAMES GADSDEN PROVINCIAL PARK*

ⓘ Moberly Marsh/ Burges and James Gadsden Provincial Park *West of Hwy 1 north of Golden; http://wlapwww. gov.bc.ca/bcparks/explore/ parkpgs/burges.htm*

Most drivers don't stop in the rush to and from Golden, but migratory waterfowl do along this stretch of Moberly Marsh between the TransCanada Hwy 1 and the Columbia River. Spot muskrats and ospreys from a 3.5-km riverbank **Dyke Trail**** in Burges and James Gadsden Provincial Park, which protects much of the marsh.

MOUNT REVELSTOKE NATIONAL PARK❖❖❖

Mount Revelstoke National Park $

Mount Revelstoke and Glacier National Parks Headquarters, 300 3rd St W (Post Office Bldg); tel: (250) 837-7500; www.pc.gc.ca/pn-np/bc/revelstoke/index_e.asp. Open Mon–Fri 0830–1200 1300–1630. Wardens at Meadows in the Sky Parkway have park information.

Giant Cedars Trail *1km west of east boundary of Mount Revelstoke National Park.*

Meadows in the Sky (Parkway) *3km east of Revelstoke in Mount Revelstoke National Park. Trailers are prohibited beyond the parkway trailer parking area 0.5km from Hwy 1.*

Unlike the Rockies National Parks, which were spurred on by the CPR and the need for an all-weather automobile route (Kootenay), this park was a result of the City of Revelstoke citizens' building a trail to the mountain's summit and lobbying for a road. That road, Meadows in the Sky Parkway, draws thousands of mid-summer visitors to the rich displays of wild flowers.

Giant Cedars Trail❖❖❖ Rainforest in the interior of BC? Eight-hundred-year-old Western red cedar trees along a 0.5-km boardwalk tell the tale. The damp, mossy streambed is dim, but vibrant with many hues of green. Virgin old-growth forest boasts standing cedars so thick with branches that little water falls through when it rains.

Meadows in the Sky❖❖❖ Stop at the elaborate archway Welcome Station entrance to the 26-km Meadows in the Sky Parkway for information. Depending on the severity of the past winter, the parkway may be closed part of the way up, even though the route is normally open early July to late September. Enjoy the winding, 16-switchback drive past fine views of Revelstoke and the Columbia River. Waterfalls plummet off rock walls covered with ferns and greenery as the parkway rises through forests of cedar, hemlock, fir and spruce. Park at Balsam Lake and take the Summit Shuttle to the wild-flower meadows or hike the colourful carpet by way of the 1-km Summit Trail to an historic fire tower at the top.

Revelstoke Viewpoint

Belvédère Revelstoke

REVELSTOKE✦

Revelstoke Chamber of Commerce Visitor Info Centre *204 Campbell Ave; tel: (250) 837-5345 or (800) 487-1493; www.seerevelstoke.com*

Snow sports *www.seerevelstoke.com/snow*

Piano Keep Gallery *117 Campbell Ave; tel: (250) 837-6554.*

Revelstoke Dam *4km north of Revelstoke; (in season) tel: (250) 814-6698, after Labour Day–late May (250) 814-6600; www. bchydro.com/recreation/ southern/southern1205.html. Open late May–Labour Day.*

Revelstoke Railway Museum $ *719 Track St West; tel: (250) 837-6060 or (877) 837-6060; www.railwaymuseum.com. Open daily Jul–Aug, 0900–2000; May, Jun, Sept, 0900–1700; Apr, Oct, Mon–Sat 0900–1700; Nov, Mon–Fri 0900–1700; Dec–Mar, Mon–Fri 1300–1700.*

No one seems to know why there are bear statues and signs everywhere in this railway hub and recreation centre in the middle of the Selkirk and Monashee Mountains. Ask and the answer is there are lots of bears around here. Trains constantly roll, click and grind through town. **Grizzly Plaza**✦ *(Mackenzie Ave, Victoria Rd and First St)* is the venue for nightly concerts in July and August. Rail and Columbia River transportation propelled Revelstoke into existence in the 1880s. The Chamber of Commerce has *Heritage Walking & Driving* and *Railway Heritage Driving Tour* brochures.

Think of the loveliest piano you've ever seen, then multiply the pleasure of the **Piano Keep Gallery**✦✦✦ dedicated to the instrument, from pre-Mozart harpsichords to modern concert grand pianos, all lovingly restored and equally lovingly explained.

BC Hydro operates **Revelstoke Dam**✦ and generating station, a must for those fascinated by waterway engineering and the intricacies of changes to the Columbia River. Get an individual talking wand at the entrance for a self-guiding tour through the two-storey visitor centre atop the powerhouse. Take a lift 175m up to the top crest of the dam and look both up and downstream.

It's not large, but the **Revelstoke Railway Museum**✦✦ is a good introduction to the challenges faced by CPR engineers and officials who encountered avalanches, difficult soil, steep grades, harsh winters and labour strife while constructing and maintaining the railway. Prized are Business Car No 4 and Mikado P-2k class locomotive No 5468, on display in a replica of Victoria's E&N Roundhouse.

Right
Revelstoke Railway Museum

Accommodation and food in Revelstoke

Many Revelstoke motels are near the noisy railway track at the west end of town.

Canyon Motor Inn $$ *1911 Fraser Dr, off Hwy 1 at Columbia River Bridge; tel: (250) 837-5221 or (877) 837-5221*, has small, very clean rooms in a quiet spot near the river.

Chalet Bakery $ *415B Victoria St; tel: (250) 837-4556*, makes European-style breads and pastries.

Frisby Ridge Teriyaki Restaurant $$ *201A 1st St W; tel: (250) 837-5449*, is one of the best few Japanese restaurants in the BC mountains.

Regent Inn $$ *112 E. 1st St; tel: (250) 837-2107 or (888) 245-5523; www.regentinn.com*, in a downtown heritage building, offers mountain bikes for hotel guests' use.

Tony's Roma Restaurant $$ *306 Mackenzie Ave; tel: (250) 837-4106*, presents huge, tasty portions of Italian specialities.

Woolsey Creek Café $ *212 Mackenzie Ave; tel: (250) 837-5500*, has delicious breakfast blueberry cornmeal and apple rhubarb muffins, and wraps and sandwiches for lunch.

ROCKY MOUNTAIN TRENCH*

Rocky Mountain Trench dividing the Rocky and Cascade Mountain Ranges from Alaska to the central USA has the Columbia River at its bottom in this area.

Astronauts say this depression between mountain ranges which extends from Alaska along the western side of the Rocky Mountains into the central US is one of the most prominent features on Earth. The rift valley separates ancient Columbia Mountains from the craggier, younger Rocky Mountains on the eastern side, with lush wetlands and cultivated farmland in between.

WINDERMERE*

St Peter's Anglican Church *Kootenay St; tel: (250) 342-6644.*

The town and its namesake lake are a resort getaway for locals, windsurfers and people from colder climes. **St Peter's Anglican Church*** was stolen in 1897, removed via a railway flatcar from Donald, 210km north, by residents who wanted a ready-made church when most Donald inhabitants moved to Revelstoke along with the CPR operations.

Suggested tour

Total distance: 310km.

Time: 2 days.

Links: South of Canal Flats on Hwy 93/95 to **The Crowsnest** (*see page 250*). At Radium Junction, go east to Kootenay National Park, or at Golden go east to Yoho National Parks in **BC Rockies Parks** (*see page 258*). At Revelstoke, continue west on Hwy 1 to the **Shuswap Lakes** (*see page 158*).

Route: From CANAL FLATS ❶, travel north through the **ROCKY MOUNTAIN TRENCH** ❷ on Hwy 93/95 along the west side of **COLUMBIA LAKE** ❸, headwaters of the **Columbia River**. The wetlands that begin here are amongst the most extensive and richest on earth, 26,000 hectares of protected space. From Canal Flats to **Donald**, north of Golden, is the least-developed section along the Columbia River. Beyond Columbia Lake's north end are the **Dutch Creek Hoodoos** looming mysteriously on the left, and **FAIRMONT HOT SPRINGS** ❹, for soaking, swimming, golfing, hiking and winter skiing with views of the Purcell Mountains to the west above the valley floor. North is **Windermere Lake**, which has **INVERMERE** ❺ on the west side and **WINDERMERE** ❻ along the highway side.

ⓘ Columbia Valley Chamber of Commerce Visitor InfoCentre *651 Hwy 93/95 Crossroads, Windermere; tel: (250) 342-2844; www. columbiavalleychamber.com. Open daily 0900–1700 summer, same hours Mon–Fri in winter.*

At **Radium Junction**, Hwy 93 splits off east from Hwy 95 to Radium Hot Springs in Kootenay National Park. Hwy 95 continues north along the Columbia River Valley to **GOLDEN** ❼, at the junction of Hwy 95 and TransCanada Hwy 1 from Yoho National Park.

Continue north on Hwy 1 past **BURGES AND JAMES GADSDEN PROVINCIAL PARK** ❽ at **MOBERLY MARSH** ❾ and **Donald**, where the CPR line first crossed the Columbia River.

Enter **GLACIER NATIONAL PARK** ❿. **Beaver Valley** has a lovely picnic spot, and wild flowers in summer. Tunnels covering the TransCanada Hwy are snowsheds, built to deflect the hideous impact of avalanches. **Rogers Pass Centre** has a roaring fire, excellent exhibit and film depictions of avalanche control and snow management, and a well-stocked bookshop. One kilometre south is the **Rogers Pass Monument** arch to the 1962 TransCanada Highway completion. The **Illecillewaet Glacier** campground and trailhead to a series of trails near the glacier are accessible from Hwy 1, not far south of the monument.

There's a 16-km gap between park boundaries. Almost immediately upon entering **MOUNT REVELSTOKE NATIONAL PARK** ⓫, stop and take the short 0.5-km **Giant Cedars Trail** for a view of BC rain forest. In May, walk the 1.2-km **Skunk Cabbage Trail** for views of the odiferous plants flowering yellow along the **Illecillewaet River**. The park's jewel is the **Meadows in the Sky Parkway**, a 42-km drive to **Balsam Lake** parking and a 2-km shuttle ride or walk to Mount Revelstoke's summit, carpeted with wild flowers in mid-summer.

Opposite
Mount Revelstoke Mountain
Meadows in the sky

Descending quickly from the park, enter **REVELSTOKE** ⓬ to visit the Revelstoke Railway Museum, Revelstoke Dam and the amazing collection at Piano Keep Gallery.

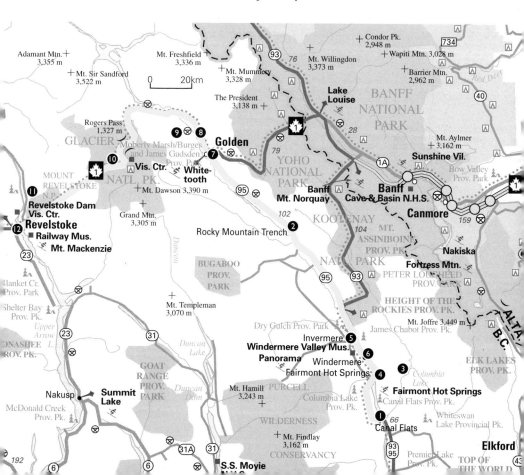

The Kootenays

Ratings

Geology	●●●●●
History	●●●●●
Mountains	●●●●●
Children	●●●●○
Outdoor activities	●●●●○
Parks	●●●●○
Architecture	●●●○○
First Nations	●●○○○

This region takes in the West Kootenays through the Purcell, Selkirk and Monashee Ranges, heaven for lovers of rugged mountains and lakes. Linked by just one highway, which follows the first track hacked from Hope to Fort Steele during the 1860s, Southern BC is more vertical than horizontal. What little flat space exists between mountain ranges is filled with water more often than not.

Ghost towns abound, no surprise in a region best known for mineral rushes in search of gold, copper, silver and lead, as do smelter ruins, decaying mine shafts and long-abandoned graveyards slowly disappearing beneath encroaching forests.

The future is as bright as the past. Urban professionals from across Canada have transformed one-time backwaters into modern enclaves surrounded by splendid opportunities for boating, hiking, fishing, skiing and other outdoor recreation.

AINSWORTH HOT SPRINGS❖❖

Ⓘ Ainsworth Hot Springs Resort $$
Hwy 31, 36km north from Balfour; tel: (250) 229-4212 or (800) 668-1171; www.hotnaturally.com

The hot springs flow from a stalactite-filled cave. Spa aficionados swear by the water, which has the highest mineral content of any natural hot springs in Canada. Everyone else swears by the stunning views across Kootenay Lake from the 45°C outdoor baths.

BOUNDARY CREEK PROVINCIAL PARK❖❖

Ⓘ Boundary Creek Provincial Park
Hwy 3, just west from Greenwood; tel: (250) 494-6500; http://wlapwww.gov. bc.ca/bcparks/explore/ parkpgs/boundary.htm. Open late May–Oct.

A slag heap and crumbling chimney are all that remain of the largest single producer of copper in the world between 1901 and 1918. The park also has pleasant camping and picnicking spots along Boundary Creek.

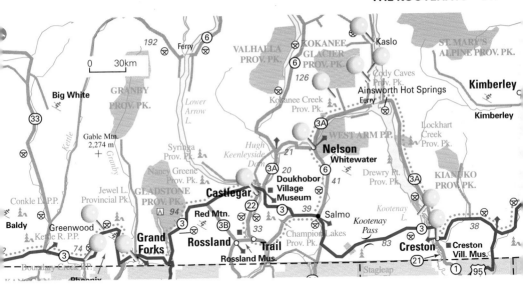

CASTLEGAR✣

ℹ Chamber of Commerce *1995 6th Ave; tel: (250) 365-6313; www.castelgar.com*

ℹ BC Hydro Hugh Keenleyside Dam *8km north of Castlegar; tel: (250) 365-3115; www.bchydro.com/recreation/southern/southern1202.html. Open Mon–Fri for self-tours.*

Brilliant Suspension Bridge National Heritage Site *Base of Airport Hill. Park at the south end of the new Kootenay River Bridge and walk 500m down the old highway.*

Castlegar Museum $ *400 13th Ave; tel: (250) 365-6440. Open Mon–Sat 0900–1700.*

Doukhobor Village Museum $ *112 Heritage Way, across from the Castlegar Airport; tel: (250) 365-6622; www.doukhobor-museum.org. Open daily May–Sept 1000–1800.*

Castlegar grew as a railway and mining town at the confluence of the Kootenay and Columbia rivers. Odorous fumes still waft from a pulp mill just below **BC Hydro Hugh Keenleyside Dam✣**, which backs the Columbia into Arrow Lakes, stretching 230km north to Revelstoke (*see page 236*). Doukhobor farms added an important agricultural element to the economy.

When local authorities ignored requests for a bridge across the Kootenay River, the Doukhobors (*see page 242*) designed and built their own span in 1913, which carried Hwy 3 traffic for decades. It forms part of the **Brilliant Suspension Bridge National Heritage Site✣✣✣**.

Castlegar Museum✣, an old CPR station, concentrates on area history from the early days of the 20th century.

Doukhobor Village Museum✣✣✣ is a reproduction of a typical village and includes the communal main house, cottages and workrooms. The furnishings, photographs and artworks are authentic, as are the costumed guides who explain traditional Doukhobor life and beliefs.

The small river island which forms **Zuckerberg Island Heritage Park✣✣✣** was named for a local Russian teacher who built an onion-dome home in the forest. Zuckerberg's home has been restored as a museum and tea room.

Accommodation and food in Castlegar

Best Western Fireside Inn $$ *1810 8th Ave; tel: (250) 365-2128; www.bestwestern.com*, is convenient and central.

Zuckerberg Island Heritage Park *9th St and 7th Ave; tel: (250) 365-5511. Open May–Aug.*

Common Grounds $ *692 18th St (Castleaird Pl); tel: (250) 365-3883,* is good for light meals and an Internet check.

Flamingo Motel $ *1660 Columbia Ave; tel: (250) 365-7978; www.rockies-bc.com/flamingo,* has a park-like setting.

The Doukhobors

The name means 'spirit wrestlers' in Russian. It's an apt name for a group of rabid pacifists who lived by the motto 'Toil and a Peaceful Life'. They successfully resisted the Russian Tsars only to be rent by internal divisions and bomb blasts.

Spiritual leader Peter Verigin led the Doukhobors to Canada, eventually settling on flat land across the Columbia River from Castlegar in 1908. Initially ignored by colonial authorities, the Doukhobors built many of the earliest bridges in Boundary Country, including the graceful Brilliant Suspension Bridge over the Kootenay River. About two dozen villages eventually filled *Ootischenia*, the 'Valley of Consolation', most of which is now occupied by Castlegar's airport and golf course.

The new immigrants planted orchards, grain and vegetables while building sawmills, jam factories, pipe works and similar enterprises, but their communal living arrangements, outspoken pacifism and vocal opposition to meat, tobacco and alcohol won few friends locally.

Verigin was killed by a bomb blast in 1924, almost certainly planted by a faction who feared that he was leading the community into mainstream Canadian society. The Doukhobors, along with Hutterites and other communal religious groups, eventually ran foul of laws designed to break up their tightly knit communities. Communal villages have disappeared, but thousands of Doukhobors still live in Boundary Country from Castlegar to Grand Forks. Many of their distinctive farm buildings are still visible along country roads, and Russian restaurants – invariably Doukhobor – are local institutions.

CODY CAVES PROVINCIAL PARK❖

Except for a few ladders, the rugged cave looks much as Henry Cody, an early prospector, first saw it a century ago. Open for guided tours only. Paths snake through forests of stalactites, stalagmites and soda straws. (**Cody Caves Provincial Park** $$ *North of Ainsworth Hot Springs; tel: (250) 353-7425; http://wlapwww.gov.bc.ca/bcparks/explore/parkpgs/codycaves.htm. Open Jul–Aug 1000–1600, guided tours only.*)

CRESTON ❖❖

ℹ **Creston and District Chamber of Commerce** *1711 Canyon St (Hwy 3); tel: (250) 428-4342; www.crestonbc.com and www.crestonvalley.com*

🏛 **Creston Valley Museum and Archives** *$ 219 Devon St; tel: (250) 428-9262; www.creston.museum.bc.ca. Open daily mid-May–mid-Sept.*

Creston Valley Wildlife Centre *$ Hwy 3, 10km west from Creston; tel: (250) 402-6900; www.crestonwildlife.ca. Open daily mid-May–Aug 0900–1700; Wed–Sun Sept–Oct 0900–1600.*

A small farming town overlooks a plain where the Kootenay River once sprawled between the Purcell and Selkirk Mountains. The river has been dyked and channelled, creating fertile grain fields. Creston's rural past appears on murals in the town centre.

Highlight of the **Creston Valley Museum and Archives**❖ is a replica of a traditional Kootenay canoe, a 'sturgeon-nosed' craft with ends pointing down into the water.

Creston Valley Wildlife Centre❖❖❖, the interpretation centre for the 7000-hectare Creston Valley Wildlife Management Area, offers guided canoe tours ($) of one of BC's richest wetland areas, also walking trails and educational displays. The area has the largest concentration of nesting ospreys in North America as well as massive bird migrations spring and autumn.

Accommodation and food in Creston

Downtowner Motor Inn $$ *1218 Canyon St; tel: (250) 428-2238 or (800) 665-9904*, is central.

Garden Bakery $ *1218 Canon St; tel: (250) 428-2740; www.crestonvalley.com/gardenbakery*, has homemade soup, sandwiches and a huge selection of cookies, cakes, tarts and pastries.

Rendezvous Restaurant $$ *1230 Canyon St; tel: (250) 428-9554*, has the best steaks.

Valley View Motel $ *216 Valleyview Dr.; tel: (250) 428-2336; www.crestonvalley.com/valleyviewmotel*, has cosy cabins near the Creston Valley Museum.

GRAND FORKS ❖❖❖

An agricultural enclave at the junction of the Kettle Valley and Granby rivers, Grand Forks boomed with the 1900 opening of the Granby Smelter. The smelter closed in 1919, but the glistening mountain of ebony-coloured slag off Granby Road, just north of town, remains.

Right
Creston Valley Wildlife Centre

Boundary Museum** houses artefacts from First Nations to Doukhobors, miners and railways. See the overview, then take a **self-guided tour**♦♦♦ of some of the 300-plus heritage buildings from the mining and railway era with a free museum map.

Mountain View Doukhobor Museum♦♦♦, in a 1912 Doukhobor communal home, overflows with period artefacts and records. Many other Doukhobor buildings are visible along Hardy Mountain Road as it twists back to Hwy 3.

The **Phoenix Forest and History Tour**♦♦♦, a back-road route between Grand Forks and Greenwood, passes many of the former mines, towns and railways that made the Boundary rich in the early 20th century.

Accommodation and food in Grand Forks

Borscht Bowl $ *258 Market Ave; tel: (250) 442-5977*, serves an interesting combination of Doukhobor and Mexican.

Grand Forks Hotel Restaurant $$ *7382 2nd St; tel: (250) 442-5944*, runs a close second to Chef's Garden and also has non-vegetarian choices.

Grand Forks Motor Inn $$ *2729 Central Ave, Hwy 3, tel: (250) 442-2127*, is central.

Spencer's Chef's Garden $$ *4405 Hwy 3 5km south, near Hardy Mountain Rd; tel: (250) 442-0257*, is one of the best Doukhobor restaurants in BC, serving vegetarian Russian cuisine.

GREENWOOD**

Greenwood Museum $ 214 S Copper St (Hwy 3); tel: (250) 445-6355; www.greenwoodheritage.bc.ca. Open May–Jun and Sept–Oct 1000–1600, Jul–Aug 0900–1700.

Lotzkar Park $ Hwy 3, just south of town.

This booming mining town nearly died after the local mines closed, but was revived as a Japanese-Canadian internment camp during World War II. Some 20 historic buildings have been restored. **Greenwood Museum***** packs a major punch in its telling of the mining boom and Japanese internment days. The museum can point out locations where some *Snow Falling on Cedars* (1999) scenes were filmed using area extras.

At **Lotzkar Park****, the best-preserved smelter ruins in North America rise above a barren ridge of black smelter slag that once glowed red hot even at noon. Locals call it a 'corner of hell gone cold'.

KASLO***

Kaslo & District Chamber of Commerce 324 Front St by the SS Moyie; tel: (250) 353-2525. Open mid-May–mid-Oct.

Kaslo was a lumber town before silver and lead strikes brought miners flooding into the Kootenays. Tourism is number one today, thanks to 60 historic buildings and spectacular hiking, mountain biking, fishing, camping and boating.

The beached and meticulously restored *Moyie*, at the **SS Moyie National Historic Site*****, sailed Kootenay Lake until 1957, and was the last sternwheeler in regular passenger service in Canada (**$** *Front St; tel: (250) 353-2525; www.klhs.bc.ca; open daily mid-May–mid-Oct 0930–1700 for self-guiding tours*).

KOKANEE CREEK PROVINCIAL PARK***

Built on the site of a former lakeside estate, the park offers hiking, boating, camping, fishing and **Redfish Creek Spawning Channel*****, an artificial spawning channel for Kokanee salmon. Best time to see the bright-red fish is mid-August to mid-September. The park also shelters a major osprey population (*Hwy 3A, 20km northeast from Nelson; tel: (250) 825-4212; http://wlapwww.gov.bc.ca/bcparks/explore/parkpgs/kokanee.htm*).

KOOTENAY LAKE***

Kootenay Lake Chamber of Commerce Visitor Info Centre next to the Crawford Bay Airstrip; tel: (250) 227-9267; www.kootenaylake.bc.ca. Open in summer.

This long, narrow lake between the Purcell and Selkirk Mountains was a major navigation route long before it became a prime recreation area. Facilities lie along Hwy 3A, north from Creston to Kootenay Bay. There you can link to Balfour by Kootenay Lake Ferry, with more facilities along Hwy 3A west into Nelson.

Crawford Bay* on the east shore of Kootenay Lake is a collection of artisans producing metalwork, brooms and similar crafts, and home to

Kootenay Lake Ferry *tel: (250) 229-4215; www.kootenaylake.bc.ca/Ferry.shtml. Year-round, 35 minutes between Kootenay Bay and Balfour. Free.*

Kootenay Lake $ *North from Creston, west to Nelson.*

Crawford Bay *Hwy 3A, 78km north from Creston.*

Glass House $ *Hwy 3A, 25km north from Creston; tel: (250) 223-8372. Open May–Oct.*

Lockhart Beach Provincial Park $ *Hwy 3A, 40km north from Creston; tel: (250) 422-3003; http:// wlapwww.gov.bc.ca/bcparks/ explore/parkpgs/lock_beach. htm. Lockhart Creek Provincial Park http://wlapwww.gov.bc.ca/ bcparks/explore/parkpgs/ lockhart.htm*

Right
Wall mural depicting Steve Martin in *Roxanne*

Kokanee Springs Golf Course ($$ *tel: (250) 227-9226 or (800) 979-7999; www.kokaneesprings.com*).

Mortician David Brown built the **Glass House**❖❖, a scenic lakeside house, from 500,000 embalming fluid bottles in the 1950s, as he explained, 'to indulge a whim of a peculiar nature'.

There's excellent camping and hiking in **Lockhart Beach Provincial Park**❖❖ and the adjacent Lockhart Creek Provincial Park.

NELSON❖❖❖

This sparkling Victorian-era mining town was the set for Steve Martin's 1986 film *Roxanne*, a modern version of *Cyrano de Bergerac*. Local painters have enshrined Martin on a mural at the end of Vernon Street. Film publicity helped Nelson re-enforce its current incarnation as a rural refuge for urban professionals who expect high-speed Internet connections and the perfect *latte* after a tough day at the computer.

The imposing **courthouse**❖❖❖ and **city hall**❖❖❖ were designed by Francis Rattenbury, who built the Empress Hotel and Parliament Buildings in Victoria. Costumed guides from the Chamber of Commerce lead walking and driving tours of the town's 350 **heritage buildings**❖❖❖ in summer, or follow self-guiding maps in any season.

Nelson & District Chamber of Commerce 225 Hall St; tel: (250) 352-3433 or (877) 663-5706; www.discovernelson.com. Open daily. **Artwalk** 560 Baker St, Ste 5; tel: (250) 352-2402; www.ndac.kics.bc.ca/artwalk.htm

Chamber of Mines Eastern BC Museum $ 215 Hall St; tel: (250) 352-5242; www.mining.kootenays.bc.ca

Nelson Museum $ 402 Anderson Street; tel: (250) 352-9813; http://museum.kics.bc.ca. Open afternoons. Call in advance, as museum will move to historic City Hall in the future.

Lakeside Park Foot of the Nelson Bridge.

Streetcar No 23 $ Downtown to Lakeside Park, daily in summer, weekends Apr and autumn.

More than a dozen galleries stage monthly shows by 100 local artists. Maps of **Artwalk✦✦✦** are available at the InfoCentre.

The **Chamber of Mines Eastern BC Museum✦** has BC's biggest mineral collection. **Nelson Museum✦**, a strictly local collection, emphasises steamboats and mines.

Lakeside Park✦✦✦ is the most popular recreation area, with sandy beaches, canoe and boat rentals, lawns, playgrounds and greenhouse.

Streetcar No 23✦✦✦ is BC's only operating historic streetcar, making regular runs the length of the city along the lakeshore.

Accommodation and food in Nelson

All Seasons Café $$ *620 Herridge Lane; tel: (250) 352-0101; www.allseasonscafe.com*, offers outstanding Northwest cuisine and the best wine list in Nelson.

Heritage Inn $$ *422 Nelson St; tel: (250) 352-5331 or (877) 568-0888; www.heritageinn.org*, has been Nelson's landmark hotel since the 1890s.

Inn The Garden $$ *408 Victoria St; tel: (250) 352-3226 or (800) 596-2337; www.innthegarden.com*, is a cheerful bed and breakfast in an historic home.

Max & Irma's Kitchen $$ *515A Kootenay St; tel: (250) 352-2332; www.maxandirmaskitchen.com*, serves Nelson's best pizza and Italian dishes.

Rickaby's Restaurant $$$ *524 Vernon St; tel: (250) 354-1919; www.rickabys.ca*, one of the venues in *Roxanne*, serves a range from seafood stuffed portobello mushrooms to blackened chicken naan.

Suggested tour

Boundary Country Tourism tel: (866) 442-2833; www.boundary.bc.ca and **Explore the Kootenays** www.explorethekootenays.com offer web links to the entire Kootenay region.

Total distance: 300km.

Time: It's possible to drive from Creston to Greenwood in one long day, but 2–3 days allows time to enjoy and explore.

Links: The **Okanagan Valley** (*see page 148*) and the **Cascade Mountains** (*see page 130*) lie west from Greenwood on Hwy 3. To the east, Hwy 3 leads to **The Crowsnest** (*see page 250*) and the **BC Rockies** (*see page 258*).

Route: The direct route follows Hwy 3 125km west from Creston past the **Creston Valley Wildlife Centre** and into the **Selkirk Mountains** to 1774m **Kootenay Pass**, the highest paved highway pass in Canada.

The west side of Kootenay Pass twists and turns across five canyons and multiple avalanche chutes. Just west is **Burnt Flat Junction** and Hwy 31, which runs 10km south to the US border at **Nelway** (*open daily 0800–2400*).

Right
Ferry SS *Nasookin* converted to a house on the shores of Kootenay Lake

Hwy 3 turns north to **Salmo**, then west to **Bombi Summit**, 1214m, with a long descent to the **Columbia River** at Castlegar. The best view of the confluence of the Columbia and Kootenay rivers is from the **Ootischenia Lookout Rest Area**, 8km from the summit on the west side of the highway.

Scenic alternative: The more interesting 150-km route to Castlegar follows Hwy 3A north from Creston along the shores of **KOOTENAY LAKE ❶**, passing **Glass House, Lockhart Creek Provincial Park** and **Crawford Bay** on the way to the Kootenay Lake Ferry at Kootenay Bay. The 35-minute crossing to **Balfour** is free, but the line-up can take most of the day, especially in summer.

Detour: From Balfour, turn north on Hwy 31 to **AINSWORTH HOT SPRINGS ❷** and **CODY CAVES PROVINCIAL PARK ❸** on the way to **KASLO ❹**. The tiny village has more than 60 heritage buildings, including the SS *Moyie*, a sternwheeler that once carried passengers on the lake. Return to Balfour.

Hwy 3A hugs the north shore of the West Arm of Kootenay Lake. The south shore is all but inaccessible except by boat. The waters between hold record-sized trout and kokanee (land-locked) salmon. What looks like a steamboat cabin perched on the north side of the highway was the upper saloon and wheelhouse of the SS *Nasookin*, once the largest steamboat on Kootenay Lake. The road crosses the bright orange **Nelson Bridge** into **NELSON** ❺, a mining town that has moved into the computer age.

Kootenay Lake empties into the **Kootenay River** just west of Nelson. The highway passes four hydroelectric dams along the river, built to take advantage of the 200m fall from Kootenay Lake at Nelson to the Columbia River at Castlegar. A lay-by 13km west of the junction with Hwy 6 offers a good view of **Lower Bonnington Dam**. A second lay-by 1500m beyond overlooks **Brilliant Dam** and, just downstream toward the Columbia River, the disused Brilliant Suspension Bridge. A modern bridge arcs over the river to **CASTLEGAR** ❻.

Hwy 3 climbs south from Castlegar, then turns west over dramatic canyons toward **Christina Lake**, an important winter range for deer and elk.

Hwy 395 leads south into Washington just beyond the lake, while Hwy 3 continues westbound into **Boundary Country**, a transition zone between the high Kootenay peaks and the drier, more fertile Okanagan Valley to the West.

GRAND FORKS ❼ is the commercial hub of the Boundary Country, an agricultural town that boomed with mineral strikes in nearby hills. Continue along Hwy 3 over **Eholt Summit**, named for an abandoned mining town, to **GREENWOOD** ❽, a one-time mine boom town, which claims modern fame as the smallest city in BC.

The Crowsnest

Ratings

Heritage	●●●●●
Historical sights	●●●●○
Scenery	●●●●○
Children	●●●○○
Museums	●●●○○
Architecture	●●○○○
Food	●●○○○
Railways	●○○○○

Perched east of the Kootenays and south of the Columbia River Valley is a microcosm of BC, with a history of coal and gold mining, lumbering, important freight railway lines and scenic ski alps, complete with a purpose-built Bavarian town. The cheerful-looking crow on Crowsnest Highway signposts belies the massacre of horse-stealing Crow warriors by Blackfoot braves who resented thieves camping in their territory, their nest. Highway 3, called the Crowsnest, spans the Alberta–BC border at Crowsnest Pass and zigzags south and west for several hundred kilometres. A circuit from Cranbrook, the regional hub, links First Nations and Gold Rush town history with scenic recreation lakes, a magnificent falls and an alpine village, famed for accordions and alpenhorns. In winter, this southeast corner of BC is transformed into a winter wonderland of mountains and icy lakes, with major ski resorts at Kimberley and Fernie.

CRANBROOK❖

ℹ Cranbrook and District Chamber of Commerce InfoCentre
2279 Cranbrook St N;
tel: (250) 426-5914 or
(800) 222-6174;
www.cranbrookchamber.com

Elizabeth Lake Sanctuary InfoCentre
1101 1st Ave S. Open
Jun–Labour Day,
0900–1700.

Aboriginal Ktunaxa lost their camping ground to White settlers in 1870 and to a member of the BC Legislature. Cranbrook became a CPR divisional point and the railway its lifeblood.

Canadian Museum of Rail Travel❖ Train buffs have a field day touring through the self-styled 'Canada's Orient Express', built in 1929 as a seven-car unit for CPR's Trans-Canada Limited for Montréal to Vancouver service. In 2004, the museum moved down Van Horne Street, so as to accommodate five sets of trains from different eras of Canada's railway history.

Canadian Museum of Rail Travel $$ *57 Van Horne St N at Baker St. (Hwy 3/95); tel: (250) 489-3918; www.trainsdeluxe.com. Open year-round. Call for hours.*

Elizabeth Lake Sanctuary Wildlife Area *1101 1st Ave S.*

Jimsmith Lake Provincial Park *5km west of Cranbrook on Jim Smith Lake Rd; tel: (250) 422-3003; http://wlapwww. gov.bc.ca/bcparks/explore/ parkpgs/jimsmith.htm. Open May–Oct.*

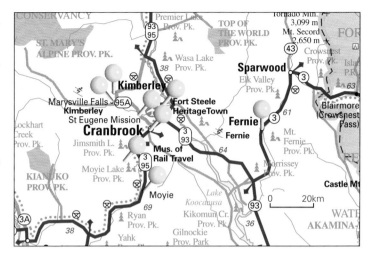

Elizabeth Lake Sanctuary Wildlife Area** A slice of the Rocky Mountain Trench protects 113 hectares of nature, with a lakeside trail, a waterfowl viewing hide and a dip-netting pond to peruse fish closely. Coots, killdeer, Canada geese, ruddy ducks, wood ducks, buffleheads and black terns share the lake with muskrats, elk, moose and turtles.

Jimsmith Lake Provincial Park* Join the locals swimming, canoeing, picnicking or camping. You can cross-country ski to the lake in winter and lace up some skates to enjoy the ice.

Accommodation and food in Cranbrook

Bavarian Chalet $$ *1617 Cranbrook St; tel: (250) 489-3305. Closed Sun.* On Thur–Sat, have the prime rib; otherwise it's a mixture of German specialities and all-Canadian.

Heritage Inn $$ *803 Cranbrook St; tel: (250) 489-4301 or (800) 663-2708.* This motor inn has 101 rooms and a very central location.

Prestige Rocky Mountain Resort $$$ *209 Van Horne St S; tel: (250) 417-0444 or (877) 737-8443; www.prestigeinn.com.* A modern, posh railway-theme hotel has 108 rooms near the railway museum.

Singing Pines Bed and Breakfast $$ *5180 Kennedy Rd; tel: (250) 426-5959 or (800) 863-4969; www.singingpines.ca,* has two rooms, a Western décor, and views of the Purcells and Rocky Mountains.

Super 8 $ *2370 Cranbrook St N; tel: (250) 489-8028 or (800) 800-8000; www.super8.com.* Across from the InfoCentre, this chain hotel is clean and comfortable at the quiet north end of town.

FERNIE**

ℹ **Fernie Chamber of Commerce Visitor Information Centre**
Hwy 3 at 102 Commerce Rd; tel: (250) 423-6868 or (877) 433-7643; www. ferniechamber.com. Open daily in summer, Mon–Fri autumn–spring or **Fernie Tourism Association** *tel: (250) 423-4395 or (888) 754-7325; www. fernietourism.com*

🅿 **Fernie Alpine Resort $$** *5339 Fernie Ski Hill Rd; tel: (250) 423-4655 or (887) 333-2339; www.skifernie. com. Open year-round, with limited spring and autumn activities. Ski season: open daily late Nov–mid-Apr.*

Mountains and tourism services are the *raison d'être* for this all-season recreational area, once known for coal mining and rum-running.

Fernie Alpine Resort, an annual 9-m snowfall creates a paradise for alpine and Nordic skiers, snowshoers and snowmobilers. Sleigh-rides and dog sledding are other winter options. Mountain bike, ride a horse, kayak, raft, hike, fly fish or take a chair-lift ride to scenic views in summer.

Accommodation and food in Fernie

Canadian Spruce Bed and Breakfast $$ *661 4th Ave; tel: (250) 423-6445 or (866) 438-5606; www.escapefernie.com.* A 1908 multistorey heritage house with fireplaces, a sitting porch and a central location.

Fernie Log Inn $$ *141 Commerce Rd, next to the InfoCentre; tel: (250) 423-6222 or (877) 733-7643; www.fernieloginn.com.* Radiant floor heating completes the cosy feeling of this log-cabin, chalet-style lodge.

Right
Living history at Fort Steele

Above
Fort Steele steam train

Jamochas Coffee House & Bagel Co $ *851 7th Ave (Hwy 3); tel: (250) 423-6977.* Cribbage, bread, coffee and atmosphere are welcome after a drive.

Wolf's Den Mountain Lodge $$ *5339 Ski Hill Rd, Fernie Alpine Ski Resort; tel: (250) 423-4655 or (866) 633-7643; www.skifernie.com.* Open all year, the 42-room lodge offers ski-in, ski-out slope access.

FORT STEELE HERITAGE TOWN✦✦✦

ⓘ Fort Steele Heritage Town $$
9851 Hwy 93/95 16km north of Cranbrook; tel: (250) 417-6000 or 426-7352; www.fortsteele.bc.ca. Open May–mid-Oct 0930–1800 (1700 May–Jun), with character actors in summer. Admission covers 2 consecutive days.

The 1864 Kootenay Gold Rush brought settlers to Galbraith's Ferry, later renamed for NWMP Superintendent Sam Steele who brought law and peace to the region. The *de facto* capital of the East Kootenays' rich mining economy lost out and declined when BC Legislator Colonel James Baker got the CPR to build the proposed divisional point in his Cranbrook holdings. The restoration is perfect, with summertime set pieces between neighbours on the street discussing the day's events and politics, all in costume. A bakery, tin-smithy, confectionery, heritage buildings, horse-drawn wagon rides and a steam train provide a well-rounded introduction to Fort Steele's golden years.

KIMBERLEY✢✢

ⓘ Kimberley Visitor InfoCentre
(moving, call for address);
tel: *(250) 427-3666;*
www.kimberleychamber.ca.
The beer-stein waving
Happy Hans statue in
lederhosen is hard to miss.

ⓑ Bavarian City Mining Railway and Sullivan Mine
tel: *(250) 427-5311.*
Open late Jun–Labour Day.

ⓢ Kimberly Alpine Resort $$ *Blackbear Crescent, off Hwy 95A S. of Kimberly; tel: (250) 427-4881 or (877) 754-5462; www.skikimberley.com, is open summer and winter.*

At 1113m, Canada's highest city was dedicated to silver, zinc and lead mining production at Sullivan Mine (Cominco), which closed in 2001. Happy Hans, the world's largest cuckoo clock, Bavarian kitsch and **Kimberley Alpine Resort** have replaced the local mining industry.

Salvaged railway cars at the **Bavarian City Mining Railway✢** now show off the countryside on the 9-km ride through the scenic countryside to the Sullivan Mine Interpretive Centre, due for completion in 2005. The mining company wanted to promote fertiliser in 1927. The resultant **Cominco Gardens✢ $** *(306 3rd Ave; tel: (250) 427-2293. Open May–Sept, dawn to dusk.* **Garden Treasures tearoom** *open daily in summer 1000–1800)* boast 48,000 blooms annually, with dedicated rose, prairie and Victorian gazebo areas.

In the **Platzl✢** *(T-shaped pedestrian street encircled by Wallinger Ave, Howard St, Kimberley Ave and Ross St)*, Bavarian architecture, restaurants, shops, wandering accordion players and depictions of the Happy Hans town mascot reflect the transition the town economy has made from mining lead to mining tourists.

Right
Marysville Falls

Accommodation and food in Kimberley

Chef Bernard's $$ *170 Spokane St, on the Platzl; tel: (250) 427-4820*. The chef is well known and locally beloved in this Bavarian *schnitzelhaus* which serves excellent pasta dishes.

Old Bauernhaus $$$ *280 Norton Ave, up the ski hill; tel: (250) 427-5133; http://kimberleybc.net/bauernhaus*. Bavaria was never so authentic as in this 350-plus-year-old building dismantled and reassembled here.

Snowdrift Café $ *on the Platzl; tel: (250) 427-2001*. Big, rich cups of *latte* and home-grown spinach salad with gorgonzola cheese, walnuts, mushrooms, carrots, and wholewheat bread reflect the quality of the menu at this fabulous vegetarian restaurant.

Wild Rose Ranch $$$ *East of Wasa Lake, north 8km on Wolf Creek Rd; tel: (250) 422-3403 or (800) 324-6188; www.wildroseranch.com*. A family-owned tourist ranch is purpose-built for horse riders and fly fishers and bird watchers in a stunning mountain-view setting.

MARYSVILLE FALLS✧✧✧

Marysville Falls $
7km south of Kimberley.

An easy 10-minute afternoon walk along rocky Mark Creek to a spectacular crashing 30-m cascade is worth a brief stop.

MOYIE✧ AND MOYIE LAKE PROVINCIAL PARK✧✧

Moyie and Moyie Lake Provincial Park $ *20km south of Cranbrook, Hwy 3; tel: (250) 422-3003; http:// wlapwww.gov.bc.ca/bcparks/ explore/parkpgs/moyie.htm*

Bears roam around the popular windsurfing and swimming lake, which nestles within the Purcell Mountains. Explorer David Thompson's party was almost swept away by Moyie River floods in 1808, but today's 200 residents point with pride to lovely buildings and a well-preserved fire hall which served when the St Eugene Mine silver/lead mine owners became rich before 1898.

ST EUGENE MISSION✧✧

St Eugene Mission
515 Mission Rd, Cranbrook; tel: (250) 489-2372.

Delta St. Eugene Mission Resort $$
7731 Mission Rd; tel: (250) 420-2000 or (888) 244-8666; www.deltahotels.com. Casino of the Rockies is adjacent to the hotel.

The 1897 white Victorian gingerbread church in the middle of farms on Ktunaxa/Kinbasket St Mary's Reserve is as immaculate inside as out with stained-glass windows and interior supports resembling a barn. Stop by nearby Ktunaxa Tribal office for information and to go inside the church. The former Kootenay Indian Residential School complex 16km north of Cranbrook is now the **Delta St. Eugene Mission Resort**, with an 18-hole championship golf course (*tel: (250) 417-3417 or (877) 417-3133, Apr–Oct*), and a base to enjoy the area's many outdoor activities. A Ktunaxa/Kinbasket Interpretive Centre is in the former school building.

Suggested tour

Total distance: 90km for a circuit from Cranbrook. Detours: 97km from Cranbrook to Fernie; 31km south to Moyie.

Time: 2 days.

Links: The **Columbia River** (*see page 230*) lies north of Wasa. Continue south and west of Moyie Lake Provincial Park on Hwy 3, the Crowsnest, to Creston and **The Kootenays** (*see page 240*). North of Fernie at Sparwood, Hwy 3 turns east to the Crowsnest Pass and enters Alberta.

Route: CRANBROOK ❶ makes a convenient base with services and facilities, but with this circuit, it's almost as convenient to stay in Kimberley.

Cranbrook's main attraction is the **Canadian Museum of Rail Travel** and the red wooden railway **Water Tower** near by, situated along the Canadian Pacific Railway line where rolling stock provides a realistic background for the historic railway carriages. A graceful reconstructed red-brick **Rotary Clock Tower** (*Baker & Cranbrook Sts*) is the focal point for a Chamber of Commerce *Heritage Tour* brochure of Cranbrook's Downtown and Baker Hill Residential Area buildings. **Elizabeth Lake Sanctuary Wildlife Area** is an utterly peaceful spot for picnicking and walking the lakeside trail accompanied by birdsong. Follow signs when crossing Hwy 3 to **Jimsmith Lake Provincial Park**, with non-powered watersports on offer.

Take Hwy 3 to the northeast end of Cranbrook and go left on to Hwy 95A. Be prepared to turn right almost immediately on to Old Airport Road to **ST EUGENE MISSION ❷** in the midst of the tribal headquarters for the Ktunaxa/Kinbasket First Nation **St Mary's Reserve**. The restored historic church is lovely. Continue along Old Airport Road to rejoin Hwy 95A.

Stop at the bridge in **Marysville** at the south edge of **KIMBERLEY ❸** and hike down Mark Creek for a view of magnificent **MARYSVILLE FALLS ❹**. Kimberley's heart is the Platzl, the Bavarian chalet-style pedestrian plaza, with a cuckoo clock that claims to be the world's largest. It chimes on the hour, revealing the ubiquitous Happy Hans yodelling. Catch the Bavarian City Mining Railway excursion train at the Platzl. A short drive up the ski hill offers vistas over the Kootenay River Valley. Before leaving town, take in the thousands of blooms at Cominco Gardens.

ⓘ Wasa Lake Provincial Park *tel: (250) 422-3003; http:// wlapwww.gov.bc.ca/bcparks/ explore/parkpgs/wasalake. htm*

Continue north on Hwy 95A past **Ta Ta Creek** and turn south at the Hwy 93/95 junction to **Wasa Lake Provincial Park** for swimming in the Kootenay's warmest lake (May–Oct). Follow Hwy 93/95 to **FORT STEELE ❺** for time travel in one of BC's best and most authentic historic site restorations. Return to Cranbrook.

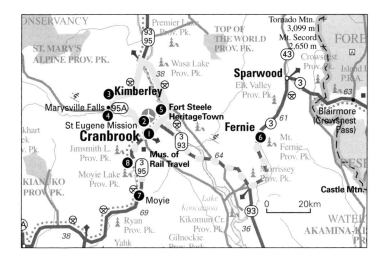

Detour to Fernie: South of Fort Steele, go east on Hwy 3/93. North of **Elko** on Hwy 3 is the **Elk Valley** traversing the Elk River, named for the numerous wapiti spotted by settlers. Coal mining boomed around 1900 from the valley into Alberta, and Fernie and the surrounding area became rich, though plagued by a legendary curse on the mines. **FERNIE ALPINE RESORT ❻** buzzes with summer and winter activity in a stunning range of mountains.

Detour to Moyie: Take Hwy 3/95 south of Cranbrook to **MOYIE ❼**, a tiny town set on a scenic hillside. **MOYIE LAKE PROVINCIAL PARK ❽** has watersports and sailing.

Demon King Coal

Fernie became rich on coal deposits, a seam which stretches across the Crowsnest Pass into Alberta at Frank Slide, site of a 1903 disaster when poor coal-mining techniques and water seepage caused 30 million cu m of limestone to slide down Turtle Mountain on to Frank Townsite.

Fernie, too, seemed cursed. Coal Creek Mine developer William Fernie, so the story goes, extracted information about coal deposits from a local Ktunaxa maiden, while pretending to woo her. When the lady was rejected by Fernie, the girl's mother placed a curse on Fernie. Curse or no, the Coal Creek Mine explosion in 1901 killed 128, followed by a 1904 fire which burned the town, and a flood in 1916. A 1964 ritual by local First Nations chiefs was enacted to counteract the curse. Since 1901, though, local people have seen the Ghostrider, said to be the spurned betrothed seated on a horse, and her mother chasing Fernie across the face of Mount Hosmer at the end of each day.

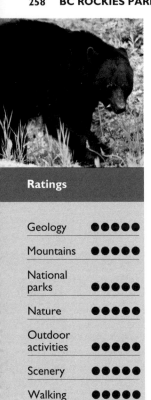

BC Rockies Parks

Ratings

Geology	●●●●●
Mountains	●●●●●
National parks	●●●●●
Nature	●●●●●
Outdoor activities	●●●●●
Scenery	●●●●●
Walking	●●●●●
Wildlife	●●●●●

The Rocky Mountains west of the Continental Divide shelter great rivers, exploding cataracts, emerald-green lakes, red-rock defiles, thick green forests and slashes of colour gushing forth from the earth. Disc-shaped trilobites, whose fossils were discovered in Yoho National Park, crawled upon this raw, breathtaking landscape half a billion years ago. Kootenay National Park's Radium Hot Springs pools soothed First Nations bathers for centuries. An enduring symbol of the Rockies, Mount Robson, dominates eastward afternoon vistas, a snow-striated massif embraced by forest at its base.

Early explorers looking for fur trade routes west followed streams and whitewater rivers to their headwaters. The mountains required feats of railway engineering when the imperative to ship goods, settlers, and tourists westward became financially irresistible. Despite a million visitors flowing through each year, there's enough high-country wilderness in the BC Rockies to leave memories of untrammelled vastness.

KOOTENAY NATIONAL PARK✦✦✦

🏛 **Kootenay National Park $**
tel: (250) 347-9615;
www.pc.gc.ca/kootenay

ℹ **Kootenay National Park Visitor Centre** 7556 Main Street East (at Redstreak Campground Rd), Radium Hot Springs; tel: (250) 347-9505. Open mid-May–Jun 0900–1700, late Jun–Labour Day 0900–1900.

Visitors who merely drive through without stopping inadvertently pay homage to the park's *raison d'être*. The Banff–Windermere Highway, Hwy 93, the route through Kootenay National Park, was built between 1912 and 1923 as an all-weather commercial transit road over the Rockies. Motorised touring and holidaymakers never looked back!

The 95-km stretch of Hwy 93 in the park follows the meanderings of Sinclair and Swede creeks to the Kootenay and Vermilion rivers. The parkway rises east from the Columbia River Valley through a red-rock canyon and passes vistas of a ridge of peaks framing the Kootenay River before winding up to the Continental Divide at the 1651-m Vermilion Pass on the BC–Alberta boundary.

The Kootenay (pronounced 'coo-teh-knee' in Canada), 'people from beyond the hills', lived and gave character and names to a region from the peaks of the Rockies to southern interior BC. Descendants of a

De Veber 7

WILLMORE WILDERNESS PARK

ROCKY

sthaven Mtn. 98 m

Mt. Chown 3,331 m

The Ranee 2,939 m

Mt. Robson 3,954 m

Resplendent Mtn. 3,426 m

Mt. Terry Fox Prov. Park

Yellowhead Pass 1,131 m

Valemount

MOUNT ROBSON PROV. PARK

Jasper

Marmot Basin

Simon Pk. 3,322 m

Mt. Edith Cavell 3,363 m

HAMBER PROV. PARK

Hallam Pk. 3,219 m

Kinbasket L.

Mica Dam

Columbia

Gordon Horne Pk. 2,885 m

Adamant Mtn. 3,355 m

Mt. Sir Sandford 3,522 m

Lake Revelstoke

Rogers Pass 1,327 m

GLACIER NAT'L PK.

MOUNT REVELSTOKE NAT'L PK.

Revelstoke Dam Vis. Ctr.

Last Spike Mon.

Herald Prov. Pk.

Yard Cr. Prov. Park

Sicamous

97A
97B

Blanket Cr. Prov. Park

Martha Creek Provincial Park

Revelstoke
Railway Mus.
Mt. Mackenzie

Shelter Bay Prov. Pk.

Mabel L. Prov. Pk.

Armstrong
Spallumcheen

Silver Star Mtn.

Lumby

Coldstream

Monashee Pass

McDonald Creek

Nakusp

Summit Lake

Windnoy

William A. Switzer Provincial Park

Brûlé Lake

Hinton

Roche Miette 2,316 m

Luscar Mtn. 2,601 m

Sirdar Mtn. 2,804 m

Jasper Tramway

Kerkeslin Mtn. 2,956 m

Mt. Balinhard 3,130 m

Samson Pk. 3,081 m

Athabasca Falls

Mt. Brazeau 3,470 m

Mt. Dalhousie 2,947 m

JASPER NATIONAL PARK

Obstruction Mtn. 3,168 m

Mt. Alberta 3,619 m

Mt. Columbia Highest Pt. in Alta. 3,747 m

Sunwapta Pass 2,035 m

Icefields

Icefield Ctr.

Mt. Cline 3,361 m

Mt. Amery 3,329 m

Cummins Lakes Prov. Pk.

Mt. Lyell 3,520 m

Mt. Forbes 3,612 m

Mt. Freshfield 3,336 m

Mt. Mummery 3,328 m

The President 3,138 m

Mt. Willingdon 3,373 m

Condor Pk. 2,948 m

Wapiti Mtn. 3,028 m

Barrier Mtn. 2,962 m

Lake Louise

BIGHORN WILDLAND

ROCKY MOUNTAINS FOREST RESERVE

Mt. Michener 2,337 m

Abraham Lake

RECREATION AREA

Clearwater

BANFF NATIONAL PARK

Sunshine Vil.

Golden

White-tooth

Mt. Dawson 3,390 m

Grand Mtn. 3,305 m

YOHO NATIONAL PARK

Mt. Norquay

Banff

Cave & Basin N.H.S.

Duncan

Mt. Templeman 3,070 m

KOOTENAY NAT'L PARK

Mt. Assiniboine

BUGABOO PROV. PARK

Dry Gulch Prov. Park

Radium Hot Springs

Invermere

Panorama

James Chabot Prov. Park

Windermere Valley Mus.

Columbia Lake Prov. Park

GOAT RANGE PROV. PARK

Mt. Hamill 3,243 m

Canal Flats Prov. Pk.

Mt. Robson 3,954 m

0   20km

MONASHEE PROV. PARK

Sugar L.

Silver Beach Provincial Park

Humamilt L.

Shuswap

Mabel L.

Upper Arrow Lake

Duncan Lake

Edson

Hornbeck Cr. P.R.A.

Nojack P.R.A.

Pembina

Brazeau

Brazeau Reservoir

Whitehorse Wildland P. P.

Right
Sinclair Canyon, Kootenay
National Park

ℹ **Kootenay Park Lodge Visitor Centre** *Vermilion Crossing, 63km northeast of Radium Hot Springs, no phone at Visitor InfoCentre. Open Apr–mid-May, Fri–Sat, mid-May–late Sept daily 1000–1800.*

linguistically unique and part Plains, part (BC) Plateau group, the Ktunaxa, Kootenae, Kootenai or Kootenay live in BC and in the USA in Montana. Foods, hunting traditions, homes, clothing and ceremonies resemble bits and pieces of neighbouring bands', but were distinct. Whatever their origins, the Kootenay gathered the brightly coloured mud running from the mountain streams and soaked weary bones in the medicinal hot springs.

Kootenay peoples called the coloured earth 'The Place Where the Red Spirit of the Earth is Taken'. Scientifically, iron oxide stains water pushing up from three springs beneath the earth red and yellow, sometimes mixing to brown or orange. The 'vermilion' for which the park's river and pass (at the Continental Divide) are named reflect the ochre paint pots' reddish colour.

Kootenays gathered the bright mud, formed and baked it into cakes, then rubbed off powder as needed and mixed it with rendered animal grease for face paint, clothing and tepee decoration and for medicine. When White entrepreneurs started a short-lived ochre mining

**Radium/Radium
Hot Springs Travel
Infocentre** *4-7585 Main
St W, Radium Hot Springs;
tel: (250) 347-9331 or
(800) 347-9704;
www.rhs.bc.ca; open
Tues–Sat 0900–1700, at
the southwestern edge of
Kootenay National Park,
serves the area's
population and services
centre. There are also
motels in the park above
the Radium Hot Springs
Pools.*

Paint Pots *85km
northeast of Radium.*

**Radium Hot Springs
Pools** $ *3km east of
Radium; tel: (250) 347-9485
or (800) 767-1611;
www.hotsprings.ca.
Open mid-May–mid-Oct
0900–2300; mid-Oct–mid-
May 1200–2100, Fri–Sat to
2200. Enquire about family
rates and hire of swimsuits
and towels. Massage and
reflexology treatments
available; tel: (250) 347-
2100. There is a
summertime poolside
restaurant for drinks,
sandwiches, burgers, ice
cream and snacks.*

operation for paint pigments in the early 1900s, they followed Kootenay trading practices by transporting the mud elsewhere, albeit by hand, to Castle Junction (Banff National Park) and on to Calgary by railway.

A 1.6-km return trail traverses varied countryside before reaching the **Paint Pots**✦✦✦, actually three main pools – one red, one yellow and one bright green. Descend from the parking area into a sub-Alpine forest with ferns and wild flowers growing beneath the trees. A swinging suspension bridge bounces and sways across the crashing blue pale waters of the Kootenay River. The land suddenly runs with rivulets of colour as the path ascends by the ruins of mining equipment to the three pots, an oasis of coloured, water-filled pockmarks surrounded by forest. A tiny wetlands offers fine bird-spotting.

The sheer golden-red walls of Sinclair Canyon shelter the site where groundwater sinking 2km down a fault in the earth returns to the surface heated to 44°C. Most of the park's 1.2 million annual visitors make a pilgrimage to the outdoor **Radium Hot Springs Pools**✦✦, to soak, swim or absorb the atmosphere of an unpretentious, not-quite-spa experience. The hot, semi-secluded soaking pool is a toasty 40°C; a lap in the swimming pool afterwards will seem almost bracing at 29°C. Mountain sheep are sometimes spotted clinging to nearby cliffs.

Radium? No, a misnomer, but there is radon, with a minuscule amount of radioactivity. Early 20th-century researchers presumed it was radium, and therapeutic, though a wristwatch emits more radium than the pools! Equally pleasant is the faint-to-odourless atmosphere distinctly lacking in the sulphur experienced in Banff's Cave and Basin National Historic Site (*see page 271*).

Accommodation and food in Kootenay National Park

Alpen Motel $$ *5022 Hwy 93, Radium Hot Springs; tel: (250) 347-9823 or (888) 788-3891; www.alpenmotel.com/html/index.htm; open Mar–Oct,* is cheerful with flower-boxes, 14 spotless, no-pet, non-smoking rooms a block from the park portal, and free mineral hot pool passes.

Kootenay Park Lodge $$ *Hwy 93 at Vermilion Crossing; tel: (403) 762-9196 or (403) 283-7482; www.kootenayparklodge.com; open mid-May–Sept.* To stay in the centre of the park in a log cabin is almost a wilderness experience. Canadian Pacific Railway built the lodge in 1923. There is a licensed restaurant; the gift-shop sandwiches are homemade and scrumptious.

Old Salzburg Restaurant $$ *4943 Hwy 93; tel: (250) 347-6553; www.oldsalzburgrestaurant.com,* matches the style of many nearby alpine-chalet-style motels with Austrian specialities such as schnitzel and goulash soup.

MOUNT ROBSON PROVINCIAL PARK◆◆◆

ⓘ Valemount Visitor InfoCentre *99 Gorse Street; tel: (250) 566-4846; www.valemount.org/Tourism/index.htm. Open mid-May–mid-Sept.*

ⓝ Mount Robson Provincial Park

Visitor Centre *at the west end of the park on Hwy 16; tel: (250) 566-4325; http://wlapwww.gov.bc.ca/bcparks/explore/parkpgs/mtrobson.htm. Open May–Oct daily 0800–1900.*

Berg Lake Trail *Car park 2km north of Visitor Centre with trailhead. Advance registration by phone, tel: (800) 689-9025, at Visitor Centre required for multiple-day hiking. 23km one-way to end; pre-book for a camp pitch en route. Carry all-weather gear and provisions. Part of trail may close to encourage caribou calving.*

The Texqakallt/Shuswap aboriginal name, *yuh-hai-has-kun,* says it all: the Mountain of the Spiral Road to Heaven. *If* Mount Robson is out from behind the often obscuring cloud cover, the sheer rise of its 3954m height is stunningly beautiful. The highest peak in the Canadian Rockies was not scaled until 1913, an ascent which continues to lure only the most experienced climbers today. Whether driving by on the Yellowhead Hwy, Hwy 16, or stopping for a look, plan on going west in the morning or east in the afternoon for the best-lit views of Mount Robson's face.

The most famous view of Mount Robson and its only slightly less high neighbour, 3426-m Mount Resplendent, is from the Visitor Centre along Hwy 16 at the park's west end. **Berg Lake Trail**◆◆◆ car park is 2km north of the Visitor Centre. From there, it's a several-day, advance-registration, 23-km hike to Robson Pass, with limited pitches for self-contained camping along the trail. Short of that is Kinney Lake at 7km, famed for still morning reflections of Mount Robson. Beyond is the Valley of the Thousand Falls and no fewer than 15 glaciers, including the advancing Berg Glacier which 'calves' blue ice into Berg Lake.

East of the Visitor Centre is a short, easy hike through forest to the sheer drop of **Overlander Falls**◆◆, named for 1862 prospectors headed for the Cariboo Gold Fields with more determination than preparation.

Midway through the park, you will spot waterfalls across Moose Lake. Canoe through the rightly named **Moose Marsh**◆◆, a likely place to find the 450kg beasts browsing. The Fraser River, which has its

Moose Marsh *Southeast of Moose Lake.*

Overlander Falls *1.5km east of the Visitor Centre.*

Yellowhead Pass *Hwy 16 at the BC–Alberta boundary.*

headwaters at Fraser Pass in the provincial park, is popular with whitewater rafters where it parallels the Yellowhead Hwy between Red Pass at the west end of Moose Lake and near the Visitor Centre, and below that spot on placid water.

The park's eastern boundary at the 1146m **Yellowhead Pass**✦ is also the Continental Divide and the provincial border with Alberta at Jasper National Park. The Yellowhead, the lowest pass in this section of the Rockies, was used for centuries by aboriginal peoples, trappers and hunters. Ironically, although it was surveyed in 1872 and known to be the best logistical engineering choice for building a railway line through the Rockies, in 1881 the CPR chose to build the railway over Kicking Horse Pass further to the south, to forestall American railroaders from stealing business from southern Canada.

Tête Jaune (*tay john*) **Cache**✦, Yellowhead's purported spot for hiding goods and furs, is at the junction of the eponymous Yellowhead Hwy (16) and Hwy 5. A few buildings and services suffice for the meeting of the roads named for trapper Pierre Hatsinaton's golden hair.

Accommodation and food in Mount Robson Provincial Park

There is a store for provisioning across from the Visitor Centre and two reservation-recommended campgrounds with 144 pitches in the park.

Mount Robson Lodge $$ *log cabins* and **Robson Shadows Campground $** *tel: (888) 566-4821 or (250) 566-4821; www.mountrobsonlodge.com,* are 5km west of the park.

Below The Fraser River

Valemount (*44km southwest of the park*) offers a range of motels.

YOHO NATIONAL PARK❖❖❖

ℹ Field Park and Visitor InfoCentre
South side, TransCanada Hwy 1, Field; tel: (250) 343-6783. Open May–late Jun, Sept, 0900–1700; late Jun–Labour Day 0900–1900; late Sept–April 0900–1600. There is an excellent selection of books and a Burgess Shale Fossil exhibit.

Above
Emerald Lake, Yoho National Park

Few places on earth have both yielded such a rich treasure trove of fossils and been the site of almost unimaginable modern engineering feats. First Nations Cree used the word *yoho* to express awe and wonder at a landscape that included rock escarpments, hanging glaciers, waterfalls, emerald lakes, crashing rivers and sheer ranges of mountains.

John Palliser's 1857 expedition took three years to scientifically survey Southern Alberta and what would become British Columbia. Geologist-naturalist James Hector was assigned to evaluate the river valley and its steep mountain pass. His skittish horse fell near Wapta Falls, knocking him out and frightening Hector's troupe. When he recovered, the relieved men named the river Kicking Horse.

Though Hector recommended against transportation across Kicking Horse Pass and in favour of the less precipitous Yellowhead Pass

Yoho National Park $ *tel: (250) 343-6783; www.pc.gc.ca/yoho*

Emerald Lake *11km north of Field.*

further north, nationalist imperative dictated that Kicking Horse be chosen as the Canadian transcontinental railway route, to show encroaching American interests that Canadians could transport their own commodities.

Brilliant, cantankerous Major Albert Bowman Rogers surveyed the passes and recommended that, despite its slope, the Kicking Horse must connect to another pass in the unexplored Selkirk Range to the West (*see Rogers Pass, page 232*) and would be viable. Canadian Pacific Railway general manager, William Cornelius Van Horne, pleasing stockholders and covering up mismanagement scandals, pushed for the Kicking Horse route. The years from 1885 to 1905 saw runaway train crashes on the 4.5 per cent grade, until the spiral tunnels were built.

A CPR engineer taking a break near the railway hub in Field probably thought he was dreaming to see some discs of stone resembling horseshoe crabs in the dirt of Mount Stephen. He had found trilobites.

Smithsonian Institution palaeontologist Charles Walcott, conducting Rockies digs on Burgess Pass within view of Emerald Lake in 1909, recognised the trilobites for what they were: fossils from the Palaeozoic Cambrian period, 500–590 million years old. The Burgess Shale has since yielded 170 fossilised species, more than 65,000 specimens of hard-shelled animals which swam and ate in the sea and underwater reef which extended inland half a billion years ago.

Emerald Lake✦✦✦ Greener than green, green enough to make blue sky pale in comparison, the glassy glacier-formed 28m-deep lake is perfect for canoeing. You can hike, or in winter (usually mid-November to mid-May) snowshoe or Nordic ski the 5-km loop around the lake. Walk clockwise from the wooden car bridge near the parking area for the best views of the President Range northward. The trail's approach to the east and south sides is more lushly forested. Veterans allow a full day to hike a 21-km triangular loop, north from the lake's north end up the Yoho Pass Trail, then south along the flanks of Wapta Mountain on the Burgess Highline Trail to Burgess Pass, then west back to the Lake Loop Trail.

Natural Bridge✦✦✦ Two kilometres up the road to Emerald Lake is one of the most accessible and beautiful attractions in the Rockies parks. A rocky outcropping forms a grey rock tunnel for the green waters of the Kicking Horse River. An afternoon stop is best for drama and photos: walk across the man-made bridge spanning the water to take in alternative viewpoints.

Takakkaw Falls✦✦✦ The winding 15-km road through the Yoho River Valley is filled with waterfalls, a Spiral Tunnel viewpoint, a lay-by for the Meeting of the Waters at the confluence of the Yoho and Kicking Horse Rivers, and a challenging switchback.

Takakkaw (the word means 'wonderful' or 'magnificent' in Cree) Falls consist of sheer, golden cliffs, tufted on the top ridge by a line of

Natural Bridge *3km southwest of Field along the route to Emerald Lake.*

Takakkaw Falls *17km northeast of Field via Yoho Valley Rd. Because of a switchback section beyond the Meeting of the Waters, trailers are prohibited. Yoho Valley Rd closed to vehicles early Oct–late Jun.*

Upper and Lower Spiral Tunnels *Lower Spiral Tunnel Viewpoint is 8km northeast of Field along TransCanada Hwy 1. Access another viewpoint along Yoho Valley Road by the Kicking Horse River interpretative sign.*

Yoho Burgess Shale Foundation $$$ *tel: (800) 343-3006; offers excellent interpretative hikes, including a long, rigorous Burgess Shale/Walcott Quarry hike and a shorter walk up Field's Mount Stephen, with numerous trilobite fossils. Access for groups limited to 15 persons is by guided tour only.*

dark green conifers, and water from Daly Glacier above exploding out into space before plunging 254m to the ground. The trail to the falls' base from the parking area crosses a bridge before winding up to a very chilly and thick misty zone, perfect for rainbows in the afternoon.

Upper and Lower Spiral Tunnels✢✢ If there's a train traversing the tunnels, you're in luck! Most of the time, the vistas of the raw landscape surrounding the 992-m Upper Spiral Tunnel and 891-m Lower Spiral Tunnel have to suffice to evoke the interpretative sign descriptions.

Imagine the Big Hill west of Kicking Horse Pass, where, because the CPR got a government-granted variance to build track on a grade over 2.2 per cent, runaway trains were common, a potential death-trap for those on the trains and those maintaining the lines.

For 20 years, death loomed any time a train went west down the Rockies' rise. In 1905, using engineering principles adapted from Switzerland's St Gotthard Railway Baischina Gorge Tunnels, the CPR completed a set of $1.5 million tunnels, so perfectly aligned when dug that the joining point varied by only 5cm.

And the innovation? Adding 7km of track in one straight and in a rough figure-8 pattern, two spirals within the mountain, reducing speed and eliminating the plunge down the 6.6km Big Hill.

Accommodation and food in Yoho National Park

The small town of **Field** has about a dozen bed and breakfasts. Enquire at the Field Visitor InfoCentre.

Cathedral Mountain Lodge $$$ *Yoho Valley Rd; tel: (250) 343-6442; www.cathedralmountain.com. Open Jun–Sept.* Log cabins with fireplaces along the pale blue Kicking Horse River and stunning views of the mountains near Field make this an alluring mid-park lodging. A grocery store is good for provisioning before Takakkaw Falls; the licensed Dining Room Restaurant serves crisp salads, tangy fresh tomato soup and delicately prepared fish.

Emerald Lake Lodge $$$ *at Emerald Lake; tel: (403) 410-7417 or (800) 663-6336; http://emeraldlakelodge.com.* Chalets surround the lodge-cum-resort, often booked out by executive conferences. The view of canoeists on the jewel-coloured lake is without equal. **Cilantro's $$** restaurant serves meals and drinks on an umbrella-decked terrace.

Kicking Horse Lodge and Café $$$ *100 Centre St, Field; tel: 250-343-6303 or (800) 659-4944; www.kickinghorselodge.net,* has 14 rooms year-round in a chalet-style building, a dining-room and lounge.

Yoho Brothers' Trading Post $$ *Hwy 1,* across from the InfoCentre, sells sandwiches, First-Nations-style souvenirs and books, and is the meeting place for the Yoho-Burgess Shale Foundation tours.

Opposite
Kicking Horse Pass

Canada's Rocky Mountain National Parks

Parks Canada provides a free tabloid-sized newspaper with a page of highlights from each of the six parks: Banff, Glacier, Jasper, Kootenay, Mount Revelstoke and Yoho. The same summaries can be found online:
www.pc.gc.ca/docs/v-g/guidem-mguide/index_E.asp

Suggested tour

Total distance: 550km.

Time: 4 days to drive; can be divided into south (Kootenay and Yoho National Parks) and north (Mount Robson Provincial Park).

Links: The Rocky Mountain Trench along the **Columbia River** (*see page 230*) at Radium is a jumping-off point for Kootenay National Park, and is the gateway to Yoho National Park at Golden. Cross over to the **Alberta Rockies** (*see page 270*) for the transit between parks via the Castle Junction and Icefields Parkway links. From Tête Jaune Cache, continue on the Yellowhead Hwy to **Prince George** (*see page 222*).

Route: From **Radium**, take Hwy 93 east through Sinclair Canyon to the **Radium Hot Springs Pools**, and follow the Banff–Windermere Hwy through **KOOTENAY NATIONAL PARK ❶**. East of the pools, traverse a red-rock defile. Shallow **Olive Lake** shimmers blue-green with fish-beloved grasses. The highway rises immediately to a superb **Kootenay Valley Viewpoint**, then descends beneath an area favoured by mountain goats to **Vermilion Crossing**. The **Paint Pots** are 22km northwest. Hike a crisscross 0.8-km trail up **Marble Canyon**. At the top of Vermilion Pass is the **Continental Divide** and the **Fireweed Trail** through a 1968 forest-fire area.

Cross into Alberta and **Banff National Park** (*see page 270*) at Castle Junction. Go north on TransCanada Hwy 1 to 3km beyond the Lake Louise exit, and continue on Hwy 1 veering left to the **Great [Continental] Divide** at the BC boundary and west into **YOHO NATIONAL PARK ❷** at **Kicking Horse Pass**. The **Lower Spiral**

Geological Rockies

Rockies' peaks and sideways-smashed mountains hint at the sliding and crashing which formed them. Inland seas lapped at the area which became the Western Rockies, silt trapping tiny lifeforms as fossils 500,000 years ago. In the Age of Dinosaurs, 160–60 million years ago, volcanoes erupted and faults thrust older rock on top of younger rock. At the bottom was granite; above was sedimentary rock, forming into the striated layers which streak faces of the Rocky Mountains.

Right
Yoho National Park

Tunnel Viewpoint is 8km west. Take the Yoho Valley Road turn-off to **Takakkaw Falls**, with the **Upper Spiral Tunnel Viewpoint** and **Meeting of the Waters Exhibit** en route. Return to Hwy 1 and descend the Big Hill to **Field Park and Visitor InfoCentre** for the Burgess Shale Exhibit. Immediately south is the road to **Natural Bridge** and **Emerald Lake**. Rejoin Hwy 1 to **Faeder Lake**, with pristine mountain reflections, hike a steep 3km trail up the **Leanchoil Hoodoos** and to **Wapta Falls**, near where Hector's horse kicked.

To continue through the Rockies, retrace the route up Hwy 1 into Banff National Park, and take Hwy 93, the Icefields Parkway, north to Jasper via Jasper National Park. From Jasper, take Hwy 16, the Yellowhead Hwy, west over **Yellowhead Pass** through MOUNT ROBSON PROVINCIAL PARK ❸, passing **Yellowhead Lake** and Moose Marsh. Canoeists paddle **Moose Lake**; rafters take to the **Fraser River**. The best views of **Mount Robson** are from the **Visitor Centre**, near the trail to **Overlander Falls**. **Berg Trail** parking is just north. Continue west to **Tête Jaune Cache**.

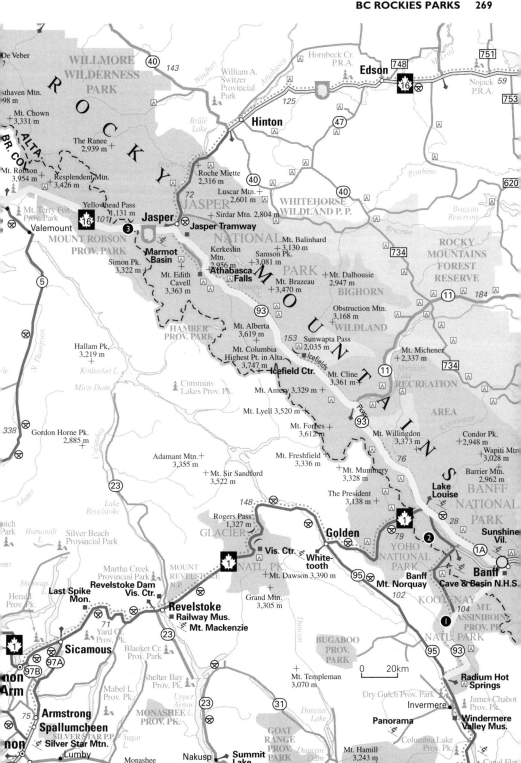

Alberta Rockies Parks

Ratings

Children	●●●●●
Mountains	●●●●●
National parks	●●●●●
Nature	●●●●●
Outdoor activities	●●●●●
Scenery	●●●●●
Walking	●●●●●
Wildlife	●●●●●

Canada's best-known natural icons don't disappoint. If anything, the peaks are higher and more pristine, the lakes a deeper aquamarine, the rivers an icier blue, the glaciers vaster and the animals more evident than seems possible.

The Alberta Rockies, primarily found in Banff and Jasper National Parks, are heaven for hikers and cyclists, canoeists, rafters, skiers and snowshoers, best when explored beyond the confines of a vehicle, motor coach or train window.

The icons also pack the parks with five million annual visitors, most driving through in July and August. They stop barely long enough to shop in Banff, stroll around the Banff Springs Hotel, walk around Lake Louise, dash to the Peyto Lake Viewpoint and haul along the Icefields Parkway. Traverse any trail to add a unique individual experience, and watch for bear, wapiti (elk), deer and Rocky Mountain sheep just beyond the next turn.

BANFF NATIONAL PARK✦✦✦

ℹ Parks Canada and Banff Visitor Centre *224 Banff Ave; tel: (403) 762-1550; www.pc.gc.ca/banff. Open late May–mid-Jun and Sept, 0800–1800; mid-Jun–early Sept, 0800–2000; late Sept–mid-May, 0900–1700.*

Banff/Lake Louise Tourism Bureau *tel: (403) 762-8421; www.bancfflakelouise.com*

Canada's first national park, established in 1885, splashes scenery around and between its two centres, the town of Banff and Lake Louise.

Banff Park Museum National Historic Site✦✦ The 1903 'railroad pagoda' exterior and Douglas-fir interior, complete with balconies around an atrium, set off this fine Victorian-style collection of stuffed park birds, insects and animals.

Banff Springs Hotel✦✦ The 1888 tourist hotel (*see page 273*) was built by the CPR to lure railway passengers to its Scottish-looking baronial manor, and some details remain. Stroll the grounds, but find the best views from Tunnel Mountain Road across the Bow River.

Cave & Basin National Historic Site✦✦ Found by CPR workers in 1883, the sulphuric hot springs were a gold mine for the Canadian government and the CPR, who both wanted to develop the area as a tourist stop. 'These springs will recuperate the patient and recoup the treasury,' commented Prime Minister Sir John A Macdonald obligingly.

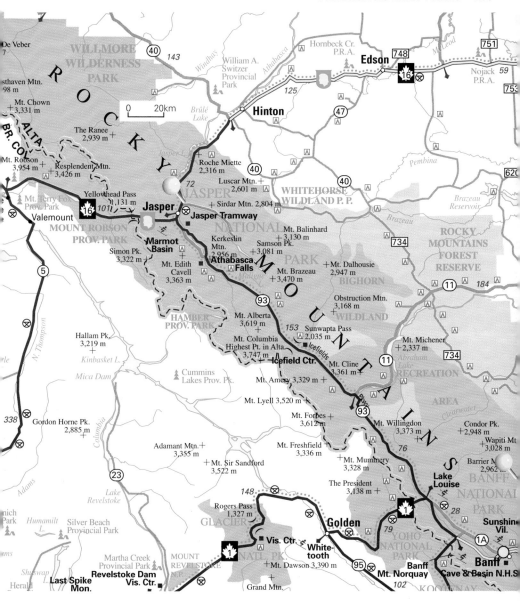

ℹ **Tourism Canmore**
tel: (866) 226-6673
or (403) 678-1295;
www.tourismcanmore.com

Banff's birthplace can be toured, but not bathed in. The free 0.6-km **Marsh Trail Loop**✦✦✦ is fine for bird-, elk- and orchid-spotting.

Lake Louise✦✦✦ Emerald water, white Victoria Glacier, red canoes, a rainbow of Icelandic poppies, a carved winter ice palace, tea-time elegance. The modernised, buff-coloured, château-style hotel stands at the east end of the lake like a sentinel. In summer, hikers take the **Lake Agnes Trail**✦✦ to one tea-house or follow the 10.5km return **Lakeshore Trail/Plain of the Six Glaciers Trail**✦✦✦ to another.

Lake Louise Visitor Centre by Samson Mall; tel: (403) 522-3833. Open early Jun–Labour Day 0900–1900; early May–early Jun, Sept 0900–1700; mid-Oct–Apr 0900–1600.

Banff Book & Art Den 94 Banff Ave; tel: (403) 762-3919 or (866) 418-6613; www.banffbooks.com, has a good selection of books on the Canadian Rockies and works by Canadian authors.

Banff Park Museum National Historic Site $ Banff Ave by Bow River Bridge; tel: (403) 762-1558; http://parkscanada.pch.gc.ca/lhn-nhs/ab/banff/index_e.asp. Open May 15–Sept 1000–1800, Oct–May 14 1300–1700.

Cave & Basin National Historic Site $ 311 Cave Ave; tel: (403) 762-1566; www.pc.gc.ca/lhn-nhs/ab/caveandbasin/index_e.asp. Open mid-May–Sept 0900–1800, and variable hours depending on day of the week Oct–mid-Jun.

Luxton Museum of the Plains Indians $ 1 Birch Ave; tel: (403) 762-2388; http://collections.ic.gc.ca/luxton. Open 0900–1900, 1300–1700 in winter.

Moraine Lake $ from Lake Louise Drive, turn south on Moraine Lake Road for 11km.

Luxton Museum of the Plains Indian✦✦✦ Plains First Nations people who followed and hunted buffalo accurately portray traditional culture in a wooden stockade museum building. Walk by the dioramas of tepee-dwellers and displays of peace pipes and elegant bead and porcupine quill clothing.

Moraine Lake✦✦✦ Ten craggy peaks surround this icy blue lake, with surreal beauty, beloved by summer canoeists. At the north end, the **Rockpile Trail**✦✦✦ boulders lead to a view of the peaks and moraine flow to the water.

Peyto Lake✦✦✦ Hike up Bow Summit through a flower carpet of Indian paintbrush and heather during July and August. Cloud patterns constantly change the colour of the lake, as it spreads long and blue before the wooden balcony viewpoint. Look left for a classic glacier flow into Peyto Lake.

Sulphur Mountain Gondola✦✦ The 8-minute ride up 2281-m Sulphur Mountain is lovely on a clear day, with unobstructed views of Banff Townsite. The short **Vista Trail Walkway**✦✦ to Sanson's Peak Observatory provides a chance to stretch your legs with fabulous views.

Accommodation and food in Banff National Park

Banff and Lake Louise accommodation does not begin to serve the millions of visitors who arrive and want to stay the night. East of the park, **Canmore**, set amid stunning snow-capped peaks, provides an ever-increasing number of motels, posh lodges and bed and breakfasts. If you are arriving from Calgary en route to Banff National Park, stop at **Travel Alberta Visitor InfoCentre** 2801 Bow Valley Trail, Canmore; tel: (403) 678-5277 or (800) 252-3782; www1.travelalberta.com. Open daily mid-May–Sept 0800–2000, Oct–mid-May 0900–1800.

Canadian Rockies Chalets $$ 1206 Bow Valley Trail, Canmore; tel: (800) 386-7248 or (403) 678-3799; www.canadianrockieschalets.com, has large, clean accommodation, cheerful owners and helpful touring advice.

The Crossing Resort $$ Saskatchewan River Crossing, Hwy 93 at Hwy 11; tel: (403) 761-7000; www.thecrossingresort.com. If you are driving between Banff and Jasper Mar–mid-Nov, this is a convenient spot to stop and refresh with lodging, a cafeteria and a gift shop.

Deer Lodge $$$ 109 Lake Louise Dr, Lake Louise; tel: (403) 410-7417 or (800) 661-1595; www.deerlodgelakelouise.com, usually has hand-hewn log décor for its 73 rooms, Victoria Glacier views from the rooftop hot-tub, and a fine restaurant serving Canadian wines with wild game, berries and local ingredients.

Fairmont Banff Springs Hotel $$$ 405 Spray Ave, Banff; tel: (403) 762-2211 or (866) 540-4406; www.fairmont.com/banffsprings, is the castle-like, 770-room icon set against the forested mountains, jammed with guests and sightseers in summer. **Willow Stream Spa** and the 27-hole

Left
Banff National Park's Johnston Canyon

Peyto Lake $ *West of Hwy 93, Icefields Parkway, 98km northwest of Banff; 40km northwest of Lake Louise.*

Banff Gondola at Sulphur Mountain Gondola $$$ *end of Mountain Ave; tel: (403) 762-2523; www.banffgondola.com. Open daily except Christmas Day and a fortnight in Jan.*

Right
Fairmont Banff Springs Hotel

Banff Springs Golf Course are enhanced by Bow Valley vistas. Intimate **Grapes Wine Bar** (mezzanine, open daily) serves delicious fondue. **Waldhaus Restaurant and Pub** *tel: (403) 762-6860*, in a Bavarian-style building near the golf course, serves hearty dishes with lager and schnitzel. For Bow Valley views, have a sundowner in the piano bar **Rundle Lounge**.

Fairmont Chateau Lake Louise $$$** *at Lake Louise; tel: (403) 522-3511; or (866) 540-4406; www.fairmont.com/lakelouise,* is a 489-room lakeside hotel with views across the lake to Victoria Glacier. In summertime, tea ($$$) is served in the aptly named **Lakeview Lounge. The 24-hour **Chateau Deli $** prepares made-to-order sandwiches. The casual **Poppy Brasserie $$** combines Lake Louise garden views with meals and a breakfast buffet.

Moraine Lake Lodge $$ *end of Moraine Lake Rd at lakeside, 15km from Lake Louise; tel: (403) 522-3733 or (877) 522-2777; www.morainelake.com. Open Jun–Sept.* While there can be snow even in summer, the 18 cabins and rooms in the lodge have spectacular mountain and lake views with complimentary tea-time pastries. Café snacks, lunches or fine dining are available in the glass-roof **Atrium $$$** during summer season.

Panorama Restaurant $$ *Banff Gondola at Sulphur Mountain; tel: (403) 762-5438; open late May–mid-Oct,* is a high dining experience at 2281m, serving breakfast and lunch buffets and dinner. The **Summit Restaurant $** serves light cafeteria fare.

JASPER NATIONAL PARK✧✧✧

ⓘ Parks Canada Jasper InfoCentre
500 Connaught Dr.;
tel: (780) 852-6176;
www.pc.gc.ca/jasper.
Open Apr–late Jun, Oct
0900–1700; late Jun–Labour
Day 0830–1900, Sept
0900–1800, Nov–Mar
0900–1600.

Icefield InfoCentre
Icefields Parkway; tel: (780)
852-6288 or (877) 423-
7433. Guided ice walks, tel:
(780) 852-5595 or (800)
565-7547. Snocoach onto
the glacier, tel: (403) 762-
6735; www.brewster.ca.
Open May–mid-Oct, daily.

Jasper Tourism & Commerce *409 Patricia*
St; tel: (780) 852-3858;
www.
jaspercanadianrockies.com.
Open daily.

ⓗ Athabasca Falls $
Icefields Parkway,
30km south of Jasper.

Columbia Icefield $$
from Icefield Centre, Icefields
Parkway; tel: (877) 423-
7433; www.brewster.ca/
attractions/icefield.asp.
Weather-dependent
Snocoach tours run mid-
Apr–mid-Oct.

Icefields Parkway $ *from*
3km west of the Lake Louise
exit, 230km north to Jasper
Townsite.

Maligne Lake $ *48km*
from Jasper via Maligne Lake
Rd.

Pyramid Lake $ *end of*
Pyramid Lake Rd.

Jasper began in 1811 as a North West Company trading post outpost and was visited by Overlander gold prospectors in 1862. The park was designated in 1907 and Grand Trunk Pacific Railway passengers arrived *en masse* in 1911. Scenic attractions outweigh shopping and dining opportunities, but who cares when wildlife roams the streets and the edge of town is a 5-minute walk away?

Athabasca Falls✧✧ Misty and mysterious, the falls descend 23m through pure quartzite. Hold on to railings to walk the 2-minute path to various viewpoints. Nordic skiers find a frozen shaft of ice and rock in winter.

Columbia Icefield✧✧✧ A huge-tyred Snocoach hauls passengers over moraine gravel to the Continental-Divide-spanning icefield, for a 20-minute walk on a glacier and a sampling of glacial water. The Icefield InfoCentre has information on Athabasca Glacier Ice Walks.

Icefields Parkway✧✧✧ The 230-km drive along Hwy 93 between Lake Louise and Jasper offers glaciers, waterfalls, wildlife and awesome vistas for several hours' drive by car or narrated Brewster Coach Tours.

Maligne Lake✧✧✧ Though Jesuit missionary Fr Pierre de Smet lost horses and goods in the river he proclaimed 'wicked', the lake at river's end is quite lovely. Take a 90-minute narrated boat tour to Spirit Island in the middle of the lake, fish for trout or canoe and kayak at this day-use lakeside retreat. En route to the lake, hike (snowshoe or ice climb) Maligne Canyon, take a look at Roche Bonhomme, a horizontal mountain profile that plausibly resembles a Native chief laying in profile, search the shores of green Medicine Lake for sunning wapiti, or join rafters bouncing downstream over Maligne River rapids.

Pyramid Lake✧✧ A close 7km from Jasper townsite, this large, crystalline lake reflects a pyramid-shaped mountain. Kayaks, canoes, sailboats and motorboats are for hire at Pyramid Lake Resort, while picnicking, horse-riding, fishing, and skating and Nordic skiing in winter are other options.

Accommodation and food in Jasper National Park

Atha B Pub $ *Athabasca Hotel, 510 Patricia St; tel: (780) 852-3386 or (877) 542-8422,* is the drinking spot for locals, with live entertainment.

Fairmont Jasper Park Lodge $$$ *tel: (866) 540-4454 or (780) 852-3301; www.fairmont.com/jasper,* has 446 rooms in chalets and log cabins, and adds a fine 18-hole golf course favoured by wandering wapiti. Splendid floor-to-ceiling views of Lac Beauvert are elegantly combined with rich meats, fish and wines in the adults-only **Edith Cavell Dining Room $$$** *tel: (780) 852-6052.* For a panoply of Canadian décor and dishes such as buffalo skillet, there's the **Moose's Nook Northern Grill $$$**.

The Glass House $$ *715 Miette Ave; tel: (780) 852-3861; www.visit-jasper.com/glasshouse.html,* complete with a solarium, is a comfortable bed and breakfast serving home-made pastries, close to the town centre.

Below
Moraine Lake, Banff National Park

Icefield Chalet $$$ *Icefield InfoCentre; tel: (877) 423-7433; www.brewster.ca; open late Apr–early Oct,* has 32 rooms on the third floor of the Icefield InfoCentre – ask for a glacier view room.